RICHARD E. GOODKIN

THE SYMBOLIST HOME AND THE TRAGIC HOME: MALLARMÉ AND OEDIPUS

JOHN BENJAMINS PUBLISHING COMPANY
Amsterdam/Philadelphia

1984

Library of Congress Cataloging in Publication Data

Goodkin, Richard E.
  The symbolist home and the tragic home.

(Purdue University monographs in Romance languages, ISSN 0165-8743; v. 13)
Bibliography: p. 199
1. Mallarmé, Stéphane, 1842-1898 -- Criticism and interpretation. 2. Sophocles. Oedipus
Rex. 3. Symbolism in literature. 4. Tragic, The. 5. Tragedy. 6. Home in literature. I.
Title. II. Series.
PQ2344.Z5G6   1984   841'.8   84-9280
ISBN 90-272-1723-8

THE SYMB OME:

PURDUE UNIVERSITY MONOGRAPHS
IN ROMANCE LANGUAGES

William M. Whitby, General Editor
Allan H. Pasco, Editor for French
Enrique Caracciolo-Trejo, Editor for Spanish

Associate Editors

I. French

II. Spanish

Volume 13

Richard E. Goodkin

The Symbolist Home and the Tragic Home:
Mallarmé and Oedipus

For B. G. and C. G.

Table of Contents

Preface

Almost inevitably, with the inevitability that the concept itself calls forth, the word "Tragedy" draws us into a history of meanings rather than yielding any simple one. To be able to define Tragedy straightforwardly would be already to transcend it, for the tragic impulse forever dreams of expressing the complex in a simple way.

Here are two definitions of Tragedy which demonstrate the thanklessness of the task of choosing one definition of it:

> Absolute tragedy exists only where substantive truth is assigned to the Sophoclean statement that "it is best never to have been born." (George Steiner, *The Death of Tragedy*)[1]

> "We believe in eternal life," exclaims tragedy. (Friedrich Nietzsche, *The Birth of Tragedy*)[2]

These diametrically opposed definitions are very much in keeping with the titles of the works which contain them, and indeed might lead us to suspect that the genitive in each title is subjective as well as objective: the death that Tragedy is, the birth that Tragedy is, might well express the two extreme views of Tragedy underlying these works.

If I were made to choose between Steiner's and Nietzsche's definitions of Tragedy (which are, admittedly, highly schematized in this brief discussion), I would take the paradoxical nature of Tragedy to heart and resort to a third definition which implicitly accepts each of the others all the while refusing both of them:

> On comprendra maintenant plus facilement ce qu'est le monde pour la conscience tragique. On pourrait le dire en deux mots: *rien* et *tout* en même temps. (Lucien Goldmann, *Le dieu caché*)[3]

The world of human existence is nothing and everything to a tragic consciousness: nothing by comparison to what that consciousness dreams of possessing (everything), and everything by comparison to that impression of nothingness.

Tragedy perpetually brings us the *other*: the other face of the coin we had not yet looked at, the other side of the question we had not gotten to. If we are happy, it makes us sadder; if we are sad, it shares our sadness and makes us happier. It is something which always works by opposition, such that the famous riddle by the man who is also the source of Goldmann's title, Pascal, might be speaking in the name of Tragedy itself in the first person, the "il" being simply "man":

> S'il se vante je l'abaisse.
> S'il s'abaisse je le vante.
> Et le contredis toujours.[4]

Thus, in the course of this study, even though I am attempting a sort of definition of Tragedy, I would like to remain aware of its elusive nature. I will use the word "tragic" not as a synonym for "sad" or "pessimistic," or even "unfortunate," but rather in a more complex way, which I hope will be defined at least in spirit by the pages that follow, but which might be stated for the moment in this way: a tragic recognition is a recognition of the limits of human existence, one which leads not only to an expression of fear and anguish over those limits, but also, in some form, to an affirmation of the value of understanding those limits, and perhaps even of fighting against them. A tragic awareness says that any attempt at understanding must come to terms with the nature of the attempt, must take account of its limits, because only if the search faces and gets over the important step of reminding itself of what it cannot do might it also become an affirmation of what it can do.

It is because they are both movements which entail the overstepping of limits that I originally became interested in linking Tragedy and Symbolism in some way and defining them in terms of each other. The tragic hero, like the Symbolist poet, reaches for an absolute which always eludes him. Both of them do so in the goal of creating a kind of hermeticism, be it that of the hero who dreams of being always and only himself, of existing in a vacuum, independently of others, or that of the poet who dreams of creating a definitive language, one which requires nothing external to it in order to yield meaning, or perhaps in order to refuse meaning. For indeed, the dream of hermeticism, tragic or Symbolist, is partially a refusal, a refusal to bear meaning by participating in a social or a socially oriented network, and yet it is a refusal which is the ultimate exaltation of the self. The tragic hero says, at least implicitly, that his life does not need to mean something with reference to other lives, because it *is* something in itself. The Symbolist poet says that his words need not carry meaning for others, because they have a life of their own; they set more than they use a linguistic standard.

Thus, in Tragedy I would like to see a movement which recognizes the limits of human capabilities both from above and from below, by perceiving both what is not possible for humans and what is possible. That Tragedy originated as a part of a religious festival would seem to mark it at least at one level as an affirmation, albeit an awe-filled and terrifying one. I see Symbolism as a movement that takes language to its limits not only to show it its shortcomings but also to celebrate its possibilities. And, as Paul Valéry has pointed out, the word "Symbolism" itself, although it is a convention, is surrounded by a kind of religious awe and mystery, felt particularly by those who attempt to define it:

> Le seul nom de *Symbolisme* est déjà une énigme pour mainte personne. Il semble fait pour exciter les mortels à se tourmenter l'esprit. J'en ai connu qui méditaient sans fin sur ce petit mot de *symbole*, auquel ils attribuaient une profondeur imaginaire, et dont ils essayaient de se préciser la mystérieuse résonance. . . . Le pouvoir excitant d'un mot est illimité. Tout l'arbitraire de l'esprit est ici à son aise: on ne peut infirmer ni confirmer ces diverses valeurs du mot Symbolisme.
> Il n'est après tout qu'une convention.[5]

If the term "Symbolism" is a convention, despite the enigma and the evocative power that reside in the word, fully defining it, like defining the complexities of Tragedy in a simple way, would be to transcend it. In the spirit of the task at hand, I have used the convention of writing "symbolism" without a capital in the more general sense of the term, and "Symbolism" with a capital when speaking of the movement, in the hopes of going beyond that convention. I would like to claim that Symbolism is simultaneously a kind of anti-symbolism and the ultimate and "proper" form of symbolism, in the sense that a "proper" name takes a capital letter. I believe it is a Symbolism which, like Tragedy, fights with and questions conventions, and perhaps loses to them, but which ultimately claims itself capable at least of affirming the struggle.

Along with the parallel movements of Tragedy and Symbolism I have tried to explore the parallel topics of the home and language, the former being a subject absolutely central to Tragedy as the latter is to Symbolism, although I would like to think that the topic of the home in some sense subsumes the other, and that is why I have worded the title as it is. I originally chose the topic of the home because of its importance for the *Oedipus Tyrannus* in particular, and for Tragedy in general. The tragic home is emblematic of every human house, since the house represents an attempt to structure and regulate human existence, and thus to lessen the gap between the human and the divine by allowing men to protect themselves, to reproduce themselves, and, especially, to recall and foresee a certain degree of stability reaching back into the past and forward into the future, the stability provided by the unchanging family name. The dilemma of the tragic home is that of every home, for the impression of stability and permanence it attempts to create is built upon the lives of creatures who are in themselves mutable and temporary. From day to day, the house hides the difference between itself as a structuring entity and its inhabitants who look to it for the structure they need, and yet it is indeed built upon that difference, and Tragedy expresses the periodic awareness of that difference that any inhabitant of a house may come to.

It is the artificial nature of the home, a nature which is exposed by Tragedy, that most closely links the home to language, another artificial structure which is equally central to human civilization. One of my aims is to draw a parallel between home and language as civilizing tools both of which attempt to impose order upon the inordinate, to structure the unstructurable so that human beings can have the impression of speaking and thinking and planning rationally about what is unspeakable, unthinkable, and unplannable, and ultimately irrational. It is here that the home is parallel in its impact on tragic heroism to the impact of language on the Symbolists: because where home provides the stable unit upon which the perpetuation of the heroic name is to be based, and thus tries to counter the passage of time and the onset of circumstance by means of a stabilizing but ultimately artificial structure providing a sense of continuity which is threatened at every moment, language provides the stable units necessary for the expression of the Symbolist dream of absolute meaning, but any consideration of language as purely stable and normative, as creating units which cannot be questioned through metaphor and syntactical ambiguity, actually prevents the poet from reaching the very goal which language is meant to allow him to reach.

Thus, home and language may be described as structures which are meant to achieve a goal but which prevent the reaching of that goal. And yet it is the search for a goal which I would most like to emphasize, and the value of that search. To fail to reach a goal may be better in the long run than to reach it and to realize that it was the wrong one. The tragic hero, unless he is really a god, cannot live a meaningful life alone, without realizing his mortal nature and accepting the various social contexts which it imposes upon him, but insofar as Tragedy itself is played out in a social context linking actors and spectators, his life can at least teach us about other lives, our own lives, and the desire to find an absolute which inhabits those lives even though we may not wish to recognize it during our waking moments, even though we may do everything to deny it exists at all. And if the Symbolist poet cannot make his words correspond to any kind of absolute meaning, he can at least allow us to realize that we are all in search of that meaning, and that we have all probably assumed at some time that language, in some form or another, can or even does provide it. It is to this extent that failure may be an affirmation, an affirmation of what we are through a recognition of what we are not but never cease to dream about being.

The comparative study that I am proposing does not mean to make any explicit comparison between Oedipus and Mallarmé. I am trying to go in search of the home that Oedipus and Mallarmé both went in search of, wishing, like them, both to keep the two halves of my *symbolon* separate and to equate them at least at some level. Undoubtedly I will have no more success in my search than my two predecessors did. My only aim in the present study is to fail in the same way that they failed.

Acknowledgments

This book was published with the assistance of the Frederick W. Hilles Publication Fund of Yale University. I also wish to thank the members of the Mrs. Giles Whiting Foundation for their generous support of this project in its early stages.

Also, four teachers in the largest and best sense of the word: Robert Roza and Gilbert Rose at Swarthmore College and Victor Brombert and Froma Zeitlin at Princeton University. My special thanks to Victor and Froma, without whose ideas, help, and encouragement this book would not have been written.

And last, but far from least, my parents, Minnie and Manuel Green, for their endless encouragement.

Introduction: Tragedy and Symbolism

Lorsqu'on emploie trop de temps à voyager, on devient enfin étranger en son pays.

Descartes
Discours de la méthode

i. Tragedy as Symbolism

It is the symbolic nature of Oedipus' quest which most centrally links the notions of Tragedy and Symbolism in the *Oedipus Tyrannus,* and that under the aegis of the concepts of home and homing. Oedipus' "homing"—his attempt to save the Thebans' (political) home in the process of which he discovers the true nature of his own (individual) home—is a kind of symbolism in the original sense of the word *symbolon*:

> Dérivé du mot *sumballein* "réunir," ce mot désigne chacun des deux morceaux d'un objet brisé, puis partagé entre deux hôtes au moment où ils se séparent. Ces moitiés doivent permettre, en s'adaptant exactement l'une à l'autre lorsque les hôtes eux-mêmes, leurs descendants ou leurs fondés de pouvoir viendront à se rencontrer, d'attester la qualité des porteurs et l'authenticité du lien qui les unit. Le *sumbolon* est un signe de reconnaissance.[1]

"Symbolism" in the first sense of the word thus describes the tracking down of a home by one who is a stranger to it but who, by the fundamentally ambiguous nature of the concept of *xenia*—the term denoting the guest-host relationship and the noun/adjective related to it, *xenos,* referring simultaneously to guest and to host, or rather to the necessarily double identity which each of them carries, host in his own land and guest in that of his corresponding *xenos* —is both outsider (searcher for what functions as a house on the road) and insider (guest received and nurtured by the house upon his arrival).

Oedipus himself remarks upon the "symbolic" nature of his search for the murderer of Laius in his first response after the parodos to the elders of Thebes who compose the chorus. Four lines into his answer to their plea to the gods for help, as a preface to the proclamations he is about to make concerning the course of action he is going to follow, we find the following lines:

ἀγὼ ξένος μὲν τοῦ λόγου τοῦδ' ἐξερῶ,
ξένος δὲ τοῦ πραχθέντος· οὐ γὰρ ἂν μακρὰν
ἴχνευον αὐτός, μὴ οὐκ ἔχων τι σύμβολον.

νῦν δ᾽, ὕστερος γὰρ ἀστὸς εἰς ἀστοὺς τελῶ,
ὑμῖν προφωνῶ πᾶσι Καδμείοις τάδε·

Things which I, a stranger to this report, will investigate,
and a stranger to what was done; for [if I were] alone
I would not trace a long path, if I had no *symbolon*. But now
as it is, since as a latecomer I join the ranks of the citizens,
I proclaim the following to all you Cadmeans. . . . 2

Sir Richard Jebb points out the intricacies of the conditional sentence which the word *symbolon* punctuates:

The chief protasis to οὐκ ἂν μακρὰν ἴχνευον is contained in αὐτός, "unaided," which is equivalent to εἰ αὐτὸς (=μόνος) ἴχνευον, *if I were tracing it alone*. . . . Now [the chief protasis] is an unreal supposition (for he is *not* tracking alone); and that makes the whole supposition unreal. . . . although, as a fact, he has *no* clue. Suppose it to be said of a man too old for work, "If he were young, he would not be doing well, if he did not work." . . . The chief protasis, (*if he were young*), being unreal, makes all the rest unreal . . . although, as a fact, he does *not* work.3

What is being contrasted here is Oedipus himself, alone (αὐτός), with the townspeople whose help he is going to require in order to be able to help them more than they alone could help themselves. As Jebb rightly explains, the only true part of the contrary-to-fact condition which Oedipus here describes is the clause including the *symbolon*, for the king does indeed have no *symbolon* insofar as the latter term denotes a perceptible clue which might lead him to a resolution of the problem at hand. But what is not true is that he is tracing alone, himself. The drift of Oedipus' sentence, which Jebb does not quite come to despite his highly analytical interpretation of it, is this: "I don't have a clue (*symbolon*) as to the identity of Laius' murderer. If I were investigating the murder alone, I could go nowhere, since I am a *xenos* to the action, a stranger to its facts. But since I am not alone (the uncontrary-to-fact condition which its opposite implies), I will trace the murderer's identity, since you, the townspeople, *will be my symbolon*."

It is thus the people of Thebes who will provide a "home," that is, the possibility of reaching the stop which only a full understanding can offer to the searcher, even though that knowledge is being sought precisely in order to save *their* home. The virtual relationship of *xenia* which links Oedipus and Thebes can be characterized only in terms of a mutuality, each member being both guest and host, needer and provider of needs. Indeed, in calling himself a *xenos* who has become a townsman of Thebes "ὕστερος," or later, as a supplement to the already-constituted citizenry, Oedipus emphasizes his own status as one who is at a distance from the crimes to be investigated but who, through the conventional conjoinment of the two halves of the *symbolon*, his externally based objectivity joining the citizens' internally based experience of the matter at hand, aims to solve the dilemma which none of the city's own could figure out.

The irreconcilable nature of the task Oedipus sets for himself in investigating Laius' murder lies in the fact that he uses convention—the two halves of the *symbolon*, here emblematic of the whole process of information gathering which is, indeed, conventional—in order to find himself beyond (or before) convention, for he discovers he is at both ends of the *symbolon* and that his very existence thus seems to go against the duality it is built upon. So that Oedipus' status is at the same time one of alterity—the very objectivity which should allow him to investigate what the townspeople themselves have not looked into sufficiently—and one of sameness—the position of insider to which Oedipus aspires only as a delegated, instituted status, *tyrannus,* but to which he falls prey as an inherited status, *basileus.*

It is in this sense that Oedipus' dilemma bespeaks a split, or rather an impossible conjunction: he is both the destination of his search and the vehicle by which that destination is to be reached, both home and the path to home, both at the foundation of his house and on the way to finding that foundation. Or, if we extend the meaning of *symbolon* to the domain of the institution of language, both the dream of a simple meaning which precedes the necessarily conventional conjoinment of the two halves of the *symbolon*—and which that conjoinment in its non-simplicity precludes—and the actuality (or actualization) of a conventional system of doubled units by which meaning must be conveyed. Oedipus is both the signified and the signifier, the meaning and the means.

It is starting from this point that we may begin to explore Oedipus as a figure exemplifying a kind of Symbolism. If the hero takes up the trappings of the investigation into Laius' murder only in order to go beyond them, to start out as an outsider in order to become (and to discover to his dismay that he has always been) an insider, he may be seen as a model of the poet who takes up the pen and the linguistic apparatus it represents only in the hope of going beyond it, of using the symbolic system of language to erase that system or at least to erase its necessary conventional aspect by taking possession of the mediating function of convention, by attempting to delegate convention himself and thus in a sense to equalize the relationship between what is to be expressed (meaning) and the system of mediation (means) by which it can be *expressed* only if there remains a distance and a distinction between means and meaning. Just as the words of a conventional symbolic system of language cannot be entirely equal to the meaning which they bear precisely because they must be equal to themselves so that they might ensure the *representation* of the meaning they protect against the dissipation of a non-expression, Oedipus as *symbolon* cannot be fully equal to his people—the represented of Thebes, who in the present crisis of the plague as in the past crisis of the Sphinx would disappear without his protection

—because in order to "signify" them and stand for them, he must be equal to himself, stand up across time in order to stand for those who alone cannot stand for themselves.[4]

It is, in fact, only the dream of a non-conventional Symbolism which desires to mobilize words that are fully equal both to themselves and to what they represent, to establish an equality of signifier and signified which goes beyond convention in that it erases the split between the two halves of the *symbolon* even as it must rely upon that split to identify the very halves which it wishes to equate and the doubled nature of which it aims to efface. The dream of a non-conventional Symbolism thus corresponds to the dream of tragic heroism: Oedipus, both outsider and insider, both leader of the investigation and its object, wishes to save the city by taking its cause as his own, and yet also to remain "other" than the citizens in order to lead them to safety. He is internal to the city's crisis insofar as he is its unknown cause, and yet he comes to Thebes as an outsider, as one whose very status as outsider might permit him to stand up for the citizens from whom he believes he is distinct, a "standing up" upon which the perpetuation of his *own* name, his heroic status ("ὁ πᾶσι κλεινὸς Οἰδίπους καλούμενος," "he who is called glorious Oedipus by all"[5]), depends.

Indeed, Oedipus is emblematic of a fundamental split in any symbolic system which the human mind can create. As Bernard Knox has so admirably demonstrated, Oedipus represents mathematical man:

> Oedipus is the equator and measurer, and these are the methods by which he will reach the truth; calculation of time, measurement of age and number, comparison of place and description—these are the techniques which will solve the equation, establish the identity of the murderer of Laius. The tightly organized and relentless process by which Oedipus finds his way to the truth is presented by the language of the play as an equivalent of the activity of man's mind in almost all of its aspects.[6]

Oedipus is first of all the eternal quantifier, the equation-maker, the political animal *par excellence*. He deals with stable units, and his belief in the power of conventional symbolic systems of tracing knowledge, in the efficacy of matching *symbolon* to *symbolon* in order to convey a piece of information, is the belief of the symbol-creating being in what he has created, the faith of the man Kenneth Burke defines as

> the symbol-using (symbol-making, symbol-misusing) animal
> inventor of the negative (or moralized by the negative)
> separated from his natural condition by instruments of his own making
> goaded by the spirit of hierarchy (or moved by the sense of order)
> and rotten with perfection[7]

in what he believes he has defined rather than in what in fact he needs in order to define himself.

Indeed, the central problem of both Tragedy and Symbolism is the question of identification and idealization: the tragic hero aims to forge a permanent identity for himself, to create an idea of himself that will never change, that will be permanently sheltered from the vagaries of time and chance and nature. To this extent he wishes to use his home as a repository, as a kind of altar which prevents the alteration of his name and his reputation and thus seems to give him a kind of idealized immortality, insofar as it allows his idea, the idea of him, forever to survive, as a sort of paradigm by which human life is to be measured. In this sense his home is what allows him to approach the permanence of divinity, which is all the more fitting as the home is itself an attempt to reach up toward the heavens, to allow human existence to aspire to certain characteristics of the divine. But it is precisely because this image of the home and the name is indeed an idealized one, a distillation, a freezing in time, that it cannot be accurate, and is by its very nature apt to separate itself from the truth of human existence. The truth in Tragedy is experienced as a recognition precisely because it is always a displacement of structures which exist to hide it more than to express it, or at least of structures which must deform it in order to express it in an acceptable form.

In this context it is useful to recall Jean-Pierre Vernant's characterization of Tragedy as being built upon a tension between a political psychology and a mythic psychology.[8] Oedipus' status as a metaphor for mathematics and all that is stable and quantifiable in any symbolic system corresponds to his political side, his role as *tyrannus,* as an outsider who comes to the city of Thebes at its time of greatest need and saves it from destruction and obscurity. To this extent it is he who stabilizes the city, who sets it aright when it is in danger of floundering; it is he who assures the city's continuity across time, who stands it on its feet when it seems to be on the point of lapsing back into a non-differentiated state, that is, of losing the individual identity as *polis* which removes its citizens from the state of nature in which they would be living without it, indeed from the state of nature which itself holds many forms of truth about mortal human existence against which the city as the creator of a form of artificial permanence never ceases to struggle.

Indeed, it is precisely the city's political identity which Oedipus maintains by counteracting the Sphinx's threat. By answering the riddle she offers as an idealization (or at least a schematization) of mortal existence, he both recognizes and counters (if temporarily) the paradox inherent in the riddle, that by which human beings with only *one voice*—i.e., a craving for a permanent, unchanging identity, political or otherwise—are in fact mutable and must submit to the changes brought on by the passage of time, must walk on four feet and two feet and three feet as well. It is by recognizing a permanent truth at this point that Oedipus temporarily counters that truth, for the recognition of what it means to be formed by—and ultimately subject to—the state of nature gains for him a reputation as a political animal, as the saver of the city. Oedipus' instantaneous and almost instinctual grasp of a painful truth at one point in time, of a truth which ever threatens the city and its artificial structures, is what leads to his own integration into those structures and, ultimately, to his own undoing at their hands.

The overriding characteristic of the riddle of the Sphinx and of the divine oracles which Oedipus follows is that in themselves they are consistent and persistent: they never change, they have only one voice; only human understanding of them changes. As a schematization of Oedipus' life, they are not false, rather, Oedipus' own idealization of them, the idea he forms of his life based on them, is in itself false, it diverges from its divine source of information even as it tries to copy it, or because it tries to copy it. His perception of the truth, first the truth of the oracle about his parents and then his interpretation of the Sphinx's riddle, a perception which therefore depends first of all on Oedipus' own purported home in Corinth and then on the city of Thebes which is his original home, reveals a kind of truth, but it is the wrong truth, just as it pushes him away from the wrong parents, and it makes him destroy the wrong monster and lose sight of the more fundamental threat about to destroy the city of Thebes, his own entry into it.

Glorious Oedipus, the killer of the Sphinx, the civilizer, the saver, he thinks, not only of his home in Corinth in which he thinks his presence would have been disastrous, but also of his adoptive home in Thebes in which his presence is in fact disastrous, bases all of his glory and his reputation on his status as a home-saver twice over, as a respecter and an approximator of the gods. And it is precisely this idealization of his identity—an idealization by which he claims to have joined the human and the divine by seeing into the gods' truth—which is the source of his downfall, because it cannot successfully counter or take into account Oedipus' ultimate enemy, *Tuche,* chance, the arbitrary, the very force he believes he has conquered, because in a totally ideal world nothing would be arbitrary.

It is because Oedipus himself overidealizes his life, that is, believes it corresponds in a stable, unchanging, and understandable way to the gods' words, it is because he takes his house as a paradigm of the house whose stability is assured by an ideal ruler, it is because of his consideration of his house as a positive paradigm or ideal that he becomes a negative paradigm. And where his aim to provide a positive paradigm of mortal existence is based essentially on the power of reason, his ultimate transformation into a negative paradigm is one which calls into question the limits of reason and essentially leaves little at all intact except a kind of faith beyond reason, as Oedipus becomes a source of reveration in the *Oedipus at Colonus.* Oedipus, the political figure, is transformed into Oedipus, the mythic figure, one who belongs in no city but whose story belongs to all cities, because it is the story of any city, of every human house.

The paradox of Oedipus thus resides in the fact that as a model for conventional symbolism and the benefits it can confer upon those who respect its boundaries and use it in their search for knowledge, Oedipus calls the system into question. He exemplifies not only a political psychology, but also a mythic psychology, if only because his search for knowledge in the interests of the *polis* tells him nothing more important—indeed, tells him nothing other—than the fact that he is a member of the *muthos* of the ruling family of Thebes, a fact which is revealed only at the crucial point of discovery toward the end of the play when "all has come clear."[9] In a political perspective, nothing "comes clear" in this play, since it tells the story of an impossible city; and in a mythical perspective, the goal is not clarity but rather the relation between appearances and forms on the one hand and underlying truths on the other. The movement of Oedipus to the status of myth is indicative of the fact that his story and that of the city require nothing more and nothing less than being told, for the telling itself, the repeated reminder of what the external forms of the city are reposing on and covering over, is the very value of myth. Oedipus' ultimate failure to save the city, at least in the way he had envisioned at the play's outset, is as much a commentary on the incompatible halves of his role as it is a result of his ignorance of his own origins. For not only does the Theban king attempt to be the city's stabilizer, its prop from the outside which assures its survival, he also ends up being an inside member of the city he is trying to protect from the outside.

Oedipus is thus the city's representative in a double and incompatible sense: he wishes to *re-place* the city's external stability, to be able, as before, to place it firmly in the vertical position (ὀρθός, "aright" or "erect") which it theoretically wants to be able to maintain forever as a combatant of obscurity and of the horizontal, the position not only of the dead man but also that of the house in ruins, since it implies a motion along the line of the Earth's surface, the direction of non-differentiation from a state of nature; but by the terms of his story, he also *replaces* the city's internal disorder with his own suffering, so that the relation which links him to the city, one which he believes to be based on a link between outside (Oedipus as representative) and inside (the city as represented) is in fact an internally motivated relation (ὀρθός, "right" or "correct" in the sense that Plato uses the term in the *Cratylus* to describe the theoretical relation of equality or resemblance which Cratylus wants to establish between words and their referents).[10]

Indeed, the tragic home and the language of the Symbolists are both ultimately caught up in the dilemma of their own double ambition of rightness: if the house must remain upright to be distinguished from the state of nature, language too must stand for what it represents: *stand* for its sake and, inevitably, *stand for* it, replace it. So that when language begins to wish to correspond in some sort of "right" way to what it represents, when it aims to be something correct and appropriate to its content as well as being something erected in order to mark the place of that content, it finds itself in the very dilemma which Oedipus, the double replacer of his city's woes, embodies.

Indeed, Oedipus, the representative of a political home in danger, Thebes, is also the representative of the very dichotomy which is at the basis of the individual home, itself an organizing unit in a symbolic system which assures the survival across time of the individual family name and all that adheres thereto. Home depends first of all upon the creation of a space within which there is no mediation or need for mediation between individuals who are related to one another by kinship and homogeneity (literally, belonging to the same family or *genos*). It depends upon the setting forth of a locality which gives the impression either of a non-differentiated space or of an infinite space, of a locus, therefore, which, despite a secondary organization of the house in terms of male and female, blood relation and affine relation, and other criteria of family, essentially relies for its cohesiveness upon the interchange-ability of its members, their belonging to an overriding paradigm which defines them first of all—in time, that is, at the beginning of their life, if not ultimately in importance—as members of that paradigm, as bearers of that family name and all that it implies.

Thus the home creates first of all a metaphorical link between its members, a link by which all individuals within the home "are like" each other and indeed "like" each other enough to function as a unit. At the same time as the home creates a unifying, metaphorical relation among its members, it also presupposes the need for a mediation between the unit which each home defines and those defined by other homes, in order for each individual home to survive as a guarantor of a fixed identity (the family name), to retain its status as an identity-creating and identity-assuring unit, and also in order to replenish the very life the mortality of which is one of the original impulses for the creation of the home.

Whence the problematic nature, for the home, of the concept of self: in its creation of a sacred space, the house seeks on the one hand to preclude the necessity for the mediation of a concept of self, since all members of a household are considered to be analogous insofar as they work to *sustain* life in common with their family members—the positive goal of the kinship bond, the mutual protection offered by the family grouping—but not to *create* life with them—the restriction which the kinship taboo implies. On the other hand, in its setting of a lasting and overriding identity purely for the purpose of the combination of its members with members of other households, that is, the creation of a system of ordering, of combination through difference, or syntax, the house seems to define "self" *only* in terms of other and self, like the concepts of *xenia* and *symbolon* in terms of a split, albeit a potentially productive one, a split whose very point of departure resides in the finite nature of the individual who must be defined as an integral "unit" (a non-divisible and clearly delineated self) only because that unit is not self-sufficient, because, precisely, its creation is a recognition of the mortality of the individual whom it forms and to whom it conforms.

Thus the boundaries of the house, like those of the self, create an illusion of infinity within them—or perhaps before them, before their existence and their necessity are recognized—all the while, by virtue of their existence, they allude to the finitude of each household member, the finite nature of mortal existence. The concept of self upon which the house must depend can be seen, like Oedipus as the representative and also the attacker of a conventional symbolic system, as existing purely in order to go beyond itself, that is, in order to transcend the very limitations upon which it depends.

Indeed, the house as an identifying unit has failed in one of its fundamental tasks if it does not send its members outside of it in order to create or to support other houses, and itself receive others from houses outside of it in order to support its own survival, a sending and a receiving which are the very essence of syntax. Those that are sent from house to house and those that are received in a home that is not their own thus continue life on the inside of a house which they must at least initially think of as other. Claude Lévi-Strauss hypothesizes an analogy between language and kinship systems as exchange networks:

> Now, these results can be achieved only by treating marriage regulations and kinship as a kind of language, a set of processes permitting the establishment, between individuals and groups, of a certain type of communication. That the mediating factor, in this case, should be the *women of the group,* who are *circulated* between clans, lineages, or families, in place of the *words of the group,* which are *circulated* between the individuals, does not at all change the fact that the essential aspect of the phenomenon is identical in both cases.[11]

That the communication system of which Lévi-Strauss speaks is one composed uniquely of *women* circulating from house of origin to house of procreation does not change the essential paradox of the home which, while it is principally thought of as a stopping place, also functions to send its members onto the road in order to find another stopping place elsewhere, since the stop (home) requires motion in order to avoid the solipsism of incest, in order to assure a communication and a "pushing forward" (pro-creation) of its meaning, the life it works to foster and protect. Indeed, that Oedipus unwittingly equates his house of origin and his house of procreation not by importing a woman who comes from another house but rather by returning himself to the house his mother has never left since her marriage—thus in a sense by negating his traveling from house (Thebes) to house (Corinth) insofar as his journey ends where it began—once again recalls the link between incest and the violations of the syntax of a normative system of communication, be it verbal or familial, since Lévi-Strauss' analogy is based upon a normative syntax of women and words which regulates and controls their movements.

The house is thus analogous to a unit of a symbolic system in that through its necessary participation in a syntax, it regularly sends its members outside of itself for the very meaning—the guarantee and continuation of a marked identity whereby life may be replenished by a combination of individuals coming from two distinct paradigms—which its existence proposes to assure. The house exists only to create elsewhere, outside of itself, and by means of a conventional conjoinment of outside to inside, the feeling that only the inside of the house, the assembler of units grouped through their sameness of identity and paradigm, thus through metaphor, can create.

Indeed, the *symbolon* is nothing other than a formal token which characterizes perfectly the relation of each individual home to other homes, a relation that is as important in terms of traveling through the various life stages by means of the various individual identities furnished by one's house of origin and one's house(s) of procreation as it is in terms of traveling on the road with the support offered by various guest-host relationships. The *symbolon*, like the tragic view of home which is presented by the *Oedipus Tyrannus*, attempts to accomplish the unaccomplishable: to base the re-creation of a home upon the very separation from home which necessitates a search for it and a return to it. The two halves of the *symbolon* exist only as a means of re-activating an ideal relationship (guest-host) by effecting an identification; it is an external criterion whereby one *xenos* recognizes another and begins his effort to make him forget what, thanks to the *symbolon,* he has just been recognized as, that is, a *xenos.* The host-*xenos* thus tries to create a home-away-from-home, a home that simultaneously *is* home by convention (the recognition assured by the two fitted halves of the *symbolon*) and is *not* home precisely because of its need for an awareness of conventions, of *comings-together* of externally joined parts.

As Jean-Pierre Vernant has pointed out in examining the tandem relation which the Greeks believed to exist between the two seemingly opposed divine forces, Hestia (goddess of the hearth) and Hermes (god of the message): "Because her fate is to reign, forever immobile, at the centre of the domestic sphere, Hestia implies in contrast and in communion with her, the swift-footed god who rules the realm of the traveller."[12] The tragic home exists as a point of departure and as a point of arrival, as an agent and a goal. And Oedipus' *symbolon* linking house to house, Thebes to Corinth and Corinth to Thebes and thus each city to itself at a double remove, confuses at least at some level the notions of departure and arrival. It is the mechanism *par excellence* which shows the dangers of "symbolizing," the dangers of any *symbolon* which, both split and unified, both double and single, mediates between two beings who are simultaneously native to each other and foreign to each other, who are connected both by a relation of necessity and by one of arbitrariness and arbitration.

ii. Symbolism as Tragedy

The enemy of the Symbolist poet as much as of the tragic hero is the arbitrary: Mallarmé's attempt to abolish "le hasard" is nothing if not a reflection of his essentially tragic goal of creating an ideal world within his poetry in which nothing is left to chance, but which is a kind of ideal transformation of the fullness and the potential that can never be realized in brute experience or in brute language, "le langage brut." And just as Oedipus' overvaluing of his own ideal system of logic—his naming of himself "the child of Chance"[13] being an indication that he wishes to govern the arbitrary by being the supreme and consummate arbiter in all things—leads to an exaltation of the human which comes dangerously close to equating it with the divine, Mallarmé's excessive ambition of determining every element within his poetic domain is yet another form of tragic heroism.

That Mallarmé in his poetic undertaking is essentially a heroic and a tragic figure has been remarked upon—although almost always in a parenthetical way, and with a great variety of meanings—by a large number of Mallarmé critics, including some of the most renowned. The word "tragic" applied to Mallarmé seems to have meant things quite as varied as it has in the minds of Steiner, Nietzsche, and Goldmann. Some critics speak of Mallarmé's tragic side in terms of hopelessness, suffering, and negation, like Georges Poulet describing Mallarmé's vision of himself in the early poem "Les Fenêtres":

> On one side of this window-glass, the poet; on the other, his image magically transformed into that of an inhabitant of the Azure: "I look at myself and find that I am an angel..." Let us not fail to recognize the tragic character of this hypostasis. It is thus that a damned person would see himself in dream in Paradise.[14]

Similarly, Maurice Blanchot speaks of Mallarmé in terms closely recalling tragic heroism: " 'En creusant le vers,' le poète entre dans ce temps de la détresse qui est celui de l'absence des dieux . . . vit dans l'intimité de cette absence, en devient responsable."[15] And Jean-Pierre Richard, against whose description of Mallarméan "happiness" Gérard Genette reacts in posing the question of "Le Bonheur de Mallarmé?" in *Figures I*,[16] sums up (and rejects) the frequent description of Mallarmé as negative tragic figure:

> Le vrai bonheur mallarméen, affirmons-le bien haut contre tant de commentaires tragiques et partiaux, n'est pas celui d'un vide en lequel le monde entier tendrait à disparaître . . . : c'est celui d'une vie qui jouit, en toute conscience, en tout savoir, de la seule grâce qui lui soit évidemment accordée, celle de vivre.[17]

Although there may be few who would fully concur with Richard's view of Mallarmé as a figure at the center of whom is an affirmation of the enjoyment of life, there are many who speak of Mallarmé and the Symbolists in terms of an affirmation similar to that of tragic heroism. A. J. Lehmann emphasizes the Symbolists' insistence upon absolute freedom, certainly an element of tragic heroism:

> In Paris in the '90's, . . . a whole group of writers and artists proclaimed that each man was a law unto himself.[18]

> [Symbolism] is a refusal to be bound by the conventions of writing.[19]

> The writer, in that complex of literary developments which we call Symbolism, was seeking his liberty as a creator, and would pay any price for it.[20]

Marcel Raymond speaks in similar terms of Mallarmé's particular search for an absolute:

> Tirer de soi, en toute conscience, un objet intangible, c'est rêver qu'on échappe "aux fatalités à son existence départies par le malheur," à la bassesse et à l'imperfection du monde, au *hasard,* et que l'on a créé un absolu.[21]

Robert Greer Cohn is one of the most important of Mallarmé critics to apply the term "tragic" to the poet's work:

> *Aboli*: one of his favorite terms, implying a tragically noble defeat.[22]

> This desperate image of a dead star which *could* have shone . . . is the tragic beauty of the swan song that runs throughout *Hérodiade.*[23]

> This eternal drama of sunset . . . is something of both Tragedy—"LA TRAGEDIE DE LA NATURE," (1169)—and Comedy. . . . Life goes on. And if he has not won the total struggle for self-expression which he, of all poets, repeatedly confronted, . . . well, that is bitterly disappointing but it cannot be helped.[24]

In Cohn's terms, Mallarmé is the tragic hero who is inevitably but nobly defeated, whose defeat essentially points out the nobility of his ambition and of his attempt. As James Lawler puts it in his description of Mallarmé: "Poetry is a tragic struggle carried on in full consciousness against the nothingness which we know to be the truth about the universe."[25] And no less a figure than Paul Valéry affirms this nobility of Mallarmé's enterprise in terms of heroism:

> Personne n'avait confessé, avec cette précision, cette constance et cette assurance héroïque, l'éminente dignité de la Poésie, hors de laquelle il n'apercevait que le hasard. . . .[26]

There is in fact no critic who speaks of Mallarmé in heroic and tragic terms as compellingly as Mallarmé himself. Implicitly, and relentlessly, Mallarmé's ambition to forge a superhuman language brings him close to the gods:

> Cette prohibition [the existence of different, "imperfect" languages and the lack of one ideal one] sévit expresse, dans la nature . . . que ne vaille de raison pour se considérer Dieu.[27]

If the necessity of speaking a "fallen" language is but one symptom of mortality, a state which refuses us the luxury of "considering ourselves God," conversely, the forging of an ideal language through poetry would result in a kind of human divinization, the very domain of the tragic hero. Indeed, Mallarmé's description of divinity as something which is never anything but itself ("La Divinité, qui jamais n'est que Soi"[28]) is remarkably appropriate to the dream of tragic heroism, the dream of being always and only oneself, defined by nothing exterior to oneself.

"Moi projeté absolu,"[29] the formula of "Igitur," is yet another definition of Mallarmé's tragic ambition, an ambition both glorious and unreachable; glorious as a "projection," a project which itself almost takes on the value of an absolute, and unreachable because a "projected" absolute, which would presumably establish a relation (and therefore a relativity) between projecting subject and projected object, would no longer be an absolute. Mallarmé's seeing himself as a projected absolute recalls his wanting to throw ("jeter") the dice one final, apocalyptic time in "Un coup de dés jamais n'abolira le hasard," in his project of "Le Livre," and, in fact, throughout his work, a throw which would put an end to all throws. And the image of these famous dice which never cease to haunt him are not so very far from the image of the *symbolon* itself: that which, divided, must be reunited with its other half in order to yield meaning; that which, a product of relativity and contingency (chance), longs to put an end to the arbitrary. The enigmatic, which is at the heart of the story of Oedipus and perhaps of Tragedy in general, is never far from Mallarmé's enterprise; as he himself says: "Il doit y avoir toujours énigme dans la poésie."[30]

Moreover, when Mallarmé describes his vision of ideal art, he does so in terms recalling Tragedy and even suggesting at times that he wishes to bring it back. In speaking of Richard Wagner's innovations in the domain of opera, Mallarmé says: "Avec une piété antérieure, un public pour la seconde fois depuis les temps, hellénique d'abord, maintenant germain, considère le secret, représenté, d'origines."[31] One wonders whether, beyond the Greeks and the Germans, Mallarmé is not envisaging a "staged secret of origins"—a wonderful description of Tragedy—for a French audience; whether, indeed, such a staging is not a secret ambition of his poetry.

Mallarmé's fascination with origins—one of the most important of concepts for Tragedy—is perhaps most apparent in his fascination with etymology, which Gérard Genette has called "cratylisme secondaire" after the Platonic dialogue featuring Socrates arguing with the proponents of two divergent views of language: Hermogenes, the Saussurian before the fact who believes in and accepts the necessity of a purely conventional link between words and things, and Cratylus, who believes that words somehow imitate things and do not simply represent them conventionally. Both Cratylus and Hermogenes believe language to be quite sufficient, each in his own conception of it; but the position of Socrates is, according to Genette, neither that of Cratylus nor that of Hermogenes, but rather one very close to that of Mallarmé:

> L'"anticratylisme" de Socrate n'est donc pas un hermogénisme. . . . Socrate est donc . . . un cratyliste déçu, et, comme on sait, *mécontent*. Sa querelle . . . annonce de manière frappante la querelle de Mallarmé. . . .
>
> Je propose de baptiser cette attitude *cratylisme* (ou *mimologisme*) *secondaire*, pour le désir presque irrésistible qu'on y éprouve de *corriger* d'une manière ou d'une autre cette erreur du nomothète que Mallarmé appelle le "défaut des langues" —et donc d'établir ou rétablir dans le langage, par quelque artifice, l'état de nature que le cratylisme "primaire," celui de Cratyle, croit naïvement y voir encore ou déjà établi.[32]

Mallarmé's desire to "correct" language is a sort of implicit criticism of the original linking of words and things, a criticism almost inevitably leveled against the *nomothetes,* the original legislator or arbiter between words and things. Even Socrates himself is forced to admit that he does not really know who or what is responsible for this original link, although he says that the Tragedians would surely know:

> That objects should be imitated in letters and syllables, and so find expression, may appear ridiculous, Hermogenes, but it cannot be avoided—there is no better principle to which we can look for the truth of first names. Deprived of this, we must have recourse to divine help, like the tragic poets, who in any perplexity have their Gods waiting in the air; and must get out of our difficulty in like fashion, by saying that "the Gods gave the first names, and therefore they are right."[33]

Socrates is here saying that for the tragic poets, the original link between words and things, that is, the rightness of original names, is attributable to the gods; which amounts to saying that if a poet like Mallarmé himself attempts to reconstruct (or to construct for the first time) the rightness of original names, he is not relying on the gods as guarantors of linguistic rightness but rather appropriating their role for himself.

Mallarmé is then not only a tragic poet—one who puts heroes onstage— but also, and more fundamentally, a tragic hero, his own principal character. As a sort of initiator into the Mysteries, Mallarmé is also a kind of initiate himself, since he must first uncover—or at least glimpse—the mystery of the non-arbitrary relation between words and things before he can reveal it to his readers. Mallarmé's going beyond the limits of human language as an ordering, intellectual tool ends up in an almost unprecedented immersion in poetic mysticism, a mysticism which requires a certain amount of faith from its followers because it does not seem to provide any real positive system of belief outside of itself, even though it is a transformation of and a paradigm for the non-ideal world.

This mystifying element of Mallarmé's poetry has often been commented on: but has it been said frequently enough that his is an essentially mythifying poetry as well? It would be difficult to overemphasize the importance of myth for Mallarmé, not of the particulars and details of any one myth, nor even a general corpus of national myths, but rather of the functions that myth fulfills. The poet himself comments on this:

[L'esprit français] répugne, en cela d'accord avec l'Art dans son intégrité, qui est inventeur, à la Légende. . . . A moins que la Fable, vierge de tout, lieu, temps et personne sus, ne se dévoile empruntée au sens latent en le concours de tous, celle inscrite sur la page des Cieux et dont l'Histoire même n'est que l'interprétation, vaine, c'est-à-dire, un Poëme, l'Ode. Quoi! le siècle ou notre pays, qui l'exalte, ont dissous par la pensée les Mythes, pour en refaire! Le Théâtre les appelle, non: pas de fixes, ni de séculaires, et de notoires, mais un, dégagé de personnalité, car il compose notre aspect multiple.[34]

Myth thus has both a positive and a negative constituent for Mallarmé: the function that it fulfills is that of revealing the underlying, unchanging sense of things, since History is nothing more than the "vain interpretation" of the fable printed on the heavenly Page. But any *specific* myth, any story which takes place with "a known time, place, and person," is not a myth at all in the positive Mallarméan sense of the term, since it, too, is a "vain interpretation," temporally and geographically bound and not eternal and universal.

It is only in the hypothesized *unity* ("mais un, dégagé de personnalité") of a newly forged, completely non-specific mythology that the *multiplicity* of human nature can be rendered, for it is only in the abstracting of all particulars of myth that the *purity* of the mythic function ("vierge de tout") can appear. To that extent Mallarmé's use of myth precisely copies his ambition to purify thought by reaching the perfect generality (and, by implication, the unity) of the Idea, an ambition which A. J. Lehmann aptly describes:

From the description he gives of the Idea, there cannot be much doubt that he is referring to something like a Platonic Idea; the recipe for reaching the "Idea" of a flower would seem to be to abstract from one's mind one by one every feature which serves to distinguish one flower from another. . . . The question remains, however, whether once these abstractions have been made, anything is left over at all.[35]

Reaching the Idea of a flower would be to reach its "sens latent," the meaning which underlies every flower, named or unnamed, but which is covered by any particular extant flower in that each individual is separated from the idea which generated it. Lehmann is quite correct to point out the similarity of Mallarmé's system to Plato's, at least at one level: in both cases the rejection of *particular* myths occurs in tandem with the embracing—perhaps unconscious— of the underlying function of myth, that is, the return to the underlying sense, the "sens latent" of the phenomenal world.

Even more central to Mallarmé's poetry than his ambition of creating a "unified" mythology and a "unified" Idea is his desire to reach a "unified" language, and here the importance of myth is absolutely capital:

> Les langues imparfaites en cela que plusieurs, manque la suprême: penser étant écrire sans accessoires, ni chuchotement mais tacite encore l'immortelle parole, la diversité, sur terre, des idiomes empêche personne de proférer les mots qui, sinon se trouveraient, par une frappe unique, elle-même matériellement la vérité . . . *Seulement, sachons n'existerait pas le vers*: lui, philosophiquement rémunère le défaut des langues, complément supérieur.[36]

What poetry aims to transcend is the *divided* nature of human language, its fallen state, its separation from a unified, underlying source. The existence of "several" languages, like the existence of many particular myths, undercuts the possibility that any one extant language or any one particular myth might reach the status of an ideal, since an ideal in this case would underlie every individual manifestation generated by it. Only if the "several" languages could be brought back to one unified and unique source could an ideal language be forged. "L'idéal serait donc de proférer, mais cette fois en pleine conscience, le mot premier, ce mot d'avant Babel d'où dérivent peut-être toutes les langues actuelles."[37] And it is here that Mallarmé's beliefs are colored by nineteenth-century events in the study of language.

The fledgling field of linguistics, which had discovered the existence of Sanskrit around the turn of the nineteenth century, provided Mallarmé with what was considered to be the "langue mère dont tous les idiomes modernes auraient procédé,"[38] thereby giving him a very central element of his own mythology of language, his belief in the existence of a seminal, originary Indo-European language. This belief is apparent as well in his semi-translation, semi-redaction of the preface to "Les Dieux antiques" entitled "Origine et développement de la mythologie," in which he attributes the *particularities* of modern languages—their individual, fallen state—to the separation of tribes who had once lived together and whose words, *like their myths,* had a common origin:

> Quelle est la conclusion à tirer . . . , sinon que les légendes de toutes ces nations ont une seule source commune? . . . Comme le temps marcha, et que les peuples

se séparèrent, le vieux sens s'oblitéra, totalement ou partiellement. Je le répète: tant que ces antiques peuplades demeurèrent au même lieu, il n'y eut pas à craindre que les termes qu'elles employaient pour parler entre elles fussent mal compris; mais le temps alla, les tribus se dispersèrent. . . . et il arriva que toutes gardèrent les noms donnés jadis au soleil et aux nuages et à toute chose, alors que la significa-tion de ces noms était presque perdue.[39]

Returning words to their "old sense" ("le vieux sens") is thus tantamount to creating a unified, "supreme" mythology.

Charles Chassé, who is one of the first to have remarked upon the centrality of the Littré dictionary to Mallarmé's poetry, also comments upon the poet's desire to re-establish in some sense the ancestral language of which modern languages are in his eyes nothing more than a pale derivative:

Un des plus magnifiques sortilèges qui pourraient lui permettre de se libérer de [sa] servitude ne serait-il pas, pour lui, de recréer la langue universelle des lointains ancêtres et de reprendre ainsi contact avec le passé?[40]

It is in this sense that Mallarmé finds himself in a double bind: on the one hand he wishes to forge an ideal language, one which manifests its relation to what is seen as a unified past and, by so doing, re-establishes the now-lost relation between words and things ("la signification de ces noms était presque perdue"). On the other hand, if language were indeed "suprême" and "univer-selle," "n'existerait pas le vers": only the fallen state of language requires (and allows) its own correction. Only the separation of the present from what is viewed as being an originary past (not simply a past which is another, equal point in time) leads the poet in search of that past. If the *symbolon* is origi-nally a device by means of which the idea of home is meant to be able to be transported and replicated away from itself, if the *symbolon* of normative symbolic systems presumes an absence from a real home and therefore the replication of an idealized home-away-from-home, a replica which brings forth the idea of the absent home while recognizing it as absent, Mallarmé's ideal language wishes to re-create with each use of each word the idea of the thing named, that is to say, have it simultaneously as an idea and as a genuine presence, not merely to call to it from a distance, but to evoke it in such a way that the words which make up each poem create a kind of ideal world as well as a sensual one, a world built out of the units of an extant, fallen language but which as a unified structure reaches the status of an ideal.

Thus one of the central paradoxes of Mallarmé's ambition is that the poet wishes to use conventional language, to use what he perceives as a scientific and systematic body of information about words—particularly their etymologies —in order to allow language to reach the status of myth; to use the particu-larities of language to return it to an absolute, ideal, generalized state. And this is precisely the procedure of Tragedy: to push reason and science to their limits, to the place at which they necessarily (and unbeknownst to themselves) rejoin belief and myth. Nietzsche, in his influential early essay "The Birth of Tragedy," speaks of the relations between scientific and tragic thought:

> If ancient tragedy was diverted from its course by the dialectical desire for know-ledge and the optimism of science, this fact might lead us to believe that there is an eternal conflict between *the theoretic* and *the tragic world view*; and only after the spirit of science has been pursued to its limits, and its claim to universal validity destroyed by the evidence of these limits may we hope for a rebirth of tragedy.... 41

It is not coincidental that this essay came to life at the same time (1872) that Symbolism was about to flourish and Mallarmé himself was entering his "hermetic" period. Though it would be difficult and ultimately unnecessary to demonstrate any direct influence of Nietzsche on Mallarmé, the phenome-non of which the former speaks in his essay is one which holds true for an entire era and the whole of industrial Europe. The *birth* of Tragedy does not of course seem to have occurred in any *obvious* way at the time; and yet its impulse, announced by Nietzsche's essay, inhabits much of the work of the end of the nineteenth century and the beginning of the twentieth, and up to our day, and indeed coexists with the very scientific impulse against which it is partially a reaction.

Indeed, Charles Chassé describes the conditions of Mallarmé's era in terms reminiscent of Nietzsche's:

> Cette hésitation entre le mysticisme et le positivisme est justement très carac-téristique des hommes de sa génération, qui, élevés dans le culte de la raison, ont assisté vers 1885 à l'éclosion du mouvement symboliste et ont senti les opinions de leur adolescence très ébranlées par le désir de croire.42

The positivistic spirit which Chassé here points to as one of the operative poles of Mallarmé's generation is in fact a part of what Nietzsche calls the "theoretic world view," a point of view which believes the world to be ultimately compre-hensible and describable, to be a locus of experimentation in which ever-increasing domains of knowledge can be circumscribed and classified, whether it be by the nineteenth- and twentieth-century revolution in science or by the philosophical revolution brought about by Socrates and Plato. And mysticism, "the desire to believe," is a succinct definition of Nietzsche's "tragic world view." The Symbolism of Mallarmé, like fifth-century Tragedy, was partially formed by the conflict between these two forces.

Jean-Pierre Vernant speaks of Tragedy in a way which clearly demonstrates its relation to scientific and philosophical thought, indeed to any mathe-matically based system:

Cette logique philosophique . . . admet que de deux propositions contradictoires, si l'une est vraie, l'autre doit nécessairement être fausse. L'homme tragique apparaît de ce point de vue solidaire d'une autre logique qui n'établit pas une coupure aussi tranchée entre le vrai et le faux . . . , puisqu'elle ne cherche pas, sur les questions qu'elle examine, à démontrer l'absolue validité d'une thèse, mais à construire *dissoì lógoi,* des discours doubles qui, dans leur opposition, se combattent sans se détruire.[43]

That Vernant is here attempting to explain Plato's hostility to Tragedy provides yet another link to the modern era: for if anything in the modern world is opposed fundamentally to *dissoì lógoi,* to doubled words which say *neither* yes nor no, it is the field of cybernetics, the unparalleled complexity of which cannot cover over the fact of being based on answering either yes or no to every bit of information given it. What Tragedy is opposed to is any binary system of thought, whether it leads to a Platonic dialogue or a computer program, any system by which yes is always or simply yes and no always or simply no; because Tragedy exists to demonstrate the insufficiency of such answers, the falseness of any simple choice.

Indeed, Nietzsche's analysis of the forces in conflict at the heart of Tragedy, the Apollonian and the Dionysian, the forces of light and darkness, or of appearance and what underlies appearance, is close to Gilbert Durand's characterization of "le régime diurne" and "le régime nocture," and both pairings are appropriate in a consideration of Mallarmé's all-important ideal of the white page:

On peut dire qu'il n'y a pas de lumière sans ténèbres alors que l'inverse n'est pas vrai: la nuit ayant une existence symbolique autonome. Le Régime Diurne de l'image se définit donc d'une façon générale comme le régime de l'antithèse.[44]

Both Nietzsche's and Durand's depictions of the relation of light to darkness go to the heart of the Mallarméan ideal of the white page. That writing necessitates the creation of a series of antitheses between the blank page and the ink that divides it up is clear, and the antitheses are of course more than simply visual: they are also what divides the timeless and infinite potential of silence from the boundedness of individual speech acts. That Mallarmé covets the blank page is indicative of an ambition that is both Apollonian and Dionysian, or perhaps of one which, like Tragedy, would merge the two deities, which would go through Apollo, the god of reason, of the sun, of law, and of *system,* to get to Dionysus, the god of delirium, of dark-colored wine, of the mysteries, and of *chaos.* Is Mallarmé's dream of the white page which, we must assume, would be re-created in a perfect poem by the black ink upon it, not essentially a tragic dream, a dream that creates or uses antitheses only to prove their limitations?

In his essay "Hamlet," Mallarmé gives what is clearly a description of himself and his own tragic spirit as much as a description of Shakespeare's famous prince, surely one of the most important and influential tragic figures of the nineteenth century:

> La nostalgie de la prime sagesse inoubliée malgré les aberrations que cause l'orage battant la plume délicieuse de sa toque, voilà le caractère peut-être et l'invention du jeu de ce contemporain qui tire de l'instinct parfois indéchiffrable à lui-même des éclairs de scoliaste. Ainsi m'apparaît rendue la dualité morbide qui fait le cas d'Hamlet, oui, fou en dehors et sous la flagellation contradictoire du devoir, mais s'il fixe en dedans les yeux sur une image de soi qu'il garde intacte autant qu'une Ophélie jamais noyée, elle! prêt toujours à se ressaisir.[45]

It is not only Hamlet who straddles the domains of folly ("fou en dehors") and hyperconsciousness ("une image de soi"), for such is also the position of Mallarmé's own poetry, perpetually on the point of leading its readers into new levels of awareness and also of lapsing into madness and non-expression by virtue of its own excessive ambition. And Mallarmé is also a figure whose often "undecipherable instinct" can lead to scholarly discoveries, a poet whose own "tragic theory," much like that of Nietzsche and that of Vernant, relies on a paradox of an antithesis which refuses to formulate itself fully, or rather on a refusal of all clear antitheses:

> Voilà une théorie tragique actuelle ou, pour mieux dire, la dernière: le drame, latent, ne se manifeste que par une déchirure affirmant l'irréductibilité de nos instincts.[46]

Mallarmé's interest in Tragedy is largely manifested through his fascination with the theater:

> Un livre, dans notre main, s'il énonce quelque idée auguste, supplée à tous les théâtres, non par l'oubli qu'il en cause mais les rappelant impérieusement, au contraire. Le ciel métaphorique qui se propage à l'entour de la foudre du vers, artifice par excellence au point de simuler peu à peu et d'incarner les héros . . . c'est bien le pur de nous-mêmes par nous porté, toujours prêt à jaillir à l'occasion qui dans l'existence ou hors l'art fait toujours défaut.[47]

If, in Mallarmé's teleology, the Book is the last and highest possible form of development, we might add that in his literary system, the highest point of development would be the theater, as Thibaudet points out: "Si tout n'existe que pour aboutir à un livre, le livre lui-même n'existe, d'un point de vue, que pour aboutir à un théâtre."[48] It would be nothing more than borrowing the poet's own words to speak of the theater of the book, of the book as a replacement for a theater which, in its present state, could not be satisfactory. And indeed, it is appropriate that the ideal of the theater, like every Mallarméan ideal, exists not to be reached, but rather to be looked at with admiration and regret as what might have been rather than as what might actually be.

It is certain that the theater of the day did not provide the apparatus necessary to express a tragic impulse, at least not in Mallarmé's perception of it:

> Avec l'impudence de faits divers en trompe-l'œil emplir le théâtre et exclure la Poésie, ses jeux sublimités (espoir toujours chez un spectateur) ne me semble besogne pire que la montrer en tant que je ne sais quoi de spécial au bâillement; ou instaurer cette déité dans tel appareil balourd et vulgaire est peut-être méritoire à l'égal de l'omettre.[49]

The expectations ("espoir toujours") of the audience and, we suspect, of the potential playwright himself will always be disappointed by the inferiority of the means at hand. Mallarmé's frustration at having to use the conventions of language would have been only magnified had he had recourse to the conventions of the theater available to him, as Thibaudet remarks: "Le théâtre actuel est une convention lourde, de même que la poésie dont a voulu se délivrer Mallarmé."[50]

Indeed, the famous Tournon crisis of 1864-65 corresponds to a large extent to Mallarmé's abandonment of the theater—and of Tragedy in particular—as a viable artistic ideal. In March 1865 the poet-dramatist could still write to his friend Cazalis: "Je me suis mis sérieusement à ma tragédie d'*Hérodiade*,"[51] and if, seven months later, he writes again saying, "Je commence *Hérodiade*, non plus tragédie, mais poëme,[52] are we to believe that the tragic conception of the piece has disappeared without leaving a trace?

In fact, in spite of his early abandonment of the two theatrical projects of *Hérodiade* and *L'Après-midi d'un Faune*,[53] Mallarmé's disappointment with the theater of his time does not result in a total rejection of theater as a medium; rather, the poet was fascinated with the theater during much of his life, as Haskell Block points out:

> It is not easy to see in this difficult and withdrawn poet the figure of a dramatist, but any overall view of Mallarmé's development must consider his continuous and intimate affiliation with the theater.[54]

Indeed, even though Mallarmé does not seem to have actualized his interest in the theater in a very concrete way, it can at least be said that he made use of a fertile confusion between the poetic and, if not the theatrical, at least the dramatic. As Block puts it:

> Dramatic poetry is not poetic drama, but the line of demarcation is fluid and imprecise. . . . drama is a permanent element of poetry. . . . Mallarmé saw . . . the separation of poetry from the theater as a misfortune that all poets should strive

to remedy. Therefore, the dramatic poem represents an effort to keep alive the ancient alliance between poetry and drama until the conditions of the theater will again make possible their dynamic interplay.[55]

Mallarmé's view of the theater makes of it a sort of go-between linking his own tragic impulse—which was never to be expressed in a conventionally theatrical mode despite his several unsuccessful attempts to write poetry for the theater—and the poetry which he in fact produced as much in the theatrical sense of "staged" or "put on" as in the divine sense of "created" or "brought to life." Thibaudet comments on the relation between Mallarmé's "Livre" and theater: "Sa doctrine du théâtre est l'efflorescence, la rêverie et comme la fumée indéfinie de sa vision du Livre."[56] And Mallarmé himself speaks of the theatrical nature of his poetry:

> [Le haut poëme] ne remplace tout que faute de tout. J'imagine que la cause de s'assembler, dorénavant, en vue de fêtes inscrites au programme humain, ne sera pas le théâtre, borné ou incapable tout seul de répondre à de très subtils instincts, ni la musique du reste, trop fuyante pour ne pas décevoir la foule; mais à soi fondant ce que ces deux isolent de vague et de brutal, l'Ode, dramatisée ou coupée savamment; ces scènes héroïques une ode à plusieurs voix.[57]

Since "festivals scheduled on the human agenda"—perhaps some future descendents of the festival of Dionysus?—would gather people around a "high poem" and not around an amphitheater, can we not speak of the tragic nature of such a poem?

Moreover, the fact that each of Mallarmé's "hauts poëmes"—certainly the Alexandrine sonnets and the longer poems—contains "plusieurs voix" is perhaps the most theatrical characteristic of his poetry, and one moreover which is once again reminiscent of Nietzsche's description of Tragedy as straddling the Apollonian and the Dionysian. Thibaudet comments on this double aspect of Mallarmé's poetry, fused in the poet's "doctrine du théâtre": "Le théâtre lui paraissait le lieu de . . . synthèse" between the two basic constituents of poetry, "la poésie du Livre, écrite pour les yeux, inclinée par là vers les images visuelles, plastiques,—et la poésie telle que ses origines sociales et sa naissance individuelle la feraient: domaine de l'ouïe, musique verbale."[58] If the visual aspect of both the play and the poem is related to the necessity of dealing in appearance, the domain of Apollo, then the musical side of both is essentially Dionysian. The visual image *lasts* and *persists* and thus seems to be eternal; it is in the realm of the individual insofar as any opaque visual image excludes all other visual images by blocking them out. But the auditive impulse not only exists in time, but also avoids the process of individuation, since tones can mix together in a harmony which is at the same time one and many. And here again we return to the ideal of the white page, which is both Apollonian and Dionysian, Apollonian in its visual aspect, in its ambition of pure appearance, and Dionysian in that it wishes to produce a feeling of unity which transcends divisions.

The problem of multiple voice in Mallarmé's poetry is important not only insofar as it indicates a struggle of the Apollonian with the Dionysian, but also as an indication of the relation between reader and writer. Georges Poulet comments on the scenic nature of Mallarmé's poetry from this point of view:

> All is finally reduced to proving that there is no authentic installation of a poetic universe, unless the place of this universe is identified with the one of the poet, and unless what happens in the poem takes place, really place, in the being of him who writes, as well as in the being of him who reads.[59]

> There is no Mallarméan poem except for the moment when there is no longer on the one side the poem, and on the other a thought, with, between the two, "the vacant space facing the stage" . . . in a spectacle which is none other than "the spectacle of Self."[60]

Once again, Mallarmé's poetry may be seen as being built upon an antithesis which it aims to overcome: the separate identity of writer and reader, the very fact of which necessitates having recourse to a conventional system of communication by which the two may come together, is meant to be abolished by the communication itself in a "spectacle of Self," of a self which, true to the conception of self which the house and the *symbolon* provide, can be *itself* only by being *another,* writer to a reader or vice versa.

If the theater of the poem requires an equalization of reader and writer at some level, it must not be forgotten that this equalization must nonetheless be built upon the superior and idealized nature of the writer and the hero of the poem, who are always to be identified with each other at some level. Indeed, one of the complaints which Mallarmé had about the theater of his day was its lack of idealization, since in its debased state it could put onstage only characters who were replicas of those watching the play, and not idealized versions of them in whom they could understand their own ideal nature, that is, the gap between their present existence and the ideals underlying that existence: "pour leur communiquer l'assurance que rien n'existe qu'eux, demeurent sur la scène seulement des gens pareils aux spectateurs."[61] Very much like the theater, the poem thus requires a gap between reader and writer, or spectators and spectacle, a gap of idealism but one which exists in order to effect an eventual communion and communication between them.

Jean-Pierre Richard comments on the liminary status of the Mallarméan hero:

> La forme théâtrale, c'est bien ce corps réel, charnel, qui se découpe sur les planches; mais ce doit être aussi l'absence, ou plutôt le départ de ce corps, sa constante irréalisation en un personnage. L'acteur, comme plus tard le mot, existe à la fois concrètement et symboliquement. Sa présence se barde de signes, qui visent à nous la rendre fictive, abstraite: mais pourtant cette présence doit demeurer pour nous opaque, fascinante. . . . Dans le langage total du théâtre, l'acteur constitue donc une

sorte de signe idéal: assez plein pour faire pénétrer en nous l'évidence de son impact, mais assez effacé pour que cette évidence puisse glisser de lui au rôle qu'il soutient.[62]

The "actor"—a term which can be applied in a large sense to the hero or heroes, explicit or implicit, of each of Mallarmé's poems—forms an integral part of the "spectacle of Self" insofar as he exists as himself only in order to exist as other than himself. He lives "concretely," as an extant being with a single corporeal identity, and also "symbolically," as one-half of a *symbolon* which must be joined in a communication with its other half, the spectator or the reader, in order to fulfill its own reason for being. As Thibaudet remarks, "Le vrai théâtre va de la scène à la salle, englobe la salle dans une scène supérieure."[63] The stage is at least figuratively *higher* than the audience—and here the analogy to the poetry is particularly appropriate, since none of its readers, in all probability, feels quite "up to it" while in the process of reading it—only to lead them to a higher truth. A truth that may, indeed, like the truth that Oedipus learns, be nothing more than a realization of the nature of their own search for the truth: "Thus poem and reader, spectacle and spectator coalesce in one selfsame thought, which is very simply reflective thought."[64]

Not the least important connection between Mallarmé's poetry and tragic theater is that it is a poetry which puts an almost unprecedented burden on its readers, a burden of interpretation which makes the reading of the poem at least as difficult and time-consuming—indeed, as all-consuming—as the writing of it, a burden which may indeed lead to a sort of catharsis, an affirmation of language through an experiencing of its limitations. If we view Mallarmé's poetry, as he did, as a *pis-aller,* as bespeaking the need to externalize an impulse which resists the distinctions of external and internal in that it pushes one to dream of perceiving oneself "simple, infiniment sur la terre,"[65] we can at least allow that poetry to re-create an internal drama, a drama inside of us, "au seul théâtre de nous-mêmes, . . . là seulement, où nous sommes tragiques. . . ."[66] To this extent perhaps the best we can do with Mallarmé's poetry is to take seriously yet another of Thibaudet's descriptions of the poem as theater:

Au théâtre il ne doit exister, à des degrés et de manières différentes, que des acteurs. L'homme ne vient pas au théâtre pour consentir librement et par fiction à une illusion, il y doit venir pour entrer et vivre, tout entier, un temps, dans une vérité nouvelle. Ainsi un poème de Mallarmé est construit pour solliciter l'activité créatrice du lecteur et se développer par elle.[67]

If we are all "actors" it is because in a tragic perspective we are all miming what we cannot be essentially and yet cannot forget: "la Divinité, qui jamais n'est que Soi." That the writer needs the poem and the poem needs readers is yet another in a long series of proofs that he cannot be "only himself." And that we as readers take up the task of playing out the dramas suggested and elicited by Mallarmé's poetry, of playing them out without expecting—although not without hoping—to reach their meaning, is proof that we have understood the task, if not the goal. Or perhaps, like Tantalus, or like Oedipus who puts together the two halves of the *symbolon,* that the means is the meaning, the task is the goal.

Interface

Thus, two texts which are separated by an almost immesurable gap of time, place, and genre, both trying to face, each in its own way—and in the way of the other—the dual but unique problem of Tragedy and Symbolism: the tragedy of any symbolic system which exists only because the mind which has conceived it has done so only because it has first conceived of its own death as itself and the need to survive, if at all, as other than itself.

I have attempted to treat each of these two texts as if it were the other one. I have analyzed the *Oedipus Tyrannus* as if it were a long poem—which, I suspect, almost no one who has read it or seen it would deny its being—and, insofar as it is in part a meditation on the nature and status of human language and other symbolic systems, a Symbolist poem. And I have tried to "produce" ("reproduce"?) six of Mallarmé's Alexandrine sonnets as if they were miniature dramas—failed Tragedies whose own failures are part of their success—which demand a kind of scenario from their readers, indeed which ask the reader to occupy the empty stage which they evoke but refuse to build.

I am not only after a "home" in this study, and indeed I suspect that home, if anything, may simply provide the point of contact of these two texts, the place where the two halves of the *symbolon* meet. It will necessarily be an artificial, reconstituted home if it is one at all. And my decision to treat the two texts in separate chapters, with only the spirit of the *other* text inhabiting each analysis, has been made partially to avoid exacerbating the artificial nature of any explicit synthesis that does not recall the split which it is trying to overcome.

Indeed, I, too, would like to have it both ways. I would like the search for home to be an affirmation of home even as it is a downright failure at many levels. Because where I believe Oedipus and Mallarmé can really face each other and recognize each other as one is in their own status as reflexive searchers, as searchers after nothing more than themselves. "All that Oedipus learns —and all that he had to learn—was that he was ignorant."[1] "Thus poem and reader, spectacle and spectator coalesce in one selfsame thought, which is very simply reflective thought."[2] What Oedipus learns about, and what

Mallarmé learns about, and what we as observers of their dramas can learn about, is learning, and learning about learning need not be a failed enterprise. Perhaps it is, after all, the most human kind of learning, one which is in harmony with Heidegger's definition of human beings:

Who is Man? He who must show what he is.[3]

It is a definition which even the Sphinx would have been proud of: man is the creature who tries to define himself.

PART ONE

Asymmetrical Equality

The House of Life and the House of Death

Jailli de l'inconnu; plus de passé, plus de modèles, rien sur quoi m'appuyer; tout à créer, patrie, ancêtres . . . à inventer, à découvrir. Personne à qui ressembler, que moi-même. Que m'importe, dès lors, si je suis ou Grec ou Lorrain?

André Gide
Œdipe

Chapter One: Asymmetrical Equality in the *Oedipus Tyrannus*

All animals are equal but some are more equal than others.

George Orwell
Animal Farm

i. Mimetic Oedipus: the city and the gods

The first occurrence of a form of the word ἴσος in the play is one which well characterizes the paradox which Oedipus as the would-be creator of a self-contained symbolic system exemplifies:

θεοῖσι μέν νυν οὐκ ἰσούμενόν σ' ἐγὼ
οὐδ' οἴδε παῖδες ἐξόμεσθ' ἐφέστιοι.

We, I and these children here, do not
sit at your hearth [judging] you equal to the gods.[1]

Even as the priest erases the equation, Oedipus equals god, he states it as a possibility, since the very fact of having to negate it allows it, indeed compels it to enter into the realm of the conceivable. As Bernard Knox puts it:

> When the priest, in the opening scene, tells Oedipus that he regards him not as "equated to the gods" but as "first of men," he is attempting, by means of this careful distinction, to clarify and correct an ambiguity inherent in his own speech and action. The beginning of the play suggests in both verbal and visual terms that Oedipus is in fact regarded as "equated to the gods." . . .
> The equation is one that Oedipus does not reject.[2]

If Oedipus is thus defined with reference to the divine by what he is not precisely but resembles closely enough to require a formal negation of his equality to it, it is that his attempt to foster a stability similar to that of the gods has never yet been disproven, and that indeed, the play can be read at one level as his final and most compelling attempt to be once again "equal" to the image of himself which has been presented to the city (and to him), an image that will crumble retroactively if it can be shown to be invalid at any time.

That the fact of being always "equal to oneself" is essentially the characteristic of a god is demonstrated by the chorus's appeal to Athena, Artemis, and Apollo in the parodos, a plea in the course of which the Theban elders ask the triply invoked divinities to come to their aid once again if ever they have done so before:

εἴ ποτε καὶ προτέρας ἄτας ὕπερ ὀρνυμένας πόλει
ἠνύσατ᾽ ἐκτοπίαν φλόγα πήματος, ἔλθετε καὶ νῦν.

If ever because of earlier catastrophes rushing against the city
you warded off the flame of suffering, come now once again.[3]

The sentence as it stands is illogical. If the apodosis turns out to be untrue, that is, if the gods do *not* come again ("καὶ νῦν"), the sentence seems to say that they never will have come before ("προτέρας"), a possibility which we may fairly assume to be untrue given the gods' history of effectiveness in the city which pays them homage. It is as if on the gods' present assistance to the city depends the summed totality of their past efficacy; as if their time-honored identity as gods benevolent to the city is called into question, is somehow attached to their being equal to the present danger rushing against Thebes. Or, to put the relation of gods to mortals in terms of a representation, it is as if the gods' incapacity (or refusal) to represent the city *at every moment* negates the relationship linking the human and the divine.

Thus, when the priest asks Oedipus to be "equal now again" ("καὶ τανῦν ἴσος γενοῦ," "also now become equal"[4]), we are faced with the superhuman resonances in his plea: he means, presumably, that he wishes the king to show *now* the same strength in defending the city as he did earlier during the crisis presented by the Sphinx.[5] But if, indeed, Oedipus is equal now again to what he was equal to before, there is a suggestion that he will be equal to more than himself, or at least to more than the mortals of whose very existence he is asked to be the guarantor.

For it is precisely the illusion that one can indeed always be equal to oneself and only to oneself that is at the root of both Oedipus' apparent power and his ultimate painful discovery, because being equal only to oneself is in fact being equal to the gods, which Oedipus in the long run cannot be ("οὐκ ἰσούμενον"). So that being "equal again" carries both a self-referential meaning ("Be equal to yourself") and an externally-referential meaning ("Be equal to more than what we are, since we cannot save ourselves"). Oedipus' quasi-god-like identity depends more than anything else on his establishment of a secure duration for the city and, by implication, for himself. If their stability seems to depend on his capacity to be "equal to himself" across time or "equal to more than the city" at any given moment, his glory depends upon his ability to assure their safety.

One of the fundamental ironies of Oedipus' situation resides in the fact that by virtue of his at least apparent resemblance to the stability of the divine, in the very act of establishing that stability, Oedipus' connection to the very humanity he wishes to represent in order to protect it becomes problematical. Oedipus' status as reflector between the human and the divine calls a genuine identification with either category into question. In calling Oedipus the first of men in life's chances and in commerce with the divine (*"ἀνδρῶν δὲ πρῶτον ἕν τε συμφοραῖς βίου / κρίνοντες ἕν τε δαιμόνων ξυναλλαγαῖς"*[6]), the priest is really doing nothing more than placing the king once again in an ill-defined middle zone between men and gods, since he is at the very forefront of the category "man," and since his two areas of expertise, each of which begins with the prefix *σύν*, "with," deal respectively with the mortal (*"συμφοραῖς"*) and with the immortal (*"ξυναλλαγαῖς"*). Even if Oedipus confronts the immortal as "other" (the *ἄλλος* element of *"ξυναλλαγαῖς"*), he must somehow be on the same footing with it in order to deal with it, just as in his dealings with the mortal he must be made analogous in some way to those whom he is representing. But his assimilation to either category, the transparency which opens up between him as representative of that category and it as represented, inevitably creates an opacity in the other direction, so that Oedipus' unstated but implicit goal—to link the stability of the undying name (the gods, the perpetual, the unforgotten and the unforgettable) to the vivacity and the flux of mortal existence—is shown to be an impossible one.

Oedipus states explicitly, although without realizing it, the fundamental incompatibility of his dual role as one who must be both equal to those he represents and greater than they through his capacity to assure their survival:

> εὖ γὰρ οἶδ' ὅτι
> νοσεῖτε πάντες, καὶ νοσοῦντες, ὡς ἐγὼ
> οὐκ ἔστιν ὑμῶν ὅστις ἐξ ἴσου νοσεῖ.
> τὸ μὲν γὰρ ὑμῶν ἄλγος εἰς ἕν' ἔρχεται
> μόνον καθ' αὑτόν, κοὐδέν' ἄλλον· ἡ δ' ἐμὴ
> ψυχὴ πόλιν τε κἀμὲ καὶ σ' ὁμοῦ στένει.

> For I know well that
> you are all ill, and being ill, there is
> not one of you who is ill on an equal footing with me.
> For your pain goes to each one alone
> for himself, and for none other; but my soul
> moans for the city and for me and for you in the same way.[7]

Even as Oedipus claims an equality (*"ὁμοῦ,"* "in the same way") between his suffering for himself and his suffering for his charges, he points out the inequality between them: for each member of the city besides Oedipus himself suffers only the pain which comes *"εἰς ἕνα μόνον καθ' αὑτόν, κοὐδέν' ἄλλον,"* "to one person, only to himself, and to none other," whereas he, Oedipus, suffers for them all.

It is precisely Oedipus' claim that he alone suffers not for himself alone but rather for others as well that puts him in a class by himself, unequal to the others he thinks he is suffering for, since they are suffering for only themselves and for no other. So that the equality becomes unidirectional only, since by establishing an equality in the direction Oedipus-representative / city-represented, it effaces the simple status by which Oedipus could be fully equal to himself, a condition which, by transgressing the reflexive law (if a equals b, then b equals a) and, ultimately, the law of identity (a equals a), erases the very definition of equality it is trying to establish.

This asymmetrical reflection which characterizes Oedipus' relationship to the citizens of Thebes is once again apparent in the king's response to Creon when the latter returns from his commission to the Delphic oracle and asks his brother-in-law and nephew whether to give the report of his findings with the citizens standing by or to go inside the house in order to speak with Oedipus in private. The king responds:

ἐς πάντας αὔδα. τῶνδε γὰρ πλέον φέρω
τὸ πένθος ἢ καὶ τῆς ἐμῆς ψυχῆς πέρι.

Speak to everyone. For I bear the pain of these people
more than [I do] concerning my own soul.[8]

The fact that Oedipus here refuses to invoke the distinction between private matters and public matters, a distinction represented by the walls of the palace whose shielding power from the citizenry the king rejects, characterizes once again his ambition to take upon himself the question of the citizens' survival, to live as his own their danger and their pain in such a way that it becomes his danger and his pain.

The construction of the second sentence quoted above, however, belies the purportedly simple nature of this ambition at the same time as it seems to express it: the enormous ambiguity of the genitive "τῶνδε" here, helped along by the word order of the sentence, allows of at least two possible constructions, each of which works to subvert any simple representation of the city by Oedipus. The most likely primary meaning of the genitive construction here would make of the pronoun "τῶνδε" an objective genitive to be construed as an object of the clause "πλέον φέρω / τὸ πένθος": as Jebb translates the phrase, "the sorrow which I bear *is for these* more than for my own life."[9] This interpretation coordinates two objects—"τῶνδε," the pain suffered *because of the citizens*, and "τῆς ἐμῆς ψυχῆς πέρι," the pain suffered *because of Oedipus' soul*—and subordinates the latter to the former: Oedipus, like any good ruler, puts the city's interests above his own, suffers more for the city *than he suffers for himself*.

But if we consider only the grouping which precedes the word "ἢ," the comparison which Oedipus is about to make seems bound to be one which coordinates not two objects, but rather two subjects, and which makes of Oedipus more a member of the very group of sufferers, "τῶνδε," for which he himself is suffering than any of the actual members of the group is, since that first clause before the "ἤ" could mean: "For I bear more of *their* suffering" —the genitive functioning as a simple possessive, and the expected complement in that case being "than they do"—or, even more tempting, "For I bear more of the suffering *than they*," the genitive functioning as the complement to "πλέον" in place of the "ἤ" to come. Once again, Oedipus' claim to a normative representation and protection of the city is undermined by the lopsided equality by which his words suggest that he is more equal to the citizens than they are equal to themselves, that he suffers for the city more than the city suffers for itself. And, ultimately, that words themselves—for we must not forget that Oedipus' story is the story of the symbolizing function as well—say more than what they are imitating.

ii. Aphasic Oedipus: Creon and Teiresias

The dual principle of unequal equality which characterizes Oedipus' link to the gods and to the city of Thebes also defines his relationship with the two men who seem to be his uneasy equals in the play, Creon and Teiresias, individuals who may be seen as representing, respectively, "la psychologie politique" and "la psychologie mythique" of which Vernant speaks[10] and the conjunction (and disjunction) of which Oedipus himself embodies. These are the two people Oedipus accuses of plotting against him, an accusation that links them not only to each other—since he thinks neither of them capable of accomplishing his overthrow alone—but also to himself, since he attacks them for the same crime, assault on a king, of which Teiresias calmly pronounces him guilty.

Even if Creon and Teiresias are not "allies" in any plot to overthrow Oedipus, we should not be surprised to discover that the king's accusation, like everything he says in the play, holds a kernel of truth: Creon and Teiresias are in fact in cahoots to the extent that they represent the two aspects of human language and human institutions which the king's story teaches us about and which are ultimately the source of his undoing: the linking of stable elements to each other (Creon), and the link between each element, seen as unstable and unintegral, and its origins (Teiresias). In language these two facets correspond to normative syntax (Creon), which can yield meaning only if it ignores the paradoxical origins of any symbolic system (i.e., how is non-integral meaning linked to integral unit or word?), and etymology (Teiresias), which, while it tells us a great deal about the origins of words and even about the workings of linguistic systems, does not in fact aim to convey a coherent meaning, and may indeed hinder understanding by showing us the overload of meaning borne by any word.

That Creon and Teiresias act as commentators on the role that language plays in Oedipus' drama is made clear by their refusal, at different times, to speak:

ΚΡΕΩΝ· ἐφ' οἷς γὰρ μὴ φρονῶ σιγᾶν φιλῶ.

Creon: For about things which I don't understand, I like to remain silent.[11]

ΤΕΙΡΕΣΙΑΣ· ἥξει γὰρ αὐτά, κἂν ἐγὼ σιγῇ στέγω.

Teiresias: For the same things will happen, even if I remain in silence.[12]

There is a striking contrast in these two refusals. Creon's phlegmaticism derives from his belief in the utter conformity of his words to his thoughts, in the adequacy of the former to express the latter. If, when he does not understand, he does not speak, then by implication when he speaks, it is that he has understood. He accepts the essential split which separates the halves of the *symbolon* and views that split as a productive, external conjoinment by which a message is conveyed, that is to say, by which words express things without further ado.

Teiresias' silence, by contrast, is emblematic of an inexpressible, implicit knowledge of the relation between words and things, and of a belief that words do not so much express things as hide them because of the unquantifiable nature of the non-simple relation connecting the two. Just as his sinister information makes us realize that an individual citizen like Oedipus may never know the true nature of the conventions that link him to his house, Teiresias calls into question the conventions demanded by the two halves of the *symbolon,* since he recognizes the split between them not as one dividing two distinct halves which come together as a fruitful double, but rather as one existing on the inside of a whole, giving it simultaneously the feeling of the need for the other half and the impossibility of ever breaking out of itself, since the split is inside of it, in its very nature. Teiresias recognizes that there is a synonymy between speech and silence: not only that silence can be a greater goad to action than speech (as he proves in his meeting with Oedipus), but also that speech can become void of all substance if one sees it as a system made up of units each of which bears no essential meaning.

Not only do Creon's and Teiresias' refusals to speak complement each other, the two men also claim the right to speak, and this they both do using the word ἴσος, "equal." Immediately after being accused by the king of planning his overthrow, Creon responds:

ἀντὶ τῶν εἰρημένων
ἴσ' ἀντάκουσον, κᾆτα κρῖν' αὐτὸς μαθών.

In place of what has been said
listen back to equal things, and then judge for yourself, having learned [them].13

If Creon is here laying claim to an equality linking him to the king, an equality which might allow him to reverse their roles momentarily and speak just as Oedipus has spoken, then it is purely a political equality. The equal things ("*ἴσα*") which Creon wants to answer back link two usages of the preposition/prefix, *ἀντί*, "in place of, in turn": in place of (*ἀντί*) what has been said, Creon asks Oedipus to listen back in turn (*ἀντί*) to what Creon will say. And what Creon will say is meant to re-place what Oedipus has said in the sense of placing it into a context that will, Creon believes, allow the two men to agree. This is the very paradigm of political exchange; equality for Creon is firmly in the domain of stable political representation.

Teiresias, similarly accused by Oedipus of attacking his royal authority, juggles Creon's subsequent words demanding permission to speak:

εἰ καὶ τυραννεῖς, ἐξισωτέον τὸ γοῦν
ἴσ᾽ ἀντιλέξαι· τοῦδε γὰρ κἀγὼ κρατῶ.

Even if you are king, you must give at least an equal right
to answer back equal things; for I also am powerful in this domain.14

Teiresias, like Creon, combines the elements *ἴσος*, "equal," and *ἀντί*, "in place of" or "back," but rather than doubling the *ἀντί* element, he doubles the *ἴσος* element, a doubling that goes to the very heart of the double nature of the equality linking Teiresias to Oedipus. Where Creon believes himself to be equal to the king with the simple equality of a citizen and the ruler who stands for him and with whom he shares certain common rights, Teiresias allows his two uses of *ἴσος*, each of which naturally implies the doubleness necessary to equate two terms, to fight with each other, for they are speaking of different things.

Indeed, as Jebb points out, Teiresias' sentence is an unconventional fusion of two others: (1) "*ἐξισωτέον τὸ ἀντιλέξαι*," "you must give equal right to answer back," and (2) "*συγχωρητέον τὸ ἴσα ἀντιλέξαι*," "you must concede to an answering back of equal things."15 As the sentence stands, the first "*ἴσος*" refers to Oedipus' political power, to his power as *tyrannus* and to the fact that he must grant Teiresias an equal right to speech. This is the same equality that Creon resorts to in his own appeal. But the second "*ἴσος*" bespeaks the very impossibility of things' being equal to themselves, for the only way that Teiresias' words can really *respond* to Oedipus' is by their very inequality not only to Oedipus' words, but also to themselves, since Teiresias' speech, a speech which understands and speaks but does not speak in understandable terms, is always double-edged. Whereas Creon's power to speak re-places Oedipus' own speech in a certain (stabilizing) context, Teiresias' words replace Oedipus' words, that is, take their place as their double as well as being double in themselves.

The first "ἴσος" thus speaks of a strictly political equality, one which links distinct, stable identities through convention and supposes that things are equal to themselves. The second "ἴσος," on the contrary, straddles the same split as Oedipus' unequal equality to his people, in whose stead he wishes to stand in their time of greatest danger (replacement through equality) and yet to whom he wishes to give a stability greater than they possess as individuals (re-placement or re-stabilization through difference). Teiresias' words, analogously, are meant to "replace" Oedipus' words ("ἀντιλέξαι"), to respond to and correct the king's misunderstanding if only by demonstrating their own brand of understanding which is beyond him (de-placement or destabilization through difference) and yet in some sense to be *equal* to those words ("ἴσα"; replacement through equality).

What Creon and Teiresias, the two aphasics who admit at least once that they cannot speak, do to equalize themselves to their interrogator is to mimic—Creon subconsciously and Teiresias in full awareness—one of his own linguistic mannerisms, one which can furthermore be seen as an ironic commentary on the nature of language itself. Oedipus, who is in this a fine example of the Greek love of speaking in terms of an opposition or a dialectic, frequently categorizes the world in terms which, even if, taken together, they are not all-inclusive, are at least, if taken separately, meant to be mutually exclusive. Eminently typical of this tendency in Oedipus is the question he poses early in the investigation as to the whereabouts of Laius at the time of his murder: "Was Laius at home, or in the countryside, or in some foreign country when the murder took place?" (vv. 112-13). Thomas Gould remarks on the importance of this listing technique: "The three suggestions, 'home,' 'countryside,' or 'foreign land' are not given for rhetorical fullness, then, but are a meticulous ticking off of the possibilities."[16] It is as if by foreseeing all eventualities in language, Oedipus believed himself capable of controlling them; his use of language becomes a kind of ritual for warding off the evil eye of the unexpected.

Oedipus' reliance upon lists as a means of categorizing and thus controlling the world is especially marked in his use of pronouns. Here is Oedipus' justification of his investigation into Laius' murder:

αὐτὸς αὐτοῦ τοῦτ' ἀποσκεδῶ μύσος.
ὅστις γὰρ ἦν ἐκεῖνον ὁ κτανὼν τάχ' ἂν
κἄμ' ἂν τοιαύτῃ χειρὶ τιμωρεῖν θέλοι.
κείνῳ προσαρκῶν οὖν ἐμαυτὸν ὠφελῶ.

I myself shall scatter this pollution from (of) myself.
For whoever was the killer of that one might
want to punish me as well with the very same hand.
By assisting that one, then, I shall be helping myself.[17]

There are three characters invoked in this drama of murder and vengeance: Laius, twice named as "ἐκεῖνος" ("κεῖνος" being a shortened form), "that one"; the murderer, referred to pronominally as "ὅστις," "whoever," and, metonymically, as "τοιαύτῃ χειρί," "with the same sort of hand"; and Oedipus himself, "αὐτός" ("myself"), "αὐτοῦ" (as Jebb states, a substitution for "ἐμαυτοῦ," "of myself"[18]), "κἄμ'," "and me," and "ἐμαυτόν," "myself." The link which Oedipus wishes to establish between Laius and himself is emphasized by the parallels "ἐκεῖνον . . . κἄμ'" ("him, me") and "κείνῳ . . . ἐμαυτόν" ("him, myself"). But the real nature of the link between Laius and Oedipus is indicated by the pronouns "αὐτὸς αὐτοῦ" which open the passage. "I of myself": what more economical way of expressing the dream of self-generation? The fact that Oedipus is himself the pollution which he is scattering ("αὐτοῦ," genitive of separation or subjective genitive, could add a second translation to the one above: "I shall scatter this pollution of myself," i.e., this pollution that I am), that he ends up finding himself guilty of the murder, is perhaps less important than the fact that by espousing Laius' cause totally, by equalizing "ἐκεῖνον" and "ἐμέ," Oedipus in effect erases Laius' independent identity. Oedipus "kills" Laius pronominally–both by becoming his own "generator" and by equalizing himself to the man he is representing–as much as he does so physically.

Oedipus' murderous equality to his defunct protégé, like the equality by which he moans equally for himself and for the city, is taken up by Creon and Teiresias in their confrontations with the king. Creon, who is a kind of caricature of the methodical side of Oedipus, adopts the technique of cataloguing with the best of faith in its power to equalize the king's interests and his own:

τοῦτ' ἀλλ', ἐάν με τῷ τερασκόπῳ λάβῃς
κοινῇ τι βουλεύσαντα, μή μ' ἁπλῇ κτάνῃς
ψήφῳ, διπλῇ δέ, τῇ τ' ἐμῇ καὶ σῇ, λαβών.

But this, if you can demonstrate that I've plotted something
in common with the prophet, don't, having proven me guilty, kill me
by a single vote, but by a double one, mine and yours.[19]

Creon's pairing of himself and the king in double accord ("διπλῇ δέ, τῇ τ' ἐμῇ καὶ σῇ") is evidence of his belief that if he is guilty, he himself will be forced to own up to it, since the truth of his guilt or innocence is in the common domain, as are all questions to be investigated and understood.

Indeed, Creon believes that his own interests and those of Oedipus must be compatible:

ΚΡΕΩΝ· οὐ γὰρ φρονοῦντά σ' εὖ βλέπω.
ΟΙΔΙΠΟΥΣ· τὸ γοῦν ἐμόν.
ΚΡΕΩΝ· ἀλλ' ἐξ ἴσου δεῖ κἀμόν.

Creon: I see well that you're not clear in your thinking.
Oedipus: I am in my own affairs.
Creon: But you must also be in mine.[20]

Creon's appeal is ultimately based upon the universal, the very universal which forms the basis of language, since it is only by universal agreement (at some level) that any word bears any meaning. A consummate Aristotelian in this respect, Creon would surely agree that "we acquire our knowledge of things only in so far as they contain something universal, some one and identical characteristic,"[21] and that the lack of that universal means a lack of equality, a lack of identity, and the inevitable terror of a lack of knowledge. To the extent that Creon equates language with knowledge, a breakdown of the consensus which binds the speaker of a language to his interlocutor ("τῇ τ' ἐμῇ καὶ σῇ," "mine and yours"; "ἐξ ἴσου δεῖ κἀμόν," "you must also be clear in *my* affairs") leads to a breakdown of the conventions upon which the *polis* is built. And that breakdown Creon is not about to recognize.

Oedipus' confrontation with Teiresias (vv. 300-462) is one in the course of which the blind seer seems to dissolve the dialectical questioning process which Oedipus has so valiantly set into motion, and upon which Creon so heavily relies. After the seer's short entrance speech (vv. 316-18), he and the king engage in a verbal duel which, with the exception of one three-line interlude (vv. 334-36), matches two-line response to two-line response for some twenty lines (vv. 320-40) in a sort of doubled stychomythia which itself adds to the impression not only that the two figures are reflections of one another but also that each is double in himself. Teiresias takes hold of Oedipus' method of categorizing the world into supposedly distinct groups simply in order to collapse the distinctions which that method attempts to create. In each of his five responses to the king in this passage, he uses Oedipus' matching technique in such a way as to create a link between the king ("τὸ σόν," "σύ"; "οὐδὲ σοί"; "τὰ σ'"; "σ'"; "τὴν σήν," at vv. 320; 324; 329; 332; and 337, respectively) and himself ("κἀγώ," "τοὐμόν"; "μηδ' ἐγὼ ταὐτόν"; "τἄμ'"; "ἐμαυτόν"; "τὴν ἐμήν," at vv. 321; 325; 329; 332; and 337).

At one level, the equality which Teiresias' pairings seem to foster, like that to which Creon appeals, appears to bespeak the common benefit which the two men would reap by Teiresias' silence. Thus at v. 332, he tells the king that he will distress neither him (Oedipus) nor himself (Teiresias): "ἐγὼ οὔτ' ἐμαυτὸν οὔτε σ' ἀλγυνῶ." Similarly, at vv. 320-21, he asks to be sent home:

ἄφες μ' ἐς οἴκους · ῥᾷστα γὰρ τὸ σόν τε σὺ
κἀγὼ διοίσω τοὐμόν, ἢν ἐμοὶ πίθῃ.

Send me home; for you will most easily bear your [affairs]
and I mine, if you obey me.

The parallel between "τὸ σόν τε σύ" ("you your") on the one hand and "κἀγὼ
... τοὐμόν" ("I mine") on the other, emphasized by the shared verb "διοίσω"
which, although it is first person singular in form, also provides the implied
action of the pronoun "σύ," creates the impression that "τὸ σόν," Oedipus'
affairs, and "τοὐμόν," those of Teiresias, are "ἴσα," equal to the extent that
both will be most easily endurable if Teiresias leaves immediately, thus preclud-
ing any real contact between him and the king.

Even in this seemingly clear-cut case of parallelism, however, there is an
underlying hint of confusion: the verb διαφέρω, of which "διοίσω" is a future
form, in addition to meaning "endure to the end" (διά as "through"), can also
mean "tear asunder" (διά as "apart"), related to the Latin *differre*, whence
"different." Thus Teiresias' words suggest obliquely that if he *does* stay and
talk to the king, not only will both of them have a harder time "enduring"
their woes but each of them will also find it more difficult to distinguish
the affairs of one from the affairs of the other. The original equality of the
two, which came out of a common interest, an equality that presupposed that
"τὸ σόν" and "τοὐμόν" were distinct but similar, becomes a collapse of one
onto the other. The longer Teiresias stays and talks, the harder it will become
to maintain integral identities. As a kind of mythic catalyst, the prophet
helps to dissolve the axioms upon which the king is relying in his investigation.

The height of the confusion which Teiresias creates in this relatively brief
interchange with the king comes when the distinction between "mine" and
"yours" goes so far as to lose all stability:

πάντες γὰρ οὐ φρονεῖτ'. ἐγὼ δ' οὐ μή ποτε
τἄμ', ὡς ἂν εἴπω μὴ τὰ σ', ἐκφήνω κακά.

For you are all misguided in your thinking. But I shall *never*
reveal my, not to mention your, misfortunes.[22]

It is impossible to decide here among three equally feasible interpretations
of Teiresias' sentence. Is he saying that he will not reveal his own misfortunes,
so as not to have subsequently to speak of Oedipus' misfortunes, which are
separate from his own but somehow related to them, so that the telling of
one might lead naturally into the telling of the other? Or that he will not
bring to light his own troubles which are indeed also those of Oedipus, the
two being equivalent? Or is he here recognizing a purely figurative linkage
between "τἄμ'" and "τὰ σ'": *my* misfortunes (which are *mine* only figuratively), not to call them *yours* (which they are literally)?

Teiresias thus emphasizes the fact that whether or not he and Oedipus
retain an independent identity, whether revealing his own misfortunes leads
to or coincides with revealing those of the king, it is in any event Oedipus'
well-being which is most centrally in question here, not Teiresias'. Teiresias'

"suffering" or "misfortune" here can only be termed as such insofar as he represents a part of Oedipus that Oedipus himself does not know or at least cannot give voice to. Teiresias' simultaneous mimicking of Oedipus' categories and collapsing of them corresponds to Oedipus' original incompatible ambitions to be equal to the people of Thebes and also equal to the task that none of them is equal to; the seer seems to be saying that he himself holds the key to what Oedipus is in search of, that the affairs of one are "equal" to the affairs of the other, but also that in his similarity to Teiresias, Oedipus is being assimilated (or will be assimilated) to a mode of knowledge which he does not presently understand, to an erasure of the very boundaries upon which he believes knowledge and language—the equality of things to themselves—to depend.

Thus, we have two characters who are somehow "equal" to Oedipus, and two types of aphasia, two types of non-speech, each of which is linked fundamentally to one aspect of language. Roman Jakobson has spoken about the relation of this illness to the dual nature of language, a symbolic system based upon "combination" and "selection":

> (1) COMBINATION. Any sign is made up of constituent signs and/or occurs only in combination with other signs. This means that any linguistic unit at one and the same time serves as a context for simpler units and/or finds its own context in a more complex linguistic unit. . . . Combination and contexture are two faces of the same operation.
>
> (2) SELECTION. A selection between alternatives implies the possibility of substituting one for the other, equivalent to the former in one respect and different from it in another. Actually selection and substitution are two faces of the same operation.[23]

Combination and selection are essentially the two halves of Oedipus' linguistic drama, embodied by Creon and Teiresias, respectively. Creon is a man who has utter faith in the workings of grammatical combination and who relies heavily upon contexts—political as well as linguistic—to support him. He is interested not in the essential nature of words or things—perhaps he assumes that he already knows their nature—but rather in using the units he assumes to be valid in order to get what he wants. He does what the French might call "combiner," plotting and planning in a political sort of way. In fact, he is a thoroughly political creature.

Teiresias, by contrast, is the "selector," the man who shows the insufficiency of any given linguistic (or domestic) unit by bringing to light its essentially metaphorical nature. Teiresias' subtle interrogation of Oedipus all the while the latter is purportedly questioning him demonstrates the non-simple nature of the units relied upon by the king in his search. By showing Oedipus that each one of his questions leads to another, prior question, that every assumption does nothing more than give the illusion of having solved a still-open question, Teiresias points up the infinitely substitutable nature of every unit in a symbolic system.

Jakobson relates these two aspects of language to two forms of aphasia, which he labels "similarity disorder" and "contiguity disorder," the former consisting of an incapacity to "select" or to find synonyms of nouns, verbs, and adjectives, and an exaggerated reliance upon connectives (pronouns, grammatical inflections, copulatives), and the latter of a gross simplification of grammatical rules, or rules of "combination," and an overuse of metaphor, often incomprehensible. Jakobson carries these two disorders even further by connecting them to the two "poles" of language. The metonymic pole, corresponding to the similarity disorder, relates things by context alone; the substitutions it produces merely provide more and more bits of information about any given linguistic unit, without giving another "whole" unit with which it might enter into a battle for meaning. As Jakobson says:

> Of the two polar figures of speech, metaphor and metonymy, the latter, based on contiguity, is widely employed by aphasics whose selective capacities have been affected. *Fork* is substituted for *knife, table* for *lamp, smoke* for *pipe, eat* for *toaster.*[24]

To say "table" instead of "lamp" is not so much to say that a lamp is a table as to say that the two things often coexist, or even that "table" can be used to modify (but not to replace) "lamp," as in the expression "table lamp." The metonymy of the similarity disorder is essentially an overvaluation of context.

This is the pole of language at which Creon is to be found, for he is the man who refuses to question meaning in any fundamental way, the man who speaks in contexts alone. Jakobson's description of a contextual aphasic might be a description of Creon himself:

> If one of the synonymic signs is present . . . then the other sign . . . becomes redundant and consequently superfluous. For the [contextual] aphasic, both signs are in complementary distribution: if one is performed by the examiner, the patient will avoid its synonym: "I understand everything" . . . will be his typical reaction.[25]

Indeed, the man who "understands everything" is the man who never questions equality and its potentially tautological nature, never sees that the equality he depends upon can provide ever-slipping redundancies rather than stable building blocks:

> Even simple repetition of a word uttered by the examiner seems to the patient unnecessarily redundant, and despite instructions received he is unable to repeat

it . . . he could not produce the purest form of equational predication, the tautology $a = a$.[26]

The metaphoric pole, attached by Jakobson to the contiguity disorder, relates things non-grammatically. It is essentially the pole which refuses to make statements, precisely because of its excessive preoccupation with individual words:

> Impairment of the ability to PROPOSITIONIZE, or, generally speaking, to combine simpler linguistic entities into more complex units, is actually confined to one type of aphasia [the contiguity disorder]. . . . There is no WORDLESSNESS, since the entity preserved in most of such cases is the WORD.[27]

Metaphor disrupts any sentence in which it is found; rather than allowing units to combine to form a proposition, it calls attention to whatever unit it is attached to. Unlike metonymy, metaphor does not give us bits of information about a word; rather, it asks us if we really know what any word means.

It is Teiresias who is to be found at this pole of language, Teiresias whose words are an endless redundancy from which Oedipus attempts to escape. Against Oedipus' ability to "put things together," and in particular to put together the pieces of the Sphinx's riddle, Teiresias stands ever ready to pull them apart, to metaphorize any inquest aiming to synthesize things into a whole which transcends its parts.

And Oedipus, as always, is to be found at both poles, for he is both Creon and Teiresias, a sufferer of both the similarity disorder and the contiguity disorder, the man who is contiguous to his similar (Jocasta). Or, to speak in terms of his father, the man who is related to his father not only metonymically, as a part emanating from a whole which subordinates its parts, but also metaphorically, as a whole which fights with the whole from which it issues and challenges its meaning.

iii. Metaphoric Oedipus: like father, like son

If, by the normative terms of kinship relations, the nurture by parents of children is balanced in later life by the nurture by children of parents, both γηροτροφία ("care of the old") and παιδοτροφία ("care of the young") are essentially a recognition of a bond based upon the interchangeability of parent and child, of the cohesion which provides the original staying power of the house as a protector of life based on a system of mutual support.[28] When at the triple crossroads Oedipus does not recognize the sameness which should link his father to himself, falling prey to what Claude Lévi-Strauss in his seminal analysis of the Oedipus myth calls the "underrating of blood relations,"[29] the fact that he is doing nothing more than replicating his father's original failure to recognize him as flesh of his flesh, worthy of nurture (life-supporting) and not worthy of violence (life-attacking), puts the relations between father and son in the register of unacknowledged sameness. For Laius' attempt to kill his son—which does nothing more than repeat his earlier refusal to nurture him—as well as Oedipus' unknowing assault on his father both effect a breaking into the integrity of the identity by which their common house should link them. And if the result of the two gestures—willful but unsuccessful παιδοκτονία matched by unwitting but successful πατροκτονία —is, on the one hand, a lack of child nurture where it should be present (Laius-Oedipus) and, on the other hand, a presence of child nurture where it should not have taken place (Oedipus-his incestuous children), it is that the refusal to recognize sameness within the house leads to the same sterility as the failure to provide a difference at the moment of its formation. While the latter leads to an infertile equality as doubling (father-brother, etc.), the former leads to a destructive equality as reduction (non-father, non-son, etc.).[30]

The first of the three occurrences of the word "ἴσος" which link Oedipus to his father comes in the midst of the king's description of his encounter with Laius at the triple crossroads, just after he has told of the old man's initial attack on him:

οὐ μὴν ἴσην γ' ἔτισεν, ἀλλὰ συντόμως
σκήπτρῳ τυπεὶς ἐκ τῆσδε χειρὸς ὕπτιος
μέσης ἀπήνης εὐθὺς ἐκκυλίνδεται.

But he didn't pay back equal at least, but all at once
having been struck by the stick from this very hand, headfirst
he rolls straight out of the middle of the cart.[31]

The inequality which Oedipus speaks of here goes far beyond its most immediate referent, that is, the fact that Oedipus' blow "outdoes" the old man's insofar as it kills him. For the exchange of blows here is a re-enactment of the entire father-son relationship and of their infraction of the normative terms of that relationship. It is only because Laius did not manage to kill Oedipus as a child that Oedipus as an adult manages to kill Laius. Just as the tandem concepts of παιδοτροφία and γηροτροφία imply reflexivity, one behavior responding to the other and validating it retroactively, those of παιδοκτονία and πατροκτονία cannot be reflexive, since if either one is successful, the other cannot be (or cannot have been). Only if you succeed in raising your child to adulthood will he care for you in your old age, whereas only if you fail to kill him might he grow up to kill you, and only if you succeed in killing him will he never grow up to kill you.

Thus Oedipus is equal to his father in the wrong sense and unequal to him in the wrong sense. He replaces his father thoroughly and in the same place where his father had been without the necessary middle term provided by the mediation of a symbolic system which orders pairings through difference, through distinct origins and identities. It is for that reason that he cannot re-place the stability provided by a following of the norms of that symbolic system, since he cannot be a creator of life equal (i.e., in the same way) to his father unless he takes to himself a partner unequal to his father's partner. It is only the joining of the two halves of the *symbolon* which provides the creative difference, the necessary transitivity of the re-creation of a home in a place other than one's own original home, the latter being one attachment to which is regulated by sameness and assimilation to it and not by difference from it and combination with it.

Oedipus, by the terms of his story, takes the givens of a normative symbolic system, one which provides mediation, a middle term distinguishing one spouse from another while conjoining them through difference, and makes of it a non-normative Symbolism, one in which the meaning is the means, the middle is the end (the goal), the *symbolon* is what the symbolic system is talking about. It is a Symbolism which does away with the split between the halves of the *symbolon* not by joining the two together while recognizing them as distinct, but by showing their essential indistinguishability such that inside and outside can no longer be named, house of procreation equals house of origin and cannot "stand for" it.

The result of Oedipus' skewed relation to his father is not only to seem to "equalize" the two men in a way they should not be equal, but also to de-equalize each to himself, to attack from inside the notion of paternity. This is made clear during the scene between Oedipus and the Corinthian shepherd, in the course of which Oedipus discovers that he is not the biological son of Polybus and Merope, but rather their adoptive son:

ΑΓΓΕΛΟΣ · ὀθούνεκ' ἦν σοι Πόλυβος οὐδὲν ἐν γένει.
ΟΙΔΙΠΟΥΣ · πῶς εἶπας; οὐ γὰρ Πόλυβος ἐξέφυσέ με;
Α · οὐ μᾶλλον οὐδὲν τοῦδε τἀνδρός, ἀλλ' ἴσον.
Ο · καὶ πῶς ὁ φύσας ἐξ ἴσου τῷ μηδενί;
Α · ἀλλ' οὔ σ' ἐγείνατ' οὔτ' ἐκεῖνος οὔτ' ἐγώ.
Ο · ἀλλ' ἀντὶ τοῦ δὴ παῖδά μ' ὠνομάζετο;

Messenger: Because Polybus was nothing to you by birth.
Oedipus: What's that you say? Didn't Polybus give me life?
M: Not a bit more than I did, but equally.
O: And how could he who gave me birth be on an equal footing with anyone
                                            who did not?
M: But he didn't give you birth, neither he nor I did.
O: But what then did he name me his child for?[32]

The two uses of the word "ἴσος" here bring into play the double-edged nature of paternity. To say that Polybus gave life to Oedipus *equally* as the Corinthian shepherd himself is to say simultaneously that Polybus was *not* Oedipus' father and that the shepherd *was* Oedipus' father. It is to recognize the fact that just as Laius did nothing to activate the father-son relationship and thus was not really Oedipus' father in a certain sense, Polybus and the shepherd were Oedipus' fathers in a certain sense. It is to destabilize the idea of paternity and to open it up to new possibilities at the same time as one calls into question the old one. As Thomas Gould points out: "OEDIPUS is surrounded by 'fathers,' especially in the great climactic scene."[33] Oedipus' literal father ("ὁ φύσας") can indeed be on an equal footing ("ἐξ ἴσου") with *anyone* who is not his literal father ("τῷ μηδενί," the negation μή here indicative of the general, categorical nature of the expression) because the failure of one specific and adequate identification of father results in a metaphorical freeing of the concept of fatherhood and the possibility of distributing it to many in the place of the one who has refused it.

When Oedipus asks, "'ἀντὶ τοῦ' did Polybus name me his son?" he is making explicit by the ambiguity of the first expression the unstable nature of paternity and identity once it has been recognized that no *one* identity corresponds to the complex "father." While the term "ἀντὶ τοῦ" clearly means "why?" as its first meaning here (as in colloquial English, "what for?"), the word "ἀντί" also retains its original impact as a preposition denoting replacement. So Oedipus' sentence can be interpreted in at least four other ways:

(1) But in place of whom did *he* name me his child?
(Who instead of Polybus should have named me his child?)

(2) But in place of whom did he name *me* his child?
(Whom instead of me should Polybus have named his child?)

(3) But in place of what did he *name* me his child?
(Instead of doing what did he name me his child?)

(4) But in place of what did he name me *his child*?
(Instead of calling me what did he name me his child?)

The series of questions that is thus generated by Oedipus' realization (or the realization of his words, at least) that either he or Polybus or the entire child-father relationship is an *Ersatz* recounts the entire motivation behind his adoption, since the answers to the questions, respectively, yield the following clear account of the adoption:

(1) *Laius* should have named me his child.

(2) Polybus had *no son* to name his child.

(3) Polybus named me his child in place of what Laius did to me, that is, in place of *exposing me on the mountainside and refusing to name me his child.*

(4) Polybus named me his child in place of calling me "ὁ μηδείς" (cf. v. 1019), *anyone who is nothing to him and not his child,* i.e., non-kin, which is what I am to him.

So that every step of the way, what is lost is what is gained, or, inversely, what is gained in the domain of fatherhood does nothing more than replace a loss anterior to it. Oedipus has two fathers (and a multitude of fathers) only because he does not have *one*: he destroys his father because his story, in breaking the chain of the orderly succession of generations by which no father and son should ever coincide on an equal footing, effects a metaphorization of the father-son relation, allows son to "equal" father by removing the pair from the temporal regulation of a succession and placing them simultaneously at the crossroads between Thebes and Delphi.

And like any metaphorization, the one which links Oedipus and Laius is based upon a struggle and a paradox: the metaphorically linked pair, insofar as they must fight for the meaning which a conventional symbolic system would stabilize by keeping the generations apart through normative syntax, but which as it is neither father nor son contains fully, must be equal both to themselves, individually, and to each other, since it is only as a pair that they bear any semantic value. Like father, like son: the case of Oedipus proves that this proverb points not only to a metaphorical link between fathers and sons, but also, almost inevitably, to a metaphorical link between any father and himself, any son and himself. A father may be at times "like" a father, and a son "like" a son, but neither is ever simply "like" what he is if he is also "like" what another is like. Oedipus and Laius, like any metaphorical pair, must fight to release their store of meaning, and this they must do because they must not contain themselves if they are to contain that meaning.

Chapter Two: The House of Life and the House of Death

"Le Tombeau d'Edgar Poe"

Je ne sais pas si l'Hôte perspicacement cironscrit son domaine d'effort: ce me plaira de le marquer, aussi certaines conditions. Le droit à rien accomplir d'exceptionnel ou manquant aux agissements vulgaires, se paie, chez quiconque, de l'omission de lui et on dirait de sa mort comme un tel.

Mallarmé
"L'Action restreinte"

Le Tombeau d'Edgar Poe

Tel qu'en Lui-même enfin l'éternité le change,
Le Poëte suscite avec un glaive nu
Son siècle épouvanté de n'avoir pas connu
Que la mort triomphait dans cette voix étrange!

Eux, comme un vil sursaut d'hydre oyant jadis l'ange
Donner un sens plus pur aux mots de la tribu
Proclamèrent très haut le sortilège bu
Dans le flot sans honneur de quelque noir mélange.

Du sol et de la nue hostiles, ô grief!
Si notre idée avec ne sculpte un bas-relief
Dont la tombe de Poe éblouissante s'orne,

Calme bloc ici-bas chu d'un désastre obscur,
Que ce granit du moins montre à jamais sa borne
Aux noirs vols du Blasphème épars dans le futur.[1]

"Un homme au rêve habitué, vient ici parler d'un autre, qui est mort."[2] Mallarmé's opening words in his lecture on Villiers de l'Isle-Adam characterize surprisingly well the relationship between living poet and dead poet which forms the foundation of "Le Tombeau d'Edgar Poe." Although the living speaker is separated by the barrier of death from the poet to whom he wishes to pay homage, their separation seems to be transcended by a link between the two men, one which equates them even in their difference. The pause provided by the comma separating "un autre" and "qui est mort" allows us to translate the sentence by providing the words which implicitly fill that pause: "A man accustomed to dreaming, comes here to speak of another *man accustomed to dreaming,* who is dead." The *other,* the object of Mallarmé's words ("parler d'un autre") in his lecture on Villiers as well as in his poem on Poe, is not only unlike the speaker by virtue of his death, he is also like the speaker in that he, too, is "au rêve habitué."

We might even go so far as to say that the sentence implicitly opposes dream to speech, that living in the habitat of dreams may not be conducive to leaving that habitat in order to formulate those dreams in words. It is in the opposition of speech to dream, or at least to non-speech, that the living poet and the dead poet are most explicitly unequal, since one of them "vient *ici* parler," while the other retains the luxury of an irrevocable distance and an imposed silence. But here again, the apparent inequality is matched by an underlying attempt at a sort of equalization between the two men: the speaker wishes not only to re-create the spirit of the deceased in the realm of the living, in a sense to resurrect him in words and therefore to transcend his mortality by immortalizing his identity through the stability of a conventional symbolic system, language, which at least seems never to change or die; he also wants to infuse that conventional symbolic system with a knowledge that only death and the possibility of a *stop,* of a becoming intransitive and immutable, can bring.

Indeed, one of the goals of the words of Mallarmé's tribute to the American poet, "Le Tombeau d'Edgar Poe," is to *link* living speech with the dead man of whom it speaks, all the while the distance separating them is retained, a distance which assures that the human words can be aimed at the superhuman state ("Tel qu'en *Lui-même*") to which Poe has attained, and also that the deceased mortal who Poe also is may be made to relive through the human, mortal words which comprise his epitaph. Mallarmé's paradox here is that of any man at odds with the conventional symbolic system which he is forced to use: Mallarmé wishes to use Poe's distance from the mortal state, his otherness, his inequality to the inhabitants of the house of life, in order to arrive at the very state of transcendence which only the distance from that state and the unattainability of it made him go in search of, and the reaching of which would imply the same distancing from the human domain and silencing of its words which characterize those beyond the grave. Mallarmé's recourse to a conventional symbolic system—the necessity of "coming to speak" of one who is departed and cannot be physically present—is coupled with his ambition of going beyond the conventions which that symbolic system presumes to be operative, beyond the distance which it assumes separates conveying word and conveyed idea—indeed, the distance which any conveyance implies—in his attempt to use that conventional symbolic system to evoke an unevocable presence, to re-create here, "ici," what is irrevocably there, "au-delà," beyond any human attempt to fix it or to capture it.

Thus Mallarmé wishes the monument he is constructing in Poe's honor to "take the place" of the departed mortal Poe who has reached his own limiting boundary, death, and thus to accept Poe's boundedness, his distance from the world of the living because of his presence in the world of the dead, by using language as a substitute for Poe's mortal existence; he also wants Poe to "take place" once again, to be resurrected through Mallarmé's own erection of a living monument to him in the human realm, to unbind Poe from the boundary separating life and death by joining the house of life to the house of death.

Indeed, the poem, since it can never be more than relatively successful, is always a sort of death, an admission of finitude by the prerequisite choosing of words that are substantial, the coming down to earth of an ethereal inspiration. Mallarmé can uncover Poe's true worth only because the American poet is, in fact, dead and has already been buried, so that his existence across time no longer creates a force resisting his naming. Conventional form is therefore to be seen as a kind of death in that even though it seems to provide an immortal stability for those mortals who use it in their search for a transcendence of their mortality, it resists, by its refusal to change, any fundamental equality to the life it is used to express and thus provides a limitation inimical to those who aspire to a perfect matching of stable form and unstable meaning.

But death may also take on the potentially benevolent features of form and therefore become, like form, not only an enemy, but also a potential ally. Death, like the process of naming, or applying epithets to attributes, that is, labels or covers to qualities that may in themselves be unstable, is seen not only as a limit to what is in perpetual flux (human existence, in the case of death; defining characteristics which become definitively defined once words are applied to them, in the case of naming); it is also the great stabilizer. It is only with death that a man's true worth can be determined, an idea that goes back at least as far as Greek tragedy, one of the commonplaces of which is that one can make no definitive judgement about a man until he has died. To this extent, the institution of the conventional word as limitation, like the acceptance of death as a boundary, is what makes possible the search for meaning in and behind that word, like the search for meaning in what death limits, life. As Pierre Beausire, speaking of Mallarmé in general and also of "Le Tombeau d'Edgar Poe" in particular, states:

> Le poëte ose considérer nettement la mort; il ne se contente pas de la prévoir et de la pressentir: il l'annonce. Il en proclame la redoutable nécessité. Elle seule donne à sa passion son sens, à son message son autorité. Il en décèle partout la présence et la puissance. Il en subit à chaque instant les coups. Il se dresse de tout son amour et de toute sa force contre cette constante et intime ennemie, dont la victoire est fatale. Mais il a partie liée avec elle.[3]

The fact that Poe turns into "Lui-même," a sort of proper pronoun which seems to lose the particularity of the mortal human at the same time as it gains the generic status of the god-like and the unchanging, moves him into the domain of what appears to be beyond the reach of the human, and indeed furnishes one of the moving forces of the sonnet: the fact that Mallarmé wishes to be Poe's equal by using the American poet's proximity to the divine to create a poem which captures the divine, the exigencies and limitations of human form notwithstanding. Gardner Davies comments with great acuity about the inversion present in the poem's first line, an inversion of epithet ("Tel qu'en Lui-même") and of the substantive the knowledge of whose identity it presupposes but actually postpones ("Le Poëte"), an inversion by which the poem's first line "paraît se détacher complètement des autres vers du sonnet."[4] It is as if the rest of the poem attempted to pin down the being named in its liminary verse and to be equal to that "Lui-même" in all of its self-sufficiency and its definitiveness, and yet also to remain equal to its own human nature, with its potential for destabilizing the god-like stability of any fixed, definitive identity.

Whence the complex relation linking—and separating—Mallarmé and Poe in the "Tombeau" poem erected by the former in the latter's name. Davies also notes the long-delayed allusion to the American poet's name, a procedure which he rightly identifies as typical, but without fully exploring its effect here:

> Le nom de Gautier n'apparaît que cinq vers avant la fin de *Toast funèbre*; de même il faut en arriver au dixième vers du sonnet avant de trouver celui de Poe.

Un examen des autres sonnets commémoratifs montre du reste que Mallarmé ne révèle jamais le nom de celui qu'il célèbre avant la fin du premier tercet.[5]

What the postponement of any specific mention of Poe's name creates here is the same sort of confusion between living poet and dead poet which the pause in Mallarmé's sentence about himself and Villiers brings out. Those commentators who speak of the ideal nature of the man who is named simply "Le Poëte" until the tenth line of the poem—like Richard who says of Poe that death "lui a ôté en somme tout ce qui définissait son relief, son angularité, tout ce qui caractérisait en lui l'individu; tout ce qui faisait de lui *un tel* ou *un tel* pour le rendre . . . à la nudité d'un pur concept"[6]—are certainly as correct as those who emphasize Poe's particular identity. But it is the conjunction of the American poet's presence throughout the poem with Mallarmé's refusal to name him until the end of the first tercet which is particularly interesting here, for it enables the double functioning of the expression "Le Poëte," referring both to the dead man addressed and to the living man who is addressing him. The capitalization of "Poëte" also makes it simultaneously a substitute for the proper noun, Poe, which it announces—and, moreover, closely resembles—and also a substitute for the idealized form which the living poet is aiming to appropriate for himself through his identification of and, ultimately, with Poe.

The poem begins with a word ("Tel") which is not only, as Robert Greer Cohn has remarked, a pun on the Greek τῆλος, "far,"[7] but is also a play on the word τέλος (*epsilon* and not *eta*), "end," the latter word appearing, in fact, in the very same line of the poem: "Tel qu'en Lui-même *enfin.*" "Tel" thus expresses both the quality (suchness, an attributive function), that is, the essence of Poe's existence, and also the finality of the epitaph/ epithet that is being applied to him, its capital importance ("Lui-même"), the claim to definitiveness which can only come with the finality of death.

If we recall Lacan's use of *symptom* as being the condition of metaphor, which is an attempt to cross the line of meaning separating signifier and signified[8] (in the sense that an equal claim to meaning is made by each signifier, so that each one competes with the others for the honor of containing the "true" meaning), and his characterization of metonymy as being, precisely, a movement forward along the line of meaning, a displacement that is a virtual admission of the non-essential meaning of each word for which it is not enough to be "equal" to itself since it must be "propped up" by a whole network of words to yield any sense, then the asymptote can be interpreted as the reaching of absolute meaning not by crossing the boundary between signifier and signified (*sym-ptoma*, a falling together), but by edging ever closer to it (*a-sym-ptote*, not falling together). Indeed, life in this conception of it is unlike metaphor as symptom, it is rather an asymptote which tends toward the barrier of absolute meaning only as it reaches its own limit, death, as quality (*tel*-ness) reaches its quantifying boundary (τέλος, "finiteness and finality"), or as the signified, made up of a certain number of qualities, tends toward the signifier, both its boundary and its limit.

The edifice of "Le Tombeau d'Edgar Poe" becomes therefore an admission and a revelation of the limitations of its architect, whose building blocks ("Du sol et de la nue hostiles, ô grief! / Si notre idée avec . . .") are made of the struggle[9] between the dream of an absolute monument as total and definitive signifier, which is seen as belonging purely to the domain of the non-human ("éternité"; "Le Poète"; "l'ange"; "la nue"), and the necessity of building a house with the materials available to a human architect ("noir mélange"; "sol"; "Poe"). It is, in fact, the human, living Poe who occupies the position of Mallarmé as living poet, and the dead Poe who represents the reaching of an absolute (death and all that is associated with it) to which the living poet can only aspire. So that the American poet occupies a sort of hinge position, equal to the stability of death and also equal to the instability of the living poet who can try to reach the ideal, absolute nature of death only through mortal and substantial tools.

Thus it is, in the first quatrain, that the dead Poe ("Poëte") has all the majesty and grandeur of an Olympian god. Not only is his title capitalized both as pronoun ("Lui-même") and as noun ("Poëte"); he is furthermore characterized as the one who is triumphant in death, or perhaps through death ("la mort triomphait par cette voix étrange"), who brings to life by his very non-living status: "suscite avec un glaive nu," a virtual oxymoron, since swords are usually meant to kill. Poe's idealized, more-than-human nature is to be used to infuse human matter and forms with new life, such that his death, his relegation of human form, serves the function of generating new meaning through that form, a kind of birth through death. The bare sword, particularly in conjunction with its homonym in v. 9 ("glaive *nu*" / "Du sol et de la *nue*"), is not only naked, but virtually insubstantial. Indeed, the rhymes in -*u* of the inner lines of the two quatrains ("nu"/"connu") are echoed by words in the first lines of both tercets ("nue," "chu"), each of which speaks of the distinction between sky and earth, between absolute, insubstantial meaning ("nue," and the -*astre* element in "désastre," falling from a star) and signification needing form ("sol" and the "calme bloc ici-bas *chu*").

If the first quatrain speaks of the Poet—and here the confusion between Poe and Mallarmé is essential—as he who is made apparent by his own death (Poe) and who, analogously, makes apparent the essential nature of existence by his ambition to constitute absolute meaning, another form of death's "triumph" (Mallarmé), the second quatrain deals with the tension between Such a Poet ("Tel"/"Poëte"/"ange"), master of the epithet/epitaph, and his human living shadow, who can only dream of "purifying" human language, whose "mots" are also his "maux" since they speak of the disjunction between form and meaning. "Mélange" contains a hint of "black angel" (μέλας, as in *melan*choly), particularly as it is preceded by "noir": it is thus the visual counterpart of the oxymoron of the resuscitating sword, since the "black" angel suggests the very perishability of human forms (black as the non-appearance of form, as well as its connection here to Poe's very mortal foible of drinking) which the divine angel must attempt to purify and make manifest. The angel, whom Mallarmé explicitly identifies as the poet in his own notes to the English translation of the poem,[10] is thus meant to transcend mortal forms by using mortal forms. The total, pure appearance of the divine angel is opposed to the "mixture" of divine aspiration and mortal form represented by the "noir mélange" just as the coveted white spaces, or silence, of the page are opposed to the black words between which they exist, as Mallarmé says:

L'armature intellectuelle du poème se dissimule et tient—a lieu—dans l'espace qui isole les strophes et parmi le blanc du papier; significatif silence qu'il n'est pas moins beau de composer que les vers.[11]

So that every human attempt to attain a superhuman state in which there is no need to speak is thwarted by the very framework ("armature") which it uses to try to reach the divine.

Indeed, the dilemma of the human "ange," the messenger (Greek ἄγγελος) whose messages are not divine and communicable by total appearance, but rather require a compromising, secular medium to house the divine word, is mirrored by an objective attributive construction which is central to the second quatrain: "[Eux] Proclamèrent très haut le sortilège bu," that is, "que le sortilège fut (or 'eut été') bu." The "mots de la tribu" of the sixth line of the poem may well be meant to be a word-play on the "mots/maux de l'attribut," for they are built upon the necessary conjunction of attribute and epithet and their ultimate irreconcilability. The keynote of the objective attribute ("attribut de l'objet," that is, an attributive construction with a verb other than "être") is that the quality or attribute in question becomes operative only given the action of the verb. In the sentence "Dieu créa l'homme cruel," it is the act of creation which gives man the "attribute" of cruelty; and if one says, "Je trouve ce vin médiocre," the implication is that the wine was mediocre not before one found it, but rather because one found it: it is in the act of finding that the identification of the mediocrity is contained.

Similarly, it is only the blasphemous word of Poe's critics and their belief that Poe's "magic" sprang from an alcoholic source which make that apparent attribute of the poet seem essential during his life, before eternity has changed him into Himself. The objective attribute thus links a quality to its fixing by a temporally, modally, and personally based verb which seems to put that quality into effect, such that it does not exist independently of its constitution in the action of the verb, which forms it (as in "créa") or formalizes it (as in "trouve" or "Proclamèrent"). The "proclamation" of the living poet protecting the dead poet, even though it is meant to euphemize the crowd's "blasphemy" and as such must be "equal" to it at some level, wishes to escape the "attribution" in all human language, for it wishes to be an eternal utterance.

The play on "ange"/"noir," furthermore, points up the ambition of the human poet to break through the boundaries between words, and thus to make of language a kind of continuum, since we may well ask whether "mél" belongs to "noir," a paradigmatic substitution in that it is its translation in another idiom and thus a sort of synonym, or to "ange," to which it is obviously attached by the normative syntax of prose. The poet wishes to deny the necessary element of difference in human language and its dependence upon the creation of a series of distinct units: "un sens plus pur" is both a purer meaning and a purer direction, an indication of the human aspiration to reaching the divine without falling back onto the humanity which is its starting point, a world in which what one drinks ("mélange") as inspiration becomes the formal bearer of the message to be transmitted ("noir ange"), interior joins with exterior, inspiration or message with expression or messenger.

Thus, if the first quatrain hypothesizes the potential existence of the ideal Poet, messenger ("ange") of death because he himself is dead and therefore unequal to the realm of human life, and if that hypothesis is tempered by a vision of the human poet who, like the tools of his trade, is substantial and can only dream of equaling the absolute status of his idealized counterpart, then, analogously, the two tercets are organized in terms of heroic hypothesis ("Si notre idée . . .") followed by human and substantial *pis-aller* ("Que ce granit *du moins* . . ."). In the first tercet Mallarmé attempts to conjoin heaven to earth in his ambition of creating a "bas-relief"—literally, something low ("bas"), or earthly, that is raised up ("relief," from *relever*) or aspiring to heaven—or an epitaph for Poe that will join heaven-reaching idea ("notre idée") to human word. The hypothetical monument to Poe will be higher than earth, "relief" implying not only height but also heightened acuity (to present something *en relief*), but presumably lower than the sky ("bas"), a liminary status that is in itself heroic.

Indeed, the "tombe de Poe" straddling heaven and earth attempts to join the two domains in the verticality which is one of the key characteristics of any house. The tomb is the house of the dead Poe, of the Poet changed into Himself, a change which implies not only a transcendence, or movement upward (the capitalization of "Lui-même"), but also a return, a movement back ("Lui-même," suggesting repetition). As such it is not *simply* a tomb— the word suggesting a movement away from the earth, as in Greek τύμβος, Latin *tumulus*, "a sepulchral mound"—but is also "tombé" from above, the downward movement made explicit in the following line by the word "chu," as Guy Michaud points out: "Le 'tombeau d'Edgar Poe' consiste en un simple bloc de granit, . . . 'chu d'un désastre obscur'; aérolithe gigantesque, il se dresse sur la terre vide, destiné à protéger la mémoire du poète."[12]

If the tomb Mallarmé builds for Poe is meant to preserve the latter's memory, it is that nothing could preserve the man himself: the tomb is a sort of transcendence of a fallen state, itself an oxymoron. Indeed, it is a transcendence only to the extent that a double negative can be a form of transcendence, since it attempts to negate Poe's own negation, that is, to raise his name high to counteract the sinking of the man himself. The last line of the first tercet is itself an "ornament," a pure decoration in that the possibility it suggests in the subjunctive ("s'orne"[13]) is that of an unrealizable dream which, if it is mentioned only in order to be negated ("*ne* sculpte" already implies the possibility that "notre idée" will *not* sculpt such a "bas-relief"), persists, nonetheless, just as the memory and the tomb of the dead poet persist after his own negation. The line thus becomes a sort of definition of the process of "ornement" as an expression of Mallarmé's artistic ideal, to the extent that his poetry re-enacts the paradoxical attempt to build an edifice in words that is totally aesthetic in the sense of the Greek word αἰσθάνομαι ("to perceive"): language making *itself* perceptible in part because it cannot make fully perceptible the meaning it is meant to resurrect. In other words, language making perceptible its *ambition* of transcending the barrier of death, which is tantamount to an admission that such transcendence is *only* an ambition.

Whence a confusion of interior and exterior: if Such a Poem (the product of Such a Poet) could, indeed, be engraved upon Poe's tombstone, it would make Poe himself appear in all his glory (and be "éblouissant"), thus linking the "inhabitant," or the inside of the tomb (Poe) to its form, or outside (the homonym of Poe, "peau"). Mallarmé once again makes use of an attributive construction here, "Dont la tombe de Poe éblouissante s'orne" (as opposed to an epithetical construction, as in "La tombe éblouissante de Poe"), one which emphasizes the fact that "la tombe de Poe" will be "dazzling" only if the verb "s'orne" actuates its potential, that is, transforms its subjunctive into an indicative.

Indeed, Mallarmé's desire to externalize attributes as they are, without losing their essence, and also to define them definitively, once and for all, to house signifieds in a transparent container and at the same time in one that will protect them against the dangers of dissipation, is nothing more than an itinerary, and makes of the "Tombeau" poem an "attribute" in the architectural sense, "emblème employé pour caractériser un édifice, donner une idée de sa destination,"[14] for the destination is never actualized. Mallarmé himself, in speaking of Poe's seemingly magical ability to use artifice by erasing the signs of its own structure, names "cette architecture spontanée,"[15] a blatant contradiction in terms which aptly describes Mallarmé's own ambition of capturing both the generative power of human structures and their potential for the stability of enduring monuments against time.

It is at the very point of the poem which finally discloses the name of the man to whom it is dedicated that the importance for the sonnet of one of Poe's own poems becomes apparent. Not only does the second tercet contain six words which are included in Mallarmé's own translation of "The Raven" ("calme," "chu," "désastre," "jamais," "vol," and "épars"[16]), but, more importantly, the paradox of the sonnet's final verse is that presented by Poe's poem. If Mallarmé's desire to erect a living but eternal monument to the dead but vitally idealized Poe is caught between the recognition of Poe's irrevocable *absence* to the house of life and the boundedness of his existence on the one hand, and the attempt to *commemorate* the departed poet eternally on the other hand, to regenerate his spirit through one of the main functions of any human house, the countering of the obscurity and the forgetfulness of the state of nature, then the French poet's desire is very much in keeping with the spirit of the American poet's masterpiece. Indeed, the Raven's unforgettable refrain, "Nevermore," speaks first of all, like Mallarmé's sonnet, of the departure of a mortal being, in the case of "The Raven," the beloved Lenore who, not unlike the tardily named Poe in Mallarmé's sonnet, seems no longer to have a human *name,* since she is, as Mallarmé's translation of the poem has the narrator say, "la rare et rayonnante jeune fille que les anges nomment Lénore: —de nom pour elle ici, non, *jamais plus!*"[17]

Furthermore, the problem of Mallarmé's sonnet, how to *name* the dead Poe in such a way that he will be forever free of the "blasphemy" that surrounded him as a mortal during his life, and also will relive in death like the century which his purifying sword brought back to life through its non-temporal, *non-secular* nature, is analogous to the narrator's nightmarish situation in "The Raven." The narrator will "nevermore" hold Lenore as a living mortal in his human house: "housse violette de velours qu'*Elle* ne pressera plus, ah! jamais plus"[18] nor, or so the Raven seems to claim, will he meet her soul in Paradise: "'dis à cette âme de chagrin chargée si, dans le distant Eden, elle doit embrasser une jeune fille sanctifiée que les anges nomment Lénore . . .' Le Corbeau dit: 'Jamais plus!'"[19] And what is even more important than Lenore's irrevocable absence is the irrevocable presence to the narrator's mind of that absence, his remembrance of her perpetual obscurity hereafter. It is indeed the pain of this very absence which the Raven's paradoxical presence serves to sharpen: "'ôte ton bec de mon cœur et jette ta forme loin de ma porte!' Le Corbeau dit: 'Jamais plus!'"[20] Neither the "forgotten lore" which the narrator seems to wish to remember at the poem's outset, perhaps precisely in order to *forget* the pain of his lost love, nor the heaven-sent nepenthe of forgetfulness, an antidote to pain,[21] are at his disposal: he may never forget that Lenore is forever absent because both potential channels of comfort, the discoveries of *science* ("forgotten lore," translated by Mallarmé as "savoir oublié") and the *divine* forgetfulness of mortality (nepenthos) are closed to him.

What Mallarmé is trying to do in the sonnet dedicated to the author of "The Raven" is to solve the nightmarish paradox of that poem's narrator, who can neither fully remember and name, or call back to the human domain, the departed Lenore, nor begin to forget her: Mallarmé wishes both to resuscitate the dead Poe and to name him, to make him equal both to a living presence in the house of life and to a stable, definitively nameable presence in the house of death. He wants both paths of communication open to him, that of human science which uses mortal boundedness to create the god-like stability of a conventional symbolic system, and that of divine wisdom, which knows no bounds but by which one might be able to *forget* the limits of mortality.

The relation between Mallarmé and Poe is not one of simple dependence, but one of symbiosis: it is a true "noir mélange," a black/white angel which links the human and the divine in a non-simple way. Mallarmé wishes to protect Poe against the "noirs vols du Blasphème"—perhaps the black flights of the Raven's blasphemous "Nevermore," the word which signals the oblivion of perishable mortals and at the same time the impossibility of forgetting those who have departed—and also to be equal to the departed mortal shadow he is attempting to bring back to life once and for all.

The last two lines of the poem—a depiction not only of the stone monument erected in Poe's memory at a specific spot on a specific date, but also of the status of Mallarmé's poem, which is "borné" and not ideal and infinite —recall the original epithetization of the Poet at the poem's outset and, more specifically, point out the limitations of the ambition to speak a definitive language: "Tel qu'en Lui-même enfin," rhyming at the *hémistiche* with "Que ce granit du moins," indicates the limited nature ("du moins") of limits ("en*fin*"). "L'éternité," in its later transformation, "à jamais," emphasizes that eternity can be conceived of for mortals only in negative terms, just as the negative "jamais" underlies the positive adverb "à jamais" which it attempts to construct.

Indeed, the granite of Poe's monument does not only show "à jamais sa borne / Aux noirs vols du Blasphème," it also shows its barrier "à jamais," to *never* itself, or to the potential obscurity of the mortal state, that is, to the subliminal but persistent reminiscence of "never" in "forever." Mallarmé's desire to write a poem that is a total reflection of the poet to whom it is dedicated, that is, equal to him—a poem which by its very insubstantiality, its transparence, its equality only to the other of which it speaks and not to itself, would not "show" its limitations, that is, its requisite character as a counter of as well as to the passing years—must forever be tempered by the limitations of mortality which say that each man, once he has died, and indeed, by the very fact that he will die, does not exist in himself, but also that not until he no longer exists in himself, as equal only to himself, will he ever be equal to more than himself and carry a symbolic value by meaning something which he himself is not. As Leo Bersani puts it, speaking of the relation between the author and his work:

> Considered alone, a book is a waste-product of self-expression, a product of psychological and historical chance. But its "ordering" or "symmetry" transcends its existence. The relations among the most apparently self-expressive elements of a single work are determined by psychologically non-expressive affinities; *the author is omitted by his structure.*[22]

If the author is "omitted by his structure," it is that any attempt at self-generation, at *spontaneity,* must learn to accept the limitations implied by structure, by the units of a bounded symbolic system, even as it wishes to go beyond the conventions of that system, for in the long run, the dreamed-of "architecture spontanée" will build an edifice that is either non-spontaneous or non-stable. It is a difficult, perhaps an impossible lesson for Mallarmé to learn: to accept the "borne," the boundary of the human units of which any symbolic system must be composed, is to have the possibility of being "born"[23] once again in a new way, both equal and unequal to oneself.

Chapter Three: The House of Life and the House of Death

"Sur les bois oubliés"

*Au lieu de tenir . . . pour arbitraire le rapport du signe et de son objet, il rêva à une sorte d'*égalité *formelle* entre *la chose et le mot chargé de désigner la chose. . . . Mallarmé rêve que le mot* crée, *et cela même matériellement, la réalité qu'il nomme. Dans l'un de ses plus beaux poèmes, il suffit pour ramener une morte à l'existence, d'un seul mot bien choisi: "le souffle de (son)* nom *murmuré tout un soir. . . .*

J.-P. Richard
L'Univers imaginaire de Mallarmé

Sonnet (Pour votre chère morte, son ami)

—"Sur les bois oubliés quand passe l'hiver sombre
Tu te plains, ô captif solitaire du seuil,
Que ce sépulcre à deux qui fera notre orgueil
Hélas! du manque seul des lourds bouquets s'encombre.

Sans écouter Minuit qui jeta son vain nombre,
Une veille t'exalte à ne pas fermer l'œil
Avant que dans les bras de l'ancien fauteuil
Le suprême tison n'ait éclairé mon Ombre.

Qui veut souvent avoir la Visite ne doit
Par trop de fleurs charger la pierre que mon doigt
Soulève avec l'ennui d'une force défunte.

Âme au clair foyer tremblante de m'asseoir,
Pour revivre il suffit qu'à tes lèvres j'emprunte
Le souffle de mon nom murmuré tout un soir."

The triangular relation of poet, deceased, and mourner in "Pour votre chère morte, son ami" is already indicated by the poem's dedication, one which uses all three possible pairings linking the three figures by two's. The dedication first speaks of a relation of poet to living mourner, since the use of the pronoun "votre" presupposes a discourse of a "je" to a "vous." To this extent the poet speaks *for* the man who has lost his wife or friend, speaks in his behalf in an effort to offer him the solace of present words to console him in the absence of his beloved. The second half of the dedication poses the relation "je"/"elle," by its use of the pronoun "son": the poet, even though he is speaking "for" the mourner, seems to be serving as a *porte-parole* for the dead woman, for the one who cannot be present to speak to her beloved directly. The poet thus plays the role of a go-between; he must be equal to the domain of the living in order to speak to the mourner of the deceased, and equal to the domain of the dead so that he might hear the message it has to send across the barrier separating the house of life from the house of death, a barrier upon which his speaking depends but which it is meant to work to efface.

The sonnet evokes two homes, one within the realm of human life, in which the living "solitaire" waits alone at night and hopes for a vision of his love to appear to him, and one beyond human existence, in which the "chère morte" is waiting for her love to join her some day ("ce sépulcre à deux qui fera notre orgueil") and access to which is cut off for him so long as he has not crossed the threshold of death ("captif solitaire du seuil"). The two homes, although they seem to be mutually exclusive—since the barrier which separates them, death, is crossable only once and only in one direction— nonetheless inform each other in the sonnet as the two lovers inhabiting them enter into what might be termed a sort of pact, or at the very least a pooling of resources. It would hardly be exaggerating the nature of the two lovers' relationship to say that it is symbiotic: just as the living member longs for a vision of his love as she used to sit in the armchair, and seems to depend upon her to advise him of the conditions under which he might obtain that vision ("Qui veut souvent avoir la Visite"), she can "revivre" only by borrowing from him "Le souffle de mon nom murmuré tout un soir." Each of the two needs something from the other, he the at least momentary appearance of an image, she the repeated utterance of a name; only the two working together can effect even a temporary transcendence of the barrier separating them, that is, the dead woman's "coming to life" at the bright hearth where her lover is waiting for her.

If the resuscitation of the dead lover, transitory though it may be, requires a collaboration of the two sorts of homes, the cooperation of forces living and dead, it is that each of them has something to contribute. Parallel to the lovers' joining forces to create a new sort of union between them is the poet's effort, which also straddles the domains of the living and the dead, to forge a poem which is an eternal, yet living monument and thus to go beyond the barrier which is always in danger of separating two fundamental aspects of language: language as eternal commemoration, with its ability as a stabilizer to counter oblivion and obscurity, and language as presence, with its evocative and generative powers. And indeed, given the poet's obvious association with the action which makes the dead lover come back to life, the almost ritual pronunciation of her name, it is not surprising that his efforts to mobilize the two aspects of language are similar to the lovers' attempts to overcome their separation by joining the power of the living home to the power of the house of death.

If language, like the couple in the sonnet, must submit to a duality of nature, both needing to be anchored in the past and to accumulate or depend upon the elements of a fixed system, and attempting perpetually to escape that past by existing in the moment, to generate a complete spontaneity of expression, this duality may partially explain the ambiguous status, in the sonnet, of flowers, suggestive not only of the sensuous, lyrical impulse which pushes the dead woman's friend or husband to wish to catch a glimpse of her form once again, even as a shadow, but also of the split between emotion and the expression of emotion, or between idea and the formulation of idea, be it through the medium of flowers placed upon a tombstone which cannot be replenished "quand passe l'hiver sombre," or through that of words, "fleurs" here recalling flowery rhetoric and its excesses which may tend to work against the regeneration of meaning: "Qui veut souvent avoir la Visite ne doit / Par trop de fleurs charger la pierre. . . ." In both cases, whether flowers are considered as belonging to the domain of physical, corporal existence which cannot stand up to the passage of time—the absence of flowers recalling the absence of the departed lover—or as being emblematic of the difficulty of poetic language which, in attempting to give external form to meaning, is in danger of placing it in a perishable body (an imperfect poem) rather than giving it eternal life, flowers, like other manifestations of form, are seen as potential enemies and potential allies.

The dual nature of perishable form is manifest in the attitude of the "captif solitaire" at the poem's outset. The paradox of the heavy bouquets' absence weighing down or even accumulating—if the etymological meaning of the term "s'encombrer," from the Latin *cumulus*, "pile," is considered—upon the grave is matched by the friend's "remembrance" of the "bois oubliés," reinforced by the inverted syntax of the opening sentence: it is as if the winter's arrival, expressed in a subordinate clause but preceding the main clause which deals with the lover's complaint, takes precedence over the human action. The chronological order of the events, or at least their cause-and-effect sequence, is thus re-enacted by the syntax of the sentence: first the forgetfulness brought about by the passage of time which darkens everything it touches ("l'hiver sombre"), then the desire to commemorate what has departed. It seems therefore that only the absence of flowers calls to mind their value, thereby setting up the lover's complaint. Just as the absence of flowers is a kind of weight, the forgetfulness of the wood as a possible expression of sentiment is a reminder of its past, and perhaps potential future value. The very value of perishable form is thus experienced only because of its limitations, can be evaluated and appreciated as what it is only once it *is* no longer: its sensuous fullness as an expression of emotion (in the case of the lovers) or of meaning (in the case of the word) becomes consciously apparent only once love as presence and language as presence have been lost.

If perishable form has an ambiguous status, then the imperishable does also. The unchanging house of the dead, "ce sépulcre à deux qui fera notre orgueil," is far more sturdy than the house of the living, the "si clair foyer" at which the dead lover trembles to sit. The sepulcher represents the only place of definitive union between the lovers; the phrase which describes the sepulcher contains the only first person plural form ("notre") of the entire sonnet—a particularly notable fact since the poem speaks principally of a couple one of whose members is the speaker—as well as the only verb in the future tense ("fera"), as opposed to several verbs which express a virtual future but only a hypothetical and uncertain one: "Avant que . . . / Le suprême tison n'ait éclairé mon Ombre," an action which could be expressed by a future perfect ("Tu ne fermeras pas l'œil tant que le suprême tison *n'aura pas éclairé* mon Ombre") but which may never come to pass; "Qui veut souvent avoir la Visite," expressing a desire which may or may not be realized; and "Pour revivre il suffit qu'à tes lèvres j'emprunte / Le souffle de mon nom . . . ," once again a potential future indicative ("Pour revivre j'emprunterai") being transformed into a subjunctive. Thus the sepulcher displays and assures an "orgueil" which is strikingly self-assured by comparison with the tentative tone of the rest of the sonnet.

But the dead lover, although she is beyond the vicissitudes of perishable form, relies upon human mortality in order to "revivre." If she has no physical existence, she does have a shadow, and it is not the reflection of a physical presence but rather a mental image in the living friend's mind; for if it were a real shadow, then lighting it up would make it disappear. The "suprême tison" here has both a qualitative and a quantitative value: the "tison," perhaps a transformation of the "bois oubliés" which are now being burnt for firewood, is the supreme revalorisation of perishable form in that it is a consumption of that form which brings light and thus demonstrates the usability of form as a medium. But the spark is "suprême" also in the way that Mallarmé often uses that adjective, as Graham Dunstan Martin remarks in his gloss on the word in Valéry's "Le Cimetière marin":

> [T]he word "suprême" means in its Latin and Mallarméan sense, "last." Man's last offering to the absolute, his last sacrifice, is his own death, after which he will be one with eternity, despising his past mortal condition. But at the same time, disturbing overtones are produced by these telescoped senses of "suprême": for they equate the poet's contemplation of the divine while he is still alive, with death.[1]

The paradoxical equality spoken of here by Martin is precisely that which underlies the relation of the house of life to the house of death: the contemplation of a transcendence of death only marks the living lover's inequality to his friend, just as it is his own mortality, his inequality to himself across time and to his beloved across the boundary of death, which is at the root of his desire for a transcendence of that boundary.

The tension between the house of life which lasts only until it has reached its last ("suprême") moment because all of its fuel has been burnt, and the house of death which cannot exist in time but which is eternally lasting ("suprême" as "above" or "highest"), is indicated in the poem by the relation of the circular to the linear. The house of death, "ce sépulcre à deux qui fera notre orgueil," is to be reached by the crossing of a threshold, a linear movement which may be seen as a progression to the extent that it will place the now-living lover in the same apparently unattackable position of pride as his dead lover is now in, but which also imprisons him in that it is a movement without return. The threshold of the house of death thus marks a position of strength, but also alienates those who are within the house as much as it houses them.

On the other hand, the home in which the "chère morte" wishes to relive, if fleetingly, is seen as a hearth ("au si clair foyer"), a center, an englobement which would surround the dead woman once again so as to include her within the context of human time and mortality. The dead lover may reappear "dans les bras de l'ancien fauteuil," benevolently surrounded by the artifacts of the house of life, the catachresis "dans les bras" suggesting also the sensuality of human love. The house of life is represented for the dead lover by a hearth, a *focus* (which is in fact the Latin word from which "foyer" comes), and not by the threshold which is not only at the periphery of the house but also nothing more than a pure quantification, an outline of the limits of the house.

It is the loss of a dimension, the lack of depth in the house of death, which may explain the importance in the sonnet of *empty* quantifiers, shown to be at odds with full human existence, just as the word seen as irrevocably stable and beyond question cannot be mobilized in the poet's attempt to generate living, vital meaning. In the first quatrain, the "sépulcre à deux" is weighted down by an emptiness, by the absence of flowers caused by the very winter with which the tomb is to be associated as another ally of death. Thus, the sepulcher is doubly empty: first, because its inhabitant, ravaged by death, is herself melting away, and secondly, because the winter has taken away the flowers that had rested upon the tomb, so that only a "lack" ("manque seul"), a kind of weighted place-holder, is now to be found on the tomb.

In the second quatrain, "Minuit," another kind of threshold in that it is the dividing line between one day and the next, is said to have thrown off its "vain nombre," "vain" here implying superfluous or empty of sense. The verb of which "Minuit" is the subject, "jeta," the only *passé simple* of the entire sonnet, is in parallel position ("qui fera" / "qui jeta," both following the *hémistiche*) to the only future form, and provides an additional link to the "sépulcre à deux," accentuated as well by the similarity of form between the two verbs (two syllables, four letters: consonant–mute *e*–consonant–*a*). Not only are both phrases, the "sépulcre à deux" and "Minuit," descriptive of potentially empty quantifiers, they both include a mathematical term as well: the "two" in "ce sépulcre à deux" may well find a resonance in its inverse, one-half, implied in "*Mi*-nuit." Just as the sepulcher brings the couple together in what may potentially be an empty union, Midnight wishes to divide and thus conquer the lover's ambition to continue his vigil across the juncture of two successive days until he has seen a vision of his lost love.

Indeed, the rhyme "Minuit"/"ennui," accentuated by the placement of the two words in the same position (immediately preceding the *hémistiche*) of their respective lines—a placement which makes them mirror images if the poem is divided in half after the quatrains and before the tercets—emphasizes the unchangeability and the boredom of invariable, empty quantifiers. Midnight, the zero hour of the night belonging properly neither to the day which precedes it nor to the day which it announces, is, like the "seuil" of the house, purely liminary, without substance but bringing out the value of the substantial units which it defines only because it is itself equal to nothing and has a purely quantifying capacity as a perfectly neutral marker of time. Like the sepulcher, its number is "vain" in that it marks a potentially empty union of two—in the case of the sepulcher, two reunited but dead lovers, in the case of Midnight, two successive days each of which is inhabited by the dead lover's absence. The verb "exalte" ("Une veille t'exalte à ne pas fermer l'œil") is a potential counter to the haughty emptiness of Midnight, since the verb, from the Latin *exaltare*, "to lift up," evokes the reaching of an altitude at which the lover might see the "suprême" (in the sense of "high") spark which would fill the emptiness of his solitude.

Even the flowers the absence of which the lover so regretted in the first quatrain are shown up to be empty place-holders in the first tercet: "Qui veut souvent avoir la Visite ne doit / Par trop de fleurs charger la pierre que mon doigt / Soulève avec l'ennui d'une force défunte." The flowers, which are originally meant to express the friend's love for his departed and thus to take the place of that love and stand for it as its expression in external form, are revealed to be pure quantity without substance. They can be lifted by a lifeless finger precisely because they are like all attempts to stabilize the flux of mortality by "holding the place" of what cannot withstand the passage of time by means of a place-holder always equal to itself but not always equal to what it is replacing; as a quantity substituted for a quality, they are in danger of killing the qualities they are meant to replace and thus of becoming empty place-holders.[2] Indeed, the rhyme "doit"/"doigt," with its "empty" letter adding nothing to the pronunciation of the first term, also furnishes a re-enactment of the uselessness of empty quantity which even a dead force can lift up, particularly if one considers that the word "doigt" may well be an echo of "vain nombre," the empty digits cast off (or perhaps thrown away, that is, wasted) by the inefficacious Midnight.

The end rhymes of the two quatrains emphasize the struggle between life as representative of mortal flux and death as representative of the attainment of an unchanging, fixed principle or identity. "L'hiver sombre," which demonstrates by its defoliating and obliterating passage the dangers of relying solely upon "flowers," has as its positive counterpart "mon Ombre," the Shadow being not obscured by the passage of time (here diurnal rather than seasonal) but rather "éclairé," lighted up by an exploitation of form (once again, perhaps the "bois oubliés" now burning in the hearth) that effects a commemoration rather than an obscuring.

The middle pair of this series, "s'encombre" / "vain nombre," once again pits seasonal time (the absence of the "lourds bouquets" being a result of winter's passage) against diurnal (or perhaps nocturnal) time, the useless stroke of Midnight. We are thus faced in the first case with an absence which is seen to be full of meaning, but an untrue or an unwished-for meaning (absence of flowers equals absence of love or absence of the physical existence of the dead lover), and in the second case with a presence which is seen to be devoid of sense, since the lover refuses to acknowledge Midnight's striking by giving up his vigil. Thus the feminine rhymes of the two quatrains move from the inevitable absenting of mortal form (wood/flowers no longer present to express love), a virtual statement of the human condition, through the unsuccessful conjoinment of form with idea ("s'encombre" evoking the absence of flowers despite the presence of love and "vain nombre" the presence of Midnight but the absence of meaning attached to its striking), toward the hoped-for elucidation of a Presence through an awareness that only a non-conventional conjoinment of form and meaning, only a complete combustion (up to the very last spark) has any chance of bringing to life, or making visible, the insubstantial idea. Giving life to the unchanging and eternal (here represented by the departed lover) with its converse, eternalizing or stabilizing the living (the surviving lover's mortal remembrance of his love as person and as emotion), are the dreams of non-conventional Symbolism.

The series of masculine rhymes in the quatrains also demonstrates the inequality of the house of life and the house of death and the dream of conjoining the two. The pair "seuil"/"fauteuil" has already been discussed, the first term indicating what holds the living lover back from the house of death and access to his love, the second suggesting what would hold the dead lover in life were she to reappear in the human house even as a Shadow. It is furthermore notable that both terms of the rhymed pair belong to the vocabulary of the house, and that "seuil" is not only peripheral and liminary, but also a place across which one moves, which in a sense pushes people into and out of the house, as opposed to the "fauteuil" which not only is in the center of the house but also immediately suggests a stop, a resting-place. That the armchair is emblematic of mortal existence and time is made even clearer by the adjective which modifies it, "ancien," both of whose principal meanings, "former" and "old," are appropriate here even though the former meaning is suggested by the adjective's placement before the noun. The armchair is not only no longer equal to an armchair for her who is no longer equal to her human self, thus recalling the temporary status of all mortal things, it is also old, suggesting the potential fullness of the passage of human time for those whose lives are marked not by empty thresholds or quantifiers, like the "vain nombre" cast off by Midnight, but rather by the full measure and value of human time by which the years, not simply a *lack,* accumulate.[3]

The other rhymed pair, "orgueil"/"œil," points up the ambition shared by the sepulcher and the living lover to *commemorate* the departed. Each speaks in terms of the fight against oblivion, the sepulcher effecting a permanence by its acceptance of a negation, its status as a *marker* and therefore a *bound* upon the existence whose former presence it announces as a present absence, and the lover resisting the inexorable passage of time by keeping up his vigil despite the forgetfulness which his human nature would lead him to. Indeed, it is not coincidental that the lover's actions in the second quatrain are both expressed in terms of a negation: "Sans écouter Minuit," "*ne pas* fermer l'œil" both are indicative not only of what the lover does, but also of what he does not do but what it would, by implication, be natural for him to do, in very simple terms, what human beings usually do at night, heed the striking of the hour and close their eyes. What the sepulcher accomplishes by its very non-living (and therefore non-dying) nature, the establishment of a permanence which is its "pride" and the pride of those sheltered under it, the lover can accomplish only by going against his nature, by being other than himself. It is the very negation of that nature, parallel to the negation of the deceased lover's existence, which is required as a marker, as the limiting outline of a stable, conventional symbolic system which is thus founded upon a series of absences and can therefore commemorate only what is no longer.

If the two quatrains concentrate upon the living lover's attempts at transcending his mortal state and thus reaching across the boundary of death to touch his departed, the two tercets focus rather upon the latter and her desire to be resuscitated into the house of life. The two lovers thus seem to be striving, each on his own side, toward the other from whom he is separated by the threshold of death. The crossing of that boundary, which is not absolutely confirmed at the end of the poem but the necessary conditions for which are sketched out ("il suffit . . ."), represents for the lovers what crossing the boundary of meaning represents for the poet: a transcendence of the human condition and of its limitations.

The dream of non-conventional Symbolism, the dream of equating form and meaning, is represented in the sonnet by the dead lover's soul becoming equated with the hearth at which it longs to come to life, "au si clair foyer" dividing its grammatical function between "m'asseoir" ("to sit at the so bright hearth") and "Ame" ("bright-hearthed soul"). Gardner Davies misjudges the poem when he comments that "L'adverb *si* ne semble guère ajouter au vers qu'une syllabe requise par l'alexandrin,"[4] since the presence of the word has at least two functions here apart from its quantitative meaning of "tellement": it indicates the hypothetical nature of the lover's reappearance at the hearth ("Soul trembling to sit at the hearth *if it is light*"), one which depends upon the success of the double venture of the poet and the separated couple. It also creates an additional equation of the soul with the hearth: "Ame, aussi clair foyer," an equation of means (hearth) and meaning (reappearance of the soul) which is precisely the goal of non-conventional Symbolism. Here the dead lover's soul is *in accord* with its potential housing, whereas the living lover complained about the dark (and not bright) winter in the sonnet's first lines. The darkness brought about by an unequal relationship between form and meaning (the absent and forgotten wood/flowers as opposed to the absent and remembered lover), and by an incompatible relationship between man and nature, is corrected to the brightness caused by an equation of exterior form and interior meaning (bright hearth / bright heart).

The equation of outside and inside, of a stable mechanism which is meant to generate an unstable meaning, is paralleled by the poem's focusing upon the *hearth* as a possible locus of the transcendence of the boundary of death. The hearth joins outside and inside, since it is fueled by wood coming from the domain of nature, from outside the house, and yet warms the interior of the house. What the hearth does is what the poet, in a sense, wishes to do: it takes the apparently dead matter of what has been ravaged by death, what is in danger of falling into oblivion, and uses it to create a living commemoration, to resuscitate meaning from it. The hearth that joins the forces of the dead with the forces of life uses a dead past to regenerate (and light up) a living presence, just as the poet uses a linguistic tradition, that is to say, "dead" words—in that their form has lost its perceptible link to meaning, or perhaps never had one—in order to re-create language as presence.

Whence the final joining of resources at the end of the poem which would be capable of crossing the barrier of meaning and the threshold of death: the murmuring, across time ("tout un soir" suggesting the plenitude of human time as opposed to "l'hiver sombre" of the first line evoking its emptiness), on the mortal lips of the living lover, of the departed lover's *name*, the unchanging construct which will forever house her memory but which, alone, cannot regenerate her presence. It is only the act of murmuring the name which joins the breath of a presence ("Le *souffle*") to the stability of a permanence ("mon nom"). And if the departed only "borrows" the life spirit she seems to desire, it is that the permanence of the tomb is incompatible with the temporality and the temporariness of all that is alive, the latter needing always to be renewed, "borrowed" once again.

The keynote here is the ritualistic value of the name's pronouncement in the last line of the poem: for ritual depends equally upon a past tradition which fixes the meaning of its symbols and upon the possibility of re-creating a genuine belief, a presence of what those symbols mean to evoke. Whence the incantatory element in the poem's last lines: the four *v*'s in v. 9, each spaced two syllables from its neighbor, make the line difficult to read without an almost imposed regularity, as does the mirroring effect, in v. 13, of "(re)*vivre*" and "*lèvres*," placed at equal distance, respectively, from the beginning of the line and from the *hémistiche*. Similarly, the almost mimetic, murmuring effect of the last line of the poem, featuring not only twelve liquid consonants and the repeated *mur* in the word "murmuré," perhaps an attempt to represent the *repetition* of the name across time, but also the miniature palindrome "mon nom," which has a similar effect.

The last line of the poem is also particular by the simplicity of its syntax. It is one of only two lines to contain neither a finite verb nor a subordinating conjunction announcing a finite verb ("Avant que," v. 7; "la pierre que mon doigt," v. 10), an unusual situation for Mallarmé, who makes spare use of verbs in many of his sonnets, tending as he does rather to nominalize action and to place noun phrases in a vague apposition linked by no verb. Here the absence of a finite verb in a sonnet of high syntactical complexity (three subjunctive forms, for example, and considerable inverted word order) is yet another attempt at creating a mortal immortality, at joining the stability of the word as timeless commemoration not pronounced in time but subsisting across time, to the generative qualities of the word uttered with all of its ritualistic potential.

Furthermore, the speaking of the name in the last line of the poem is in contrast with several other actions: with the living lover's earlier utterance of a complaint ("Tu te plains"), as complex syntactically by the rhetoric of the opening lines as the final murmur is simple; with the sepulcher's "orgueil," also the reporting of a name but one the self-assured insistence and monotony of which is in strong contrast with the lover's quiet but effective murmur; with Midnight's empty striking which, like the lover's murmur, is formed out of a repetition, but which, unlike his repetition of the name, is to no avail; and with the forgetting of the woods at the poem's outset, described by the only other past participle of the entire sonnet, and the placement of which mirrors almost exactly that of the murmured name, with which it rhymes ("les bois oubliés," v. 1, and "mon nom murmuré," v. 14).

For the lover's murmur is not syntactically complex precisely because it attempts to go beyond syntax, beyond the joining of inert units of meaning to each other, in its ambition to recapture the essential meaning and spirit of the individual name, its relation to itself—whence the repetition of the name creating a syntax of self-perpetuation—and its link to meaning as it stands alone, the potential equality of name and named by which the former might bring the latter across the boundary of death. The boundary of death is not only the line separating the two lovers, but also the essential negation which is the underlying mechanism by which any name must exclude the named which it cannot be precisely because at one level it must be itself in order to stand for what it names.

Thus, at the end of the sonnet, the lover's ambition matches the poet's as much as the poet writes on behalf of the lovers in an attempt to rejoin those whose present separation and inequality to each other allow him as well as compel him to break into speech, both to initiate its movement across the page and to refuse to respect its integrity. The house of life and the house of death can be equalized—if at all—only instantaneously, at a zero point in time, because their separateness is not only a prerequisite for the functioning of a conventionally based speech trying to fill a lack (the dead lover's absence as well as the absence of the named presumed by the presence of the name), it is also the very reason for the presence of that speech, a presence trying to fill an absence upon which its own existence depends. The two halves of the *symbolon,* in their admission that home is to be searched for, take away by the very terms of their conjoinment what they are trying to construct as a presence, for each half searches for a home in the half which it is not. It is only by the dream of a non-conventional Symbolism that the name can be both equal to itself and equal to what it is trying to represent as a presence, equal to the unchanging house of death and to the house of life which spends its life in a search for an immortality, for an enduring existence which by its very nature it cannot contain.

Chapter Four: The House of Life and the House of Death

"Le vierge, le vivace et le bel aujourd'hui"

*L'Art demeure pour lui la plus sublime opération du Moi,
lui-même identique au non-être dont it est émané.*

Antoine Orliac
Mallarmé tel qu'en lui-même

Le vierge, le vivace et le bel aujourd'hui
Va-t-il nous déchirer avec un coup d'aile ivre
Ce lac dur oublié que hante sous le givre
Le transparent glacier des vols qui n'ont pas fui!

Un cygne d'autrefois se souvient que c'est lui
Magnifique mais qui sans espoir se délivre
Pour n'avoir pas chanté la région où vivre
Quand du stérile hiver a resplendi l'ennui.

Tout son col secouera cette blanche agonie
Par l'espace infligé à l'oiseau qui le nie,
Mais non l'horreur du sol où le plumage est pris.

Fantôme qu'à ce lieu son pur éclat assigne,
Il s'immobilise au songe froid de mépris
Que vêt parmi l'exil inutile le Cygne.

Ah! à l'exprès et *propre* usage, du rêveur se clôture, au noir d'arbres, en spacieux retirement, la *Propriété,* comme veut le vulgaire: il faut que je l'aie manquée, avec obstination, durant mes jours—omettant le moyen d'acquisition—pour satisfaire quelque singulier instinct de ne rien posséder et de seulement passer, au risque d'une résidence comme maintenant ouverte à l'aventure. . . . [1]

In this passage taken from "Conflit," Mallarmé speaks of a conflict central to his enterprise of creating a home in language, a conflict which is also essential in the sonnet "Le vierge, le vivace et le bel aujourd'hui." It is a fight between property and properness, between the "virginity" of a hermetically sealed, tomb-like place of meaning and residence and the "vivacity" of the world of the constant regeneration of meaning. The "Property" of the dreamer-poet is closed to "proper" usage not only because poetic property is "improper," that is, non-conventional, but also, and more importantly, because any relegation of characteristics or qualities (properties) to a single and fixed form (Property) is a closing off, a "clôture," which puts an end to those properties in themselves. The "conflict" in effect results from a contradictory desire, from the wish to have a property, a home, as a protection against the vagaries of existence, and at the same time "to possess nothing and simply to pass on," the latter term ("passer") suggesting a life made up simply of unconnected moments, an unmarked and unresisted movement toward death. The "property" evoked in "Conflit" is thus a source both of death and of life, since it embodies a conflict between the dream of a permanent, final housing of meaning ("du rêveur se clôture . . . la Propriété") and an ever-momentary but potentially dissipated generation of it ("une résidence comme maintenant ouverte à l'aventure").

The parallel between "Conflit" and "Le vierge, le vivace et le bel aujourd'hui," aside from the sharing of a surprising number of key terms,[2] thus resides in a similarly equivocal attitude toward two elements which may constitute home: if "Conflit" hesitates between the always potential rebirth of interest offered by a residence "open to adventure" and the peace of a "spacieux retirement," the sonnet attempts to merge these two elements and to have them both. It attempts to evoke a presence, to turn "un cygne d'autrefois" into a "cygne d'aujourd'hui," to bring about a regeneration of seemingly lost properties ("Magnifique"), a kind of rebirth of all that is "vivace" through a tearing ("déchirement") open of the surface of frozen forms. But it also wishes to create a proper noun, to change the "cygne d'autrefois" into "le Cygne," a proper Swan, not merely (and perhaps no longer) a living and present one, but one whose identity transcends the passage of time, a creature existing outside (and against) temporality. This double ambition might well be described as a conflict between time and space: it is because the passage of time "de-spatializes" mortals that they attempt to counter time by creating the spatial stability of the house; but once the structure of the house has seemingly stopped time, it may then go on to strangle it, to fight against the necessary role of time as a useful bringer of new things.

The sonnet begins with the depiction of an "aujourd'hui" which itself straddles the domains of time and space. Normally a temporal adverb, the word becomes transformed, through the use of the definite article and the string of adjectives modifying it, into a noun, the subject of the long sentence which comprises the first quatrain. By moving the word from one grammatical function to another, Mallarmé has in a sense stabilized it, given it a title; as Emilie Noulet expresses it, the article, which largely serves the function of making a substantive of the adverb, is a "signe apparent de sa dignité."[3] Whereas the adverb would be a complement to the sentence (Latin *adverbium*, "added to the verb"), the noun is its subject and thus is absolutely central to it, a transformation which, according to Edward Bird, is typical of Mallarmé: "l'expression mallarméenne est caractérisée . . . par l'affaiblissement de la fonction du verbe et par l'importance croissante de celle de l'adverbe."[4] The temporal complement, a mere adjunct in a conventional sentence, is thus drawn into the center of focus as a non-conventional subject.

And indeed, because of the syntax of the first sentence of the sonnet, it is as if the word "aujourd'hui," normally descriptive of a point in time, is no longer a mere indicator of a present moment but rather has become "spatialized" by its nominalization. The effect of the long, untraditional, but typically Mallarméan inversion of the noun and the three adjectives modifying it is to create a very large unit of meaning, since the subject of those three adjectives is in doubt until the end of the first line, as Noulet remarks:

> Cet éloignement de l'article engendre ainsi cette légère hésitation sur la nature des quatre mots en les faisant prendre tour à tour pour le substantif attendu et donne ce rythme qui semble imiter le départ quatre fois renouvelé de l'élan.[5]

This thrice abortive "departure" of the sentence, which can only get moving once its subject has at last been identified on the fourth try, has the effect of slowing things down considerably. This is a "today" which seems to exist not in a single moment of time, but rather across time.

The welding together of a rather unorthodox unit of meaning in the first line of the sonnet, including a word which is itself a "welding together" of several words, "au-jour-de-hui," has the effect of placing at the head of the poem a sententious block of meaning: "the today," not simply an evoker of presence here, seems, like Poe in his poem, to be given the authority of a permanent, lasting title as well as a certain responsibility for action ("va-t-il nous déchirer"). Guy Michaud notes the immediate value of this periphrastic future: "le poème s'ouvre, comme une brusque déchirure, . . . se projette par bonds successifs vers l'avenir,"[6] and Thibaudet remarks upon the tension already fully present in the first quatrain between the stability of the spatial element and the utter immediacy of the desire to create a presence:

> Mais ce premier quatrain, isolé, ici, suffit, je crois, à nous montrer juxtaposés, un peu hostiles, les deux ordres d'images et de figures qui en se distinguant se mettent l'un l'autre en valeur dans la poésie de Mallarmé. D'un côté une ampleur de passé à forme d'espace, de l'autre une pointe d'instant, un visage vivant. . . .[7]

The spatial element of the today is further developed by the action it may be executing: its tearing apart of the forgotten lake is the reverse of the process by which it is joined together with the other words of the first line, as well as with itself ("au-jour-de-hui").

The ripping of the "lac dur oublié" is a metaphorical breaking apart of the surface of words in order to dip into their meaning, to re-explore what has been "forgotten" and what cannot "dure" as presence so long as it is "dur," "solid." Thus, in the parallel position to the amalgamated term "aujourd'hui," we find in the second line "d'aile ivre," repeated aurally in the second line of the second quatrain in an "amalgamated" form, "délivre," the meaning of which also underlies its homonym in the first quatrain: will the beautiful today tear into the hard lake and deliver, or liberate, the meaning that is frozen under the surface? The phrase "d'aile ivre," in its torn apart form, may be seen in part as the result of the very action ("déchirer") of which it is a complement. It is breaking the surface of "common" words, "unhousing" the words of everyday speech and thus at least momentarily realizing their dream of freedom from the protection the house has to offer, that allows them to take flight: the "coup d'aile ivre" is meant to carry out the action which has been neglected by the stationary, confined "vols qui n'ont pas fui," that is, the process of indefinitely prolonged generation of associations that Mallarmé's "langage essentiel" is meant to execute.

What the "déchirement" would reveal underneath the frozen lake's surface, were it to be successful, would be "Le transparent glacier des vols qui n'ont pas fui," the piling up of unsuccessful attempts at birthing new meaning, a spatialized chronicle of the poet's tries at parenting through the perfect poem. The image of the iceberg suggests the accumulation of days during which no poem came to life, before the appearance of the "successful" poem, which is the tip of the iceberg in that its physical manifestation, like the actual moment of birth, reveals only a minute fraction of the time and effort that went into its creation. But the iceberg is "transparent" as the poem cannot be, for the former reveals itself as being in the process of "parenting"–"transparent"–whereas the latter can show only the final product which necessarily creates an opaque property and not simply a transparence.

Mallarmé's desire to join the stability of the word as an always-erect, inherited property to the potential of generating through the destabilization of metaphor a perpetually corrected, "proper" meaning is analogous to the process by which the "lac dur oublié" at some indefinable juncture turns into the water underneath its frozen surface. Even if temperature can be conceived only as a continuum, for every liquid substance there exists one temperature which effects a transformation, an indefinable jump that breaks the continuum and creates a contiguity rather than a continuity even within the essential sameness of the substance which changes from gas to liquid to solid, as Thibaudet remarks in his comments about the sonnet: "la même eau compose et la glace et les vapeurs qu'élève une haleine de soleil."[8]

Indeed, the solidity of the ice, reminiscent of the unchangeability of inherited form, can only "express" its content, water, by relegating its solidity, and conversely, as the water reaches the surface, it becomes fixed within a form which alone is visible, which hides latent or underlying meaning even though that meaning may be made consistent with the surface covering it through a constant back-and-forth motion between the solid and the liquid state. The paradoxical nature of home for the swan resides in the "lac dur oublié" that could but does not allow him either to settle down on it or to take flight from it. The lake is neither completely liquid, liquidity implying an absence of any fixed self-equality and thus of any resistance to a constant regeneration, nor completely solid, since its purportedly solid state cannot escape being haunted by the freer state which its present surface only covers over. Thus the lake allows neither a metaphorical flight of redefinition nor a metonymical setting forth of boundaries by which the lake's surface could simply be "taken for" its underlying parts.

The solidity and hence the impenetrability of the frozen water of the lake as opposed to the transparence of what the solid surface covers are parallel to the realization made by the "cygne d'autrefois," an animate counterpart of the "bel aujourd'hui" as well as its understood metaphorical partner in the first quatrain ("coup d'aile"): a realization that his own existence represents a disjunction, a contiguity and not a continuity. The iceberg of the first quatrain may be echoed in the near homonyms "autrefois" / "eau très froide," reinforced by the identical position of the words "autrefois" and "glacier" in two contiguous lines. The swan, like the various forms of water which are present in the first quatrain, finds that his identity, an illusory sign of continuity, covers over the change he has undergone within the false stability of that name. Like the water in solid and liquid form "sous le givre," the swan discovers a part of himself underneath the surface, the *sou-* element in "se souvient" recalling the geography of the "lac dur oublié."

The swan's "coming to himself from underneath" ("se souvient"), his remembering of what he really is, can be seen as being analogous to the today's tearing of the surface of the frozen lake: both actions involve a transgression of the integrity of the name in order to explore its value. The swan discovers his fundamental and essential quality ("Magnifique") underneath his proper (conventional) but improper (inessential) title, the demeaningly unspecific pronoun "lui." And that discovery leads to the entire movement of the rest of the sonnet: a movement toward the creation of an improper (non-conventional) and proper (particular and essential, and therefore capitalized) title, "le Cygne." From "Magnifique," a mighty quality applied to a thoroughly vague and general pronoun, the swan becomes "the Swan"; it is as if the adjective "Magnifique," derived from the Latin *magnus,* "great," led to the creation of a "majuscule," from a diminutive of the comparative form of *magnus, majusculus,* "a bit greater."

The homonym "cygne"/"signe" points up the fact that the swan's drama is essentially the drama of language itself: of language which, in order to be proper (accepted by its everyday users), must be improper (untrue and unequal to what it is representing). Ferdinand de Saussure speaks of the distinction between "sign" and "symbol":

> The word *symbol* has been used to designate the linguistic sign, or, more specifically, what is here called the signifier. Principle I [the arbitrary nature of the sign] weighs against the use of this term. One characteristic of the symbol is that it is never wholly arbitrary; it is not empty, for there is a rudiment of a natural bond between the signifier and the signified.[9]

The first realization of the swan ("cygne") in the sonnet is that he is a sign ("signe") and not a symbol: that he has lost every "rudiment of a natural bond" between his name and his essence. This is not something which has happened all at once, in one moment of disillusionment, but rather a process: if the swan *has not* sung of a home to live in during the winter ("Pour n'avoir pas chanté la région où vivre"), it is that his realization of the inessential nature of such a song, and of such a home, has been gradual; the present "se souvient" is only the tip of an iceberg of dissatisfactions. If the swan had fully accepted the difference between unimpressive outside ("cygne"/"lui") and glorious inside ("Magnifique"), if he had been content to let one express the other without being equal to it, he would perhaps have been able to find a conventional home in language, to sing—or to construct as a functioning sign—a "région où vivre," a home in which to store meaning. But in so doing he would have had to give in to the arbitrary relation between outside and inside as well, that is, to the very character which allows the outside (boundary of the property, "clôture") to protect the inside (properties) by being essentially different from it.

Jacques Derrida, in commenting upon Saussure's distinction between sign and symbol, says that the movement between symbol and sign is in fact not a punctual, circumscribed change, but a generalized movement, the very movement of language itself: "In Saussurian language, what Saussure does not say would have to be said: there is neither symbol nor sign but a becoming-sign of the symbol."[10] It is when he realizes that he is a "cygne," a common noun, a mere sign, that the swan realizes that he is already losing the potential of his symbolic nature, for the awareness of his conventional identity is at odds with his capacity to dream of a conjunction of form (title) and meaning (qualities). And once he has made that realization, the swan spends the rest of the sonnet fighting against it, or against its consequences; fighting, that is, to regain—or perhaps not fully to lose—his symbolic potential.

Like the lake forgotten because it has been frozen in time by a solid representation, the homeless swan is "haunted" by his non-song, and this in an etymological sense: Littré says that the word *hante* comes either from the Scandinavian *heimta*, from *heim*, "home," the essential meaning of the verb being to think of repeatedly, to yearn for as one would for a home (cf. the English noun *haunt*, "a place of frequentation"), or from the Latin *habitare*, "to inhabit."[11] The closest that the swan can come to home is in his being inhabited by the idea of a non-home, that is, by the thought of the limitations of any home he could sing into existence; and it is in fact only as a haunt ("Fantôme") that he will at last be pinned down to one locale ("à ce lieu").

The last two tercets of the sonnet are a form of swan song, a dying struggle accompanied by a song (the shaking of the swan's neck suggesting that he is emitting a sound as well as trying to get rid of the snow on his head), a conflict of a creature wishing to survive as himself, without a home, without the protection of an insufficient identity, of an improper property. It is of course a final struggle, as a swan song must be, a closing into a property ("se clôture . . . la Propriété"). But the swan, a wintry counterpart of the fiery phoenix, dies only to be reborn because of his struggle, to be reborn both different from and equal to himself.

The keynote of the swan's struggle is redundancy: because he is fighting against the disjunction between outside and inside, he has no home, and it is for this reason that he seems to melt into his surroundings. This is a fight of transparency, not the fertile transparency of parenting, or making apparent, but the transparency of non-identity, of dizzying non-differentiation, of white (the swan's neck) fighting its apparent equal (snow). "Agonie" here retains at least partially its etymological sense of "struggle"[12] and also suggests— especially given its rhymed counterpart, "nie," which it swallows up ("ago-nie"[13])—the English word *ago*: the "cygne d'autrefois," the swan of long ago, the swan who has realized what it means to be a sign, that is, who has understood that to be a sign of a swan is no longer to be a swan, is engaged in a struggle with temporality itself, the temporality which the sign apparently counters (artificially) and ultimately gives in to (by needing to counter it).

In his attempt to eliminate difference, the difference which is the basis of the house, the swan thus thoroughly confuses himself with his surroundings. The action of the first line of the first tercet can be seen as tautological, given the very likely echo of *cou* in "secouera": the swan's collar will "collar" itself ("se couera"), its apparently frenzied movement being in fact a non-movement, since the purported mover and the space through which he is moving are not distinct. The *se-* element of "secouera" further recalls the fact that three of the other actions the swan executes are reflexive ("se souvient," "se délivre," "s'immobilise"); his reflexivity now seems to become amalgamated to the verb expressing his action, almost as a grammatical re-enactment of his own absorption into his surroundings, his lack of a distinct identity which lends even his actions upon the outside world a certain reflexivity, since that world is not fully distinguishable from him. Finally, the implied future of the first quatrain ("Va-t-il nous déchirer"), an immediate, almost present future full of promise and the hope of a genuine change about to take place, is in contrast to the amalgamated future form ("secouera"), which in fact describes a fully circumscribed movement, a non-change.

What the swan learns about in his struggle of white against white, in this scene of non-differentiated layers, is the two dangers of fighting against home: first of all, the danger of dissipation and non-identity. The swan, by abolishing the distinction of outside and inside, has so come to resemble his surroundings that it is as if he had written himself out of existence, or rather refused to write himself into it. The struggle of white against white is a kind of incest, a denial of the difference necessary to found any identity, a denial of the separation from self and from home required by any home, a denial of the necessity of writing which alone gives the white page its power to communicate. If in fact the creation of a home is in some sense concomitant with a form of writing, or using signs, the swan's struggle shows that not using signs leads to the terror of pure space, "l'espace infligé," the white of the blank page inflicted upon the poet who refuses to divide its infinite potential into regions of meaning.

But what finally puts an end to this scene of tautological repetition is the swan's horrible realization of the other danger of not having a home: "l'horreur du sol." Home exists not only as a necessary separation of outside and inside, a storage place for meaning through difference, but also as a protection against difference itself, "l'horreur du sol où le plumage est pris," presumably the slowly appearing mud around the edge of the thawing lake where the swan has been caught. The swan's revolt against home is largely a revolt against inequality, against an inequality of expression and meaning; the end of his revolt is signaled by his perception of the horror of his own difference, the difference brought on by the passage of time, the difference of mortal creatures to themselves, in the long run. It is the horror of mortality itself, the blackness of ink which must be committed to the page if anything is to be commemorated, the blackness of mud which signals the terrifying "renouveau"[14] of winter's end, the blackness of the soil upon which any house must be based and to which mortal creatures must return, their aspirations to the divine ("plumage") imprisoned ("pris") by their mortal state.

It is at this moment, in the space between the two tercets, that the swan "dies," but he dies only to reappear as the "Fantôme" of the following line. For him, death is not so much a disappearance as an appearance, a fixing in form, a resignation to the necessary element of the house of death in any house based on convention. The "cygne d'autrefois" loses his fight against the necessity of home itself because of his own mortality, the reason home exists. As a common swan he is ultimately undone by immobilization ("s'immobilise") and localization ("à ce lieu"), what Derrida calls the "becoming-unmotivated of the symbol"[15] corresponding to the creation of the locus of meaning of the swan/sign, the signal of his own death as himself and of a house of representation as death. It is only as a ghost ("Fantôme") that the swan is at last "booked" ("Fantôme" as "Fan-tôme"), called to justice by a sign ("assigne"), imprisoned by the limits of conventional writing ("le plumage est pris," the feather indicating both the wing's dream of a transcendent flight of meaning and the quill's need to commit ink to the page), undelivered (the opposite of "se dé-livre," to "unbook" oneself[16]). The common swan is defeated by his desire to win both sides of the conflict, to be "pur éclat," a combination of the "vierge," "pur," and the "vivace," "éclat," a kind of shattering or tearing.[17]

But out of the fight waged by the common swan against the home as a sign and not a symbol, or against language as a conventional symbolic system and not a transcendent Symbolism, is born the proper Swan, and it is in this reincarnation beyond the flesh that we might reverse Derrida's description of language as the "becoming-sign of the symbol" into the "becoming-Symbol of the sign," or the becoming "Cygne" of the "cygne." As an offspring born into the house of death of his deceased namesake ("cygne"), the proper Swan goes beyond the distinction between the house as life and the house as death which haunted his progenitor. Like the deceased Poe whose death at last brings his essential nature to life, the swan, through his transfiguration in death, finally becomes Himself, no longer "lui," but "le Cygne."

This Swan takes up where the other swan left off. If he is an exile ("Que vêt parmi l'exil"), it is not because he has been thrust out of his home, but because he has seen home for what it is, that is, a structure which requires its inhabitants to call it endlessly into question, to go outside of it and to reach beyond the boundaries that seem to contain and imprison them as well as protect them. The Swan's exile is "useless" ("inutile") not in a negative sense, not because he will learn nothing from it, but in a positive sense, because he has nothing to learn from it; because it is an exile which is in itself a kind of transcendence of home. The swan's denial ("nie") of space as a sufficient locus for home is countered by the Swan's affirmation of another kind of home, a home that is airborne, held up by dreams ("songe froid"), a home from whose heights one can look down ("mépris") on mortals, a "nid" rather than a "nie." Like the dead lover in "Sur les bois oubliés," the proper Swan can look down upon the house of life with a kind of disdain, a feeling of pride or superiority based both on sameness and on difference, for he, like the dead lover, has passed beyond the house of life only by knowing it for what it is, only by seeing himself (in the form of the common swan) engage in the very struggle he has now transcended.

The transfigured Swan has not eliminated the dilemma of home; rather, because he is born of the struggle against the limits of home, he is exempt from them. If the common swan vainly fought the cold of the white snow with his unprotected white neck in a struggle against difference, the proper Swan simply puts on the cold wrap of dream, as if his very source of protection were his knowledge of a coldness he no longer feels. The unsung homing song of the common swan ("la région où vivre") as well as his dying swan song together become the "songe froid de mépris" of the Swan, a merging of the house of life and the house of death, with a possible word-play on the English *song* and the French *songe*: the Swan need only dream of language, rather than trying to use it, for he represents the dream of non-conventional Symbolism, the closing off of the dreamer's property without losing the dream it is meant to protect.

That dream is the dream of transmitting meaning in a way which neither home nor language habitually provide for, in a way which would leave meaning both alive and immortal and which would eliminate the negativity—and thus the difference—inherent in any mortal conception of immortality, the barrier between mortal swan and immortal Swan. Mallarmé himself is both swans, the frenzied, living struggler and the distant, god-like dreamer, and the relation of "mépris" which links the two swans is emblematic of the poet's relation to himself and of the relation of ideal to real. That relation is not simply one of "mépris," "disdain," but is also one of "méprise," "misunderstanding": of misunderstanding not simply in the sense of a non-expression, but also in the sense of a freedom to attempt expression again and again, a refusal to be caught ("pris") in the superficiality of a simplified comprehension. Writing the poem of the two swans, like writing the poem of the two poets and the poem of the two lovers, may be nothing more than describing the two components of the writer himself, and saying that one will never fully understand their relationship: the mortal who lives in order to dream, and the dreamer whose dreams can never be fully contained by their mortal author.

PART TWO

Proximity and Approximation

The Earthly Home and the Celestial Home

Il y a deux manières hétérogènes d'effacer la différence entre le signifiant et le signifié: l'une, la classique, consiste á réduire ou à dériver le signifiant, c'est-à-dire finalement à soumettre le signe à la pensée; l'autre . . . consiste á mettre en question le système dans lequel fonctionnait la précédente réduction. . . . Car le paradoxe, c'est que la réduction métaphysique du signe avait besoin de l'opposition qu'elle réduisait.

Jacques Derrida
L'Ecriture et la différence

Chapter Five: Proximity and Approximation in the *Oedipus Tyrannus*

παρά and the Search for Home

There are two tragedies in life. One is not to get your heart's desire. The other is to get it.

G. B. Shaw
Man and Superman

i. Paradoxical Oedipus

It is Oedipus himself who first uses the word παρά in the play, and in so doing establishes one of the fundamental oppositions which the word entails. Shortly after the king has arrived onstage, he speaks the following words to the suppliants gathered around him:

ἀγὼ δικαιῶν μὴ παρ' ἀγγέλων, τέκνα,
ἄλλων ἀκούειν αὐτὸς ὧδ' ἐλήλυθα.

Things which I have come here to hear myself, children,
since I deemed it right not to hear them beside other messengers.[1]

Oedipus thus announces immediately that one of his goals is to replace one intermediary or middle term on his road to learning the truth: he wishes to hear the facts not through the mediation of a go-between ("μὴ παρ' ἀγγέλων"), but rather himself ("αὐτός"). That he wishes, by being a fully *present* listener, to erase the distance which a messenger would imply is also indicated by the very first finite verb of the play which has Oedipus as its subject: "ἐλήλυθα," "I have come, here I am."

What Oedipus here opposes to the παρά of agency is indeed his very presence, "αὐτός." That the real contrast here is between παρά as indicative of the need to pass through the mediation of others—or of a conventional symbolic system designed to communicate with others—and the self as an ultimate presence and an overriding identity measuring others by its own criteria, not beside (παρά) the source of transmission of knowledge but itself the unchanging and self-contained transmitting and distinguishing mechanism, is made clear by the addition, which Jebb recognizes as redundant, of "ἄλλων," ostensibly modifying "ἀγγέλων" ("messengers") but in fact, as Jebb points out, "serving to contrast ἀγγέλων and αὐτός, as if one said, 'from messengers—at second hand.'"[2] "Other" messengers are thus not to be thought of as "additional" messengers added to original ones, but rather as messengers who in themselves are "other" ("ἄλλων") as opposed to self ("αὐτός").

Indeed, if the *Oedipus Tyrannus* explores the paths of communication by which human understanding is (and is not) reached, the term παρά—considered both as a preposition and as a verbal, adjectival, and nominal prefix—is indicative of the two components which that understanding involves, and which are shown to be at odds in the tragic world which the play presents. On the one hand, παρά speaks of the movement from one entity to another which any *communication* must entail, and of the syntax by which words are combined with other words in order to transmit a meaning which they convey together, collectively. On the other hand, παρά is used as a prefix to a word which is uttered by the chorus in speaking of Oedipus at a very crucial moment of the play: "παράδειγμα" (v. 1193) or "paradigm," a word which, as Bernard Knox observes, speaks of "the existence and authority of divine prescience and of the fundamental ignorance of man,"[3] that is, of the stable and unmoving state beyond question and challenge which each unit of information (e.g., a word) must possess within itself, the undetachable consecration which establishes the right to signification and without which no means of communication has any meaning, no author of an utterance any authority.

The second meaning of παρά thus turns the tables on its first meaning. If the first meaning is indicative of the movement toward a goal, the second meaning speaks of the goal, the paradigm toward which one moves: the noun "παράδειγμα," related to the verb παραδείκνυμι, literally means a thing beside (παρά) which one shows (δείκνυμι) another, that is, that to or by which a thing is compared, the implication being in order to make the two compared terms *match*. Thus, if the approximating agent could fully coincide with its model, the distance separating the two would disappear as would the distinct identities of the traveler toward a goal and the goal which is traveled toward. The movement (παρά) of words toward meaning or of any human follower after a non-human model could reach a stop only if the modeler reached the model; but the model is itself identifiable as a model distinguishable from its seekers only insofar as it cannot be reached.

The word παρά embodies the same duality in the play as ἴσος, for each of the two words exemplifies a tension between a need and an ambition. There is first of all the largely political need to participate in a community by being "equal" to others or by going through the intermediary of others in order to reach a state of consensus. But striving against the recognition of that need is the heroic ambition of being always equal to oneself in order to approximate the stability of the gods through the unchanging glory of one's name, of being or reaching a paradigm that creates a sort of standard to which humanity is to be compared and, implicitly, by which it is to be measured. Just as the first meaning of the word παρά describes the desire to chase after a meaning which is perpetually elusive and the quest for a measurement of that meaning such that man, to add a letter to Protagoras' famous phrase, might be the measurer of all things, the second meaning of the term describes the attempt to install the divine in the mortal realm. In its self-awareness, heroic ambition, recognizing the limitations of any human measuring stick composed of indissoluble units created by convention and refusing to combine units with other units none of which is adequate, stops instead and looks again at the original convention linking quantifying unit to qualifying meaning, the foundation of each of the models which any syntax must set into motion.

The opposition embodied by παρά is particularly important for the presentation of home in the play. In its first meaning, that of transmission and transitivity, the word is related to the combination of the house seen as a unit-creating mechanism with other houses that do not coincide with it but with which it can create a community, the very texture which assures the functioning of the *polis*. Just as information may be transmitted "beside" a messenger who is necessarily "other," human life must be renewed "beside" another, not only the partner coming from another house with whom one procreates, but, more importantly, the new being (and unit, or individual citizen) which together two partners create. Jocasta herself makes clear the necessarily contiguous status of offspring by her not unconventional use of the preposition παρά in speaking of the oracle concerning the child born to her and to Laius:

ὅστις γένοιτ' ἐμοῦ τε κἀκείνου πάρα.

Whoever would be born beside me and that one [Laius].[4]

The "παρά" here refers not to Jocasta's being "beside" her husband (as in the English expression, to have a child "by" someone), but rather to both parents "beside" whom the child is born, the subordination of both "ἐμοῦ" and "ἐκείνου" to "παρά" being emphasized here by the coordinating copula "τε καί" linking the two pronouns. The child—Oedipus of course being an exception because of the skewed nature of his generational "progression" —carries forward the "meaning" of the parents, transmits it to subsequent generations who, in order to keep alive the family name, must themselves participate in the perpetual forward motion of the house's procreational process.

In the second meaning of παρά, that of paradigm, the word may be used to describe the exploration of the individual house and its relation to its foundation. As opposed to the syntactical function of the house, one by which an existing and palpable form combines with another one to create a new form which is also existing and palpable, the paradigmatic function explores the relation of existing forms and their underlying meaning, a relation which is the organizing principle of the house considered as paradigm (identity-creating unit) and which is essentially irrational, dealing not with the combination (*ratio*) of two integral units with each other but rather with the irrational conjunction by which a necessarily integral unit (house, word) is attached to a necessarily multiple and fractional meaning which it cannot hope to be but which it can only house.

We are reminded of Aristotle's comments about words and things:

> For we cannot discourse by carrying things themselves, but rather we use names in place of things as *symbols*, we believe what takes place ["τὸ συμβαῖνον," literally "what comes together"] in names also takes place in things, just as for *those who calculate by arithmetic*. But it's not the same; for names and the multitude of words can be brought to an end, but things are infinite as to their number. So it is necessary for the same word and one single name to mean more [than they themselves are].[5]

What Aristotle implicitly contrasts here are the ideas of *symbol*, "σύμβολα," and of purely quantifying cipher, "ψῆφος," the latter being that by which one can take a precise count of things. The ψῆφος, which is originally an abacus-like pebble which corresponds to each thing to be counted—and which belongs to the political domain as much as to mathematics, since it was also used to cast votes—differs from the σύμβολον in that the other half of the ψῆφος is the thing itself, not a necessarily unquantifiable and ultimately irrational idea of the thing such that one *symbolon* (the host's house) attempts to represent its other half (the guest's own house) only across the distance which necessarily separates and distinguishes the two halves of the *symbolon*. What "comes together" in arithmetic also comes together in the physical world which calculation by ψῆφοι refers to, since each thing counted corresponds to its place-holder or ψῆφος in a perfect fit. What seems to "come together" in language does not come together in the world of which it speaks, because there is no single convention—from Latin *convenire*, like the Greek συμβαίνω in the above citation—that links one word to *only* one meaning.

Thus it is that Oedipus' *paradox*—another παρά word which serves to express the irresolubility of the term's other two meanings—resides in the fact that he uses a conventional symbolic system, the series of information sources "beside" which he learns the truth, as well as his own all-important movement as a young man in search of the truth, in order to find that the truth lies in himself, not in "convention" or coming-together but rather in the very searcher who is attempting to bring together questions and answers, in the individual whose own characteristics—his insistence on knowing the truth, his quick intelligence, indeed, his belief in the ultimate power of the human to understand the divine—are the real guiding principles of the play. As Bernard Knox puts it, "All that Oedipus learns—and all that he had to learn—was that he was ignorant."[6] Oedipus' message-gathering movements do nothing, ultimately, but call the very process of the quest for knowledge into question. And the result of this calling-into-question is, for both the investigator and what he is investigating, a stop, one which says that *this* paradox cannot be resolved, but that at best its story can be told.

ii. Paralysis and analysis: the bound and the unbound

The story of Oedipus' moving—by convention, by rationalization, by syntax; by a seemingly stable and transitive symbolic system—into the domain of non-movement—that of divine meaning, of underlying motivations, of exploring and destabilizing foundations and assumptions which may or may not be true and solid—is one which calls into question not only the king's own identity and the future position of the city which he governs, but also the locus of humanity, its proper site straddling the domain of the gods and the domain of the subhuman. Early in the play, the priest, speaking for the terrified citizens of Thebes, mentions the Sphinx twice as an example of an earlier menace which had shaken the seemingly stable foundation of the city, and he shows by his double use of παρά the city's bipolar orientation, reaching not only up toward the celestial sphere of divine stability and uprightness but also down toward the subhuman sphere of obscurity, chaos, and constant change:

ὅς γ' ἐξέλυσας, ἄστυ Καδμεῖον μολών,
σκληρᾶς ἀοιδοῦ δασμὸν ὃν παρείχομεν.

You who indeed came to the Cadmean city and unbound
the harsh singer's tax which we had beside us.

ἀσφαλείᾳ τήνδ' ἀνόρθωσον πόλιν.
ὄρνιθι γὰρ καὶ τὴν τότ' αἰσίῳ τύχην
παρέσχες ἡμῖν, καὶ τανῦν ἴσος γενοῦ.

Set the city unfailingly aright.
For you held good fortune beside us then with an auspicious
bird-sign; now again be equal.[7]

The double use of παρέχω ("to have or hold beside"), the first having the citizens of Thebes ("we") as its subject and the second referring to Oedipus' action, combines the negative and positive elements inherent in the proximity (παρά) of the human and the superhuman. It is the presence of the Sphinx's "tax," her refusal to go away, which poses the threat to the city she is devouring bit by bit; it is as if she embodied the relentless question which any human aspiration to the divine brings down: "What is man?" But rather than giving the stable quantity, the name, and asking for its qualities, its essence, the Sphinx poses the riddle in the other direction: given the seemingly disparate nature of this curious creature ("two feet and four feet and three feet as well"), how does one name him? How can a creature which has so many different quantities of feet have, as the riddle states, only one voice? How can one find a single answer to what is not simple, give an immutable mask to what is mutable, a single signifier to so many signifieds?

The Sphinx's presence thus represents in part the dangers of dissipation, of dispersion, and of non-presence. Her presence is as divisive as the tax which she exacts from the citizens of Thebes, a δασμός, related to the verb δατέομαι, "to divide or distribute." By naming the name, "man," the single answer to the complex question, that puts an end to the Sphinx's fractioning up of the city—and it is furthermore noteworthy that she poses the question not to the citizenry as a whole, but to each individual member of it, yet another source of division and dispersion—Oedipus implicitly accepts the limitations in both a positive and a negative sense, the boundedness which that one name places on the infinity of states—even though only three of them are named explicitly here—which it covers. For in rendering whole, standard, and standing—in short, erect and fixed—what is fractional, multiple, and constantly in motion, Oedipus says yes to the protection of the linguistic house of Thebes, and by so doing, he cannot avoid also saying yes to the approximation, the inevitable gap of inaccuracy left by any mere proximity, any solution by proxy, which that naming requires.

One side of the Sphinx thus represents the dangers of chaos and obscurity; her other side represents suffocation, as her name indicates, Sphinx, related to σφίγγω, "to bind tight or fast." The Sphinx's relentless presence ("δασμὸν ὃν παρείχομεν," "the tax which we had beside us") also represents the boundedness of human existence as opposed to divine existence. Even though the Sphinx herself is obviously not immortal, which Oedipus' answering of the riddle is quick to show, the enigma she embodies is a never-ending, inescapable one. For it is by finding an apparent answer to her question and thus accepting the irrational relationship linking linguistic unit and what it represents that Oedipus binds himself to the possibility that the divine pronouncements previously uttered in his regard do not cover *only* the meaning he had thought was theirs. By his "analysis" (from ἀνάλυσις, "an unbinding"), or unloosing of the riddle, he "loosens" ("ὅς γ᾽ ἐξέλυσας") the "bonds" of the "binder" ("Sphinx"), but in so doing, not unlike Prometheus who attempts to gain god-like benefits for mankind, he himself becomes bound.[8] Oedipus falls prey to the Sphinx to the extent that he wishes to make use of the bounds necessitated by the creation of a conventional symbolic system and at the same time to enjoy the freedom which only unboundedness to any set standard could afford.

iii. A pair of allies

Indeed, in the course of the drama, Oedipus does a great deal of cognitive traveling, of moving from side to side and from source to source simply to discover what at one level seems to have been always true. His investigative moves in the present crisis are matched by the entire course he has traveled since his birth; his present search for the truth of the gods is thus mirrored—although in a curiously unequal way—by his past attempt and that of his parents to avoid the truth of the gods, to escape their pronouncements. And while none of the earlier movements of the king were delegated to others, but were rather all traced out by Oedipus himself, the present investigation is conducted largely by proxy, Oedipus at first sending *for* information at Delphi through Creon, then sending *for* a source of information, Teiresias, after which point he can hardly keep up with the solicited and unsolicited flow of information converging upon him.

The double and related nature of the two circuits of movement in the play, one tracing Oedipus' search for the truth about the plague and about Laius' murder, the other tracing his own movements and identity, is made virtually explicit by the dual role played by each of the two shepherds who are the transmitting sources for the child Oedipus exposed by his parents on Mount Cithaeron. Each of them is involved both with the storage of a message concerning Oedipus' father—in the case of the Theban shepherd, the Θεράπων, a piece of evidence about the death of Oedipus' biological father, Laius, and in the case of the Corinthian shepherd, the ἄγγελος, the news of the death of Oedipus' adoptive father, Polybus—and with the transmission of Oedipus himself to "safety" when as a child his death warrant had already been sealed. The bearers of the message of death for Oedipus' two fathers, the two shepherds who do as much to bear witness to those deaths as they do to bear Oedipus from the rejecting hands of one to the accepting hands of the other, are also the bearers of the responsibility of Oedipus' life. In this way they may be seen as representing the unboundedness of the wild, the instability and potential freedom which lie just beneath any fixed symbolic system and just beyond the walls of any city.

Thus the shepherds, who guide Oedipus' seemingly beneficial wandering away from his city's hostile presence as much as Eumaius, Odysseus' swineherd, helps to guide the Ithacan king's wandering back into his city,[9] are doubly messengers. They undo the apparently stable message they are meant to transmit between Laius and the child whom his orders would have disappear into the oblivion of Mount Cithaeron, and they attach the child whose life they have saved to the hope for a new possibility of meaning, a new circuit of movement. So that Oedipus, by bringing the two shepherds together once again and thus re-establishing the internal connection which has been undone, brings to a halt a life which should have been stopped before it began but which has nevertheless been spent in movement.

It is first of all the question of source which concerns those who would receive the double message of the Corinthian messenger: Jocasta's question, "παρὰ τίνος δ' ἀφιγμένος;" ("From whose side do you come?"[10]), one which pinpoints the potentially untrustworthy nature of any message-bearing unit, not unlike one half of a *symbolon* which only the other half, the sure identification of a source, can vouch for, is matched by Oedipus' query— infinitely more anxious, but of an identical nature—as to the source of the child which the messenger-shepherd long ago transmitted to the Corinthian king: "ἦ γὰρ παρ' ἄλλου μ' ἔλαβες οὐδ' αὐτὸς τυχών;" ("So you took me from another's side and didn't get me yourself?"[11]). In both cases, whether the transmission be of a message or of a child, it is only the distance between emitting source and message which seems to be the source of Oedipus' salvation: his distance from the now-dead Polybus in Corinth, the source of the message at hand, is what he has relied upon since his visit to Delphi as the guarantor of his non-fulfillment of the oracle he received there; and his distance from Laius, the gap across which the Corinthian shepherd received him, is what allowed him to live.

Oedipus survives because of the non-neutral nature of the transmitting agents which move him out of one house and into another, because of an interference of means (messenger-shepherds) into the domain of meaning (Laius' death order) which is in this case benevolent. But in other cases, such an interference might not be benevolent; the distance between means and meaning can act as a hindrance to something one wants as well as a hindrance to something one fears. Oedipus' final re-establishment of the internal link (the meeting of the two shepherds) which connects Thebes to Corinth and ultimately Thebes to Thebes results not only in the *symbolon*-like recognition of a place which can be called home, but also in the understanding of the doubly exclusive nature of home. Like the site of the linguistic utterance, one must be separated from home before one has gained any first-hand understanding of its nature—for such information, like an incestuous relationship, keeps its gatherer from ever breaking out of himself and leaving the place where he may not remain forever—separated by the distance between means and meaning, between signifier and signified, and by the re-cognition through two fitted *symbola* of home only away from home; and one can never return home once one has gained an understanding of it from a distance, as ἄλλος ("other") rather than as αὐτός.[12]

The establishment of the internal link is reflected by the ambiguous use of παρά with reference to the two shepherds. If the Theban shepherd, the Θεράπων, does not happen to be present (παρά) in the house—a fact which is indicated by Oedipus' question to Jocasta: "ἦ κἂν δόμοισι τυγχάνει τανῦν παρών;"[13]—it is that he did happen to be present at the scene of Laius' murder, and upon returning to the city and discovering who was king, begged the queen to be allowed to live *away* from the city.[14] The ambiguity of the Theban shepherd's presence and absence, or rather his double presence, present in the distant past at Laius' murder and to be made present in the near future at Oedipus' house, is felt when the chorus, attempting to cheer the king up, tells him:

ἕως δ' ἂν οὖν
πρὸς τοῦ παρόντος ἐκμάθῃς, ἔχ' ἐλπίδα.

So until you find out
from the one who was there / will be here, have hope.[15]

Indeed, the desire to make present the sought-after information, which only the shepherd's presence at the scene of the murder and at the scene of the assassin's coronation can constitute, is what accounts to a large extent for Oedipus' increasingly marked desire to hasten the speed of the investigation, beginning with his annoyance at Creon's apparently delayed return from Delphi,[16] and not culminating until his reversion to threats of violence upon the person of the Θεράπων,[17] but reaching a curious sort of high point in the almost magical response of Jocasta to Oedipus' impatient order to bring the one witness of Laius' murder to the palace:

ΟΙΔΙΠΟΤΣ · πῶς ἂν μόλοι δῆθ' ἡμῖν ἐν τάχει πάλιν;
ΙΟΚΑΣΤΗ · πάρεστιν.

Oedipus: Well then, how might he get back here quickly?
Jocasta: It is possible / He is here.[18]

Even the Scholiast, who does not generally seem to relish ambiguity, glosses Jocasta's "πάρεστιν" metaphorically: "Think of him as being right here ('παρόντα'), that's how easy it is to get him here"[19]—an explanation which certainly does not negate what seems to be the primary meaning of the word in this context, affirmed by Jebb[20] and others, "It is possible [to get him here quickly]."

Oedipus' very enterprise, his search for the truth, explores the possibility of making the two halves meet, of bringing two kinds of presence into contact with each other. It is as if his expressed wish to make the man who *was* present become the man who *is* present, to bridge the gap and know the unknowable, removed the limitations of time and place and seemed to make possible the materially impossible. Indeed, the king does not simply gather information from the presence of each of the two shepherds separately, he brings the two of them into contact with each other:

ΟΙΔΙΠΟΤΣ· τὸν ἄνδρα τόνδ' οὖν οἶσθα τῇδέ που μαθών;
ΘΕΡΑΠΩΝ· τί χρῆμα δρῶντα; ποῖον ἄνδρα καὶ λέγεις;
ΟΙΔΙΠΟΤΣ· τόνδ' ὃς πάρεστιν.

Oedipus: Then do you know this man [the Corinthian messenger], having observed
                                                                    him here?
Servant: Doing what? Which man do you mean?
Oedipus: This one who is here.[21]

Gould notes very astutely that the Theban shepherd's question at v. 1129
shows his confusion as to the referent of "τὸν ἄνδρα τόνδ'," in v. 1128; "The
HERDSMAN is horrified by an ambiguity in OEDIPUS' question: 'this man'
could mean 'me.' . . . Was the king about to ask him if he had witnessed him
abroad (literally 'somewhere there')?"[22]

All three "presences" thus interact here: the Theban shepherd must have
been at some earlier time in the presence of the Corinthian shepherd, since
he passed Oedipus along to him in what he thought was a saving gesture; the
Theban shepherd was present when Oedipus killed his father; and it is by
bringing all three men into each other's presence once again that Oedipus
constitutes the most fundamental understanding, the hitherto hidden meaning
of the means of transmission he has undergone in the course of his movements.
It is by re-presenting these three presences to each other that Oedipus attempts
to represent his life as a whole, that is, to bind all of its crucial time periods
together and make them constitute a whole.

When, at the climactic point of this, the play's climactic scene, it is absolutely and irrevocably clear who Oedipus is and where he has been, the king
postpones his lamenting just long enough to ask the Theban shepherd why he
gave the child Oedipus to his Corinthian companion. The shepherd replies:

κατοικτίσας, ὦ δέσποθ', ὡς ἄλλην χθόνα
δοκῶν ἀποίσειν, αὐτὸς ἔνθεν ἦν.

Because I'd taken pity on you, master, thinking that he would
bring you to that other country, where he himself lived.[23]

The very supposition that the movement *away* from the decree of Laius, the
displacement toward an *other* ("ἄλλην χθόνα") by means of a saving
*alli*ance, could prevent the fulfillment of the oracle stands as a condition
not only for Oedipus' survival but also for all of his subsequent movement
toward the thing he was meant to avoid. Indeed, the Corinthian messenger
"unbinds" Oedipus from his anxiety about Polybus and the oracle that
Oedipus himself received: "Let me *untie* you [ἐξελυσάμην] from that fear," he
says to the king, using the very word used of Oedipus to describe his "unbinding" of the Sphinx's curse.[24]

But the source of this "unbinding," the messenger-shepherd who attempts to move Oedipus away from the gods' decrees by means of a euphemizing mediation, is also the source of binding together the moments of Oedipus' life, the very capacity for linking together (or allying) that constitutes that life. In the end, the first circuit of information-gathering movements which Oedipus follows in the play, one which seems to have clearly defined limits ("Who killed Laius?") and to be fully in accordance with the gods' commands, does nothing but lead the king to a knowledge of the unfixable nature of divine pronouncements. Where the two shepherds err with respect to the effectiveness of geographical boundaries, and where Oedipus errs with regard to the discretion of his investigation and even of his own life stages—since his house of procreation does coincide with his house of origin—is where both Oedipus and his two "saviors" err with regard to the discretion, the fixedness together and apart in space, of the gods' words and their meaning. Even though the gods' speech never changes in its most fundamental meaning, running toward or away from that meaning and trying to make an ally of it leads to a realization of the meaning of the word *ally*: one who, even if he purports to be benevolently disposed, is unremittingly ἄλλος, irrevocably *other*.

iv. Apparent enemies: the problem re-paired

The part of the play which focuses on the apparently simple matter of finding Laius' murderer rather than on the movements of Oedipus himself comprises the prologue, the parodos, and the first episode, in the course of which Oedipus speaks with the priest, with Creon newly returned from Delphi, and with Teiresias. It is the latter who closes this information-gathering circuit by bringing up, unsolicited, the very question of parentage which Oedipus himself had once put to the oracle at Delphi:

ΤΕΙΡΕΣΙΑΣ· ἡμεῖς τοιοίδ᾽ ἔφυμεν, ὡς μὲν σοὶ δοκεῖ,
             μῶροι, γονεῦσι δ᾽, οἳ σ᾽ ἔφυσαν, ἔμφρονες.
ΟΙΔΙΠΟΤΣ· ποίοισι; μεῖνον. τίς δέ μ᾽ ἐκφύει βροτῶν;

Teiresias: So we were born mad, as you seem to think,
             but as for your own parents' opinion, those who gave you birth, we
                                                  were born wise.
Oedipus: Who? Wait! Who among mortals gave me birth?[25]

It is thus the first series of investigating movements which establishes the importance of the second circuit, that of Oedipus' own life-long movements, for the city of Thebes and its present crisis, the starting point for the first investigation.

In fact, Teiresias' presence actually seems to create a further distance between Oedipus and the answer he is searching for in the city's name. Teiresias is like the Sphinx in that the attempt to bind his words to a stable meaning results in the launching of a new enterprise undertaken in the supposition that a true "fit" between word and meaning has been established, the assumption of the Theban throne by Oedipus upon his "solving" of the Sphinx's riddle matched by the renewed search into the questionable nature of his parentage which seems to be one of the only things which the king even marginally understands in his discussion with the Theban seer.

This link between the enigmatic speech of the Sphinx and that of Teiresias, a speech which in both cases points to the distance separating stable word and unstable meaning, is made far more explicit by Oedipus than the king himself realizes when he questions Teiresias about the latter's comments concerning Oedipus' parents:

ΟΙΔΙΠΟΥΣ · ποίοισι; μεῖνον. τίς δέ μ' ἐκφύει βροτῶν;
ΤΕΙΡΕΣΙΑΣ · ἥδ' ἡμέρα φύσει σε καὶ διαφθερεῖ.
ΟΙΔΙΠΟΥΣ · ὡς πάντ' ἄγαν αἰνικτὰ κἀσαφῆ λέγεις.

Oedipus: Who? Wait! Who among mortals gave me birth?
Teiresias: This day will give you birth and will destroy you.
Oedipus: Why must you always speak in riddles and confusion![26]

Not only does Oedipus use a word, "αἰνικτά," "things enigmatic," which is a clear reference to the Sphinx, but he does so in response to a statement made by Teiresias which is more than a little reminiscent of the Sphinx's riddle: in both cases, the *answer* which Oedipus seeks will only be found by putting things together and making them fit. Oedipus' finding the single answer, "man," which binds together the seemingly disparate qualities in the Sphinx's question corresponds to his "joining" the day of his birth—that is, the discovery of who gave him life—with the day of his destruction. He will realize—both execute and become aware of—the full measure of his mortal bounds, will become the answer to the Sphinx's riddle, a man, only by joining the day of his beginning with the day of his end and constituting the mortal limits which set the boundaries for his search for knowledge.

The connection between Teiresias and the Sphinx is further emphasized by the repetition of foot imagery referring to both figures, imagery which itself points to the distance to be covered between the truth and any searcher for the truth. Oedipus, in asking Creon why no conclusive investigation into Laius' murder was conducted at the time of his death, is told that the Sphinx put a distance between the city and the investigation:

ΟΙΔΙΠΟΥΣ · κακὸν δὲ ποῖον ἐμποδὼν τυραννίδος
οὕτω πεσούσης εἶργε τοῦτ' ἐξειδέναι;

ΚΡΕΩΝ · ἡ ποικιλῳδὸς Σφὶγξ τὸ πρὸς ποσὶ σκοπεῖν
μεθέντας ἡμᾶς τἀφανῆ προσήγετο.

Oedipus: But when the king's rule had toppled in that way,
what evil impeded [literally, blocking your feet, kept you away from]
a thorough investigation?

Creon: The many-songed Sphinx led us to give up the unclear
and look to what was at our feet.[27]

The Sphinx's presence, all the while it impedes the all-important investigation of Laius' murder and brings it to a halt, also leads Oedipus to bring the city's suffering to a halt by his own apparent stabilizing of the situation. Similarly, Oedipus, finally despairing of ever getting a comprehensible answer from Teiresias, spits out this reproach at the seer:

κομιζέτω δῆθ' · ὡς παρὼν σύ γ' ἐμποδὼν
ὀχλεῖς, συθείς τ' ἂν οὐκ ἂν ἀλγύναις πλέον.

Yes, let him take you away; because by being here beside me underfoot
you cause more trouble, and far away you couldn't bother [me] more [than you
do close by].[28]

Teiresias' presence ("*παρών*") is an impediment to Oedipus' further forward movement, since the seer brings no comprehensible information to the king, just as the Sphinx's presence was an impediment to a backward-looking investigation into a recent but extremely important past event, Oedipus' fateful journey from Delphi to Thebes. Just as the Sphinx moved Oedipus' career "forward" and placed an artificial boundary onto an investigation of his past—and indeed, how else but by accomplishing an exploit like that of ridding the city of her menace could Oedipus have avoided such an investigation before receiving the throne of Thebes?—Teiresias moves the king's investigation backward, as if to prove the illusory nature of the "progress" he has made thus far.

Teiresias' special relation to the divine and to divine knowledge, one which Oedipus may be seen as breaking into by his search for information which Teiresias is loath to impart, is demonstrated by the chorus's description of the seer when, unaware of the fact that Oedipus has already sent for the prophet, they suggest to the king that he do so:

ἄνακτ' ἄνακτι ταῦθ' ὁρῶντ' ἐπίσταμαι
μάλιστα Φοίβῳ Τειρεσίαν, παρ' οὗ τις ἂν
σκοπῶν τάδ', ὦναξ, ἐκμάθοι σαφέστατα.

One lord I know above all who sees as much as another lord,
I mean Teiresias [who knows as much] as Phoebus, [Teiresias] beside whom someone
searching for these things, lord, might find them out most clearly.[29]

The proximity of the two forms of ἄναξ, "lord," which are used to describe Apollo and Teiresias, and their indistinguishability until the names are provided in parallel cases but in an inverted order (accusative-dative, then dative-accusative) which fosters further confusion, seem to create a special relationship between god and prophet. The two pairings "ἄνακτ᾽ ἄνακτι" (reinforced as well by the elision of the final alpha of ἄνακτα) and "Φοίβῳ Τειρεσίαν" are balanced by the distance separating each pair from the other, as if each of the beings here named attached less importance to a relationship connecting each of them to an earthly name or label than to a relationship linking each to the other. As Kamerbeek states: "The chiasmus elegantly rounds off the equalization of the two ἄνακτες,"[30] and even the Scholiast observes that the equality of names is meant to equal an equality of vision.[31]

The pairing of seer and god needs no παρά to indicate its proximity; indeed, making that proximity explicit would undermine its unspeakable nature. Creon, by contrast, upon return from Delphi, says to Oedipus:

λέγοιμ᾽ ἂν οἷ᾽ ἤκουσα τοῦ θεοῦ πάρα.

I would report what I've heard beside the god.[32]

This is the only occurrence in the play of the word παρά directly connecting a human searcher with a divine agent, but the very fact of saying that link as if it were a direct, simple one (παρά as "close to") is evidence of its remote nature (παρά as "to the side of"). Oedipus himself is relegated to the category of intruders by the word παρά, for according to the words of the chorus which follow their description of the relationship of Apollo and Teiresias, his presence beside Teiresias ("Τειρεσίαν, π α ρ᾽ οὗ τις ἂν . . . ἐκμάθοι," "Teiresias, *beside* whom one might find out") might be seen as being "beside" the point, as an impairment of a pairing which admits no human intrusions and allows no human comparisons.

v. Apparent success: the problem "repaired"

It is indeed Teiresias' self-enclosed words to Oedipus which lead in an indirect way to the closing of the "simple" investigation into Laius' murder (the first circuit of movement) and the opening of the inquiry into the king's own past movements (the second circuit), for it is Teiresias' puzzling accusation of Oedipus which ignites the king's argument with Creon and ultimately elicits Jocasta's story[33] about the momentous oracle delivered to her and Laius, a story which sends the king onto the path of his new investigation:

οἷόν μ' ἀκούσαντ' ἀρτίως ἔχει, γύναι,
ψυχῆς πλάνημα κἀνακίνησις φρενῶν.

What a wandering of my soul and an agitation of my mind
take hold of me at what I just heard from you, my lady![34]

Jebb notes that this is indeed the juncture which sends the movement of the play back toward a past which had seemed beside the point at hand: "πλάνημα denotes the fearful 'wandering' of his thought back to other days and scenes."[35] Again, an attempted movement of stabilization, represented by Jocasta's desire to convince her husband once and for all of the unreliability of the oracles, leads to an unexpected wandering, a wandering back to a terrain which had seemed to be closed and inventoried.

The attempt to draw clear boundaries between the human and the divine as a sort of insurance of the rectitude of human assumptions becomes explicit with a triple conjunction of παρά words, when Oedipus and Jocasta are speaking of the death of Oedipus' father (Polybus) and the nullification of the oracle it seems to have effected:

ΟΙΔΙΠΟΥΣ · τὰ δ' οὖν παρόντα συλλαβὼν θεσπίσματα
            κεῖται παρ' Ἅιδη Πόλυβος ἄξι' οὐδενός.
ΙΟΚΑΣΤΗ · οὔκουν ἐγώ σοι ταῦτα προύλεγον πάλαι;
ΟΙΔΙΠΟΥΣ · ηὔδας · ἐγὼ δὲ τῷ φόβῳ παρηγόμην.

Oedipus: But Polybus lies *beside* Hades, having taken with him
         the oracles *as they stand,* worthy of nothing.
Jocasta: Didn't I tell you those very things [that the oracles would come to
                                              nought] long ago?
Oedipus: Yes, you did; but I was *led aside* by fear.[36]

Oedipus' double use of παρά in his musing over his father's invalidation of the oracle characterizes the latter as a bridge between the human and what is beyond the human. The oracles are "worthy of nothing" because they are now beside Polybus who is beside Hades; their presence with him seems to effect a distancing from the other man, the still-living Oedipus, whom they seemed to involve in their message. The participle "παρόντα" thus refers not only to Oedipus' attempt to make the oracles figuratively, if not literally, true ("Unless he perished from missing me, and in that way died at my hands"[37]), the participle in that case being translatable as "being in their present form"; it also speaks of an irrevocable distancing between the land of the living and the land of the dead, the land of existing and changeable human knowledge and the land of knowledge which death has irrevocably fixed. Polybus' presence in the underworld seems to make the oracles, which held their power of affecting human action only so long as both Polybus and Oedipus were living, worthless, "παρόντα ἄξι' οὐδενός," existing only in the realm of the dead and therefore absent from the understanding of the living.

And it is this very absence of understanding which is the real source of Oedipus' being "led aside" or astray ("παρηγόμην"); not the fear which no soothing on Jocasta's part could assuage, but rather the relaxing of the fear which the oracle justly inspired and which the king thinks he has justly observed, a relaxing which becomes manifest at the moment of the announcement of Polybus' trip to Hades, but which in fact has all along been one of the main factors in Oedipus' approximation of the oracle's truth, his missing the mark. For the king "relaxes" the vigil which the oracle seems to bid him to set up only because he thinks he is no longer "beside" the people the oracle seems to speak of. Oedipus' relieved and somewhat sheepish admission to Jocasta that fear had led him astray until Polybus was well and truly gone is analogous to what must surely have been the "relief" he felt as a young man upon leaving Corinth (and danger) apparently behind him. And the absenting ("παρ' Ἅιδη") of his apparently endangered parent leads to the series of events which culminates in Oedipus' realization (too late) of a far less apparent but far nearer danger to his other parent.

vi. A parent's peril

If Oedipus' movement toward the realm of the gods' truth is one which ultimately distances him from the domain of conventional human life and knowledge, the king's movement toward non-movement is prefigured by that of his wife, who at least intuitively feels the truth before her husband does and leaves the domain of human life before him. Shortly before the arrival of the Corinthian messenger and the double message he bears concerning both Polybus' death and Oedipus' birth, Jocasta makes double use of the word παρά in the curious passage which opens the third episode:

ὅτ' οὖν παραινοῦσ' οὐδὲν ἐς πλέον ποιῶ,
πρὸς σ', ὦ Λύκει' Ἀπολλον, ἄγχιστος γὰρ εἶ,
ἱκέτις ἀφῖγμαι τοῖσδε σὺν κατεύγμασιν,
ὅπως λύσιν τιν' ἡμῖν εὐαγῆ πόρῃς.

Since I am accomplishing nothing more by advising him [Oedipus],
toward you I come as a suppliant, Lycean Apollo, for you
are closest, with these votive offerings,
so that you might bring us some non-polluting [or conspicuous] solution.[38]

The queen's effort to "move aside" ("παραινοῦσ'") Oedipus' search[39] is a failed effort which results in creating a distance between the royal couple. The word "παραινοῦσ'," by which she describes her attempt at putting her husband off what must appear to her to be an ever more dangerous track,

contains an echo of the Sphinx and her *enigma*—the latter word having the
same origin as the verbal component, αἰνέω, of Jocasta's "παραινοῦσ'"—and
thus suggests that the queen's failure to stop Oedipus will have results as
disastrous—and as enigmatic—as the Sphinx's failure to stop the king, for in
both cases the apparent success (the reaching of a new point of understanding)
will lead to the discovery of a more fundamental failure.

Jocasta's own failure to turn Oedipus away from his search turns her toward
the gods, toward Apollo whom she describes as "closest" not only, we suspect,
because his altars are the closest of all the gods', but also—a far more startling
fact here—because his distance to her seems to be at least potentially "closer"
than Oedipus' distance to her at this moment. Whence Jocasta's opening
words of the episode, words which follow immediately upon the chorus's
lament that "ἔρρει τὰ θεῖα,"[40] the closeness between men and gods is slipping
away:

χώρας ἄνακτες, δόξα μοι παρεστάθη
ναοὺς ἱκέσθαι δαιμόνων.

Lords of the land, the idea stood beside me
to come to the temples of the divinities.[41]

As Gould points out, the verb παραστατέω is "sometimes used for the presence of a god by one's side."[42] If Jocasta's proximity to the gods seems to
counter the general condition of distancing from them deplored by the
chorus, it is not that the gods are coming closer to the human realm, but
rather that Jocasta is slowly wandering away from it. Whence the double
movement of the two verbs ἀφῖγμαι, "I have arrived," and πόρῃς, "so that
you might find a path," a suitable wish to counter Jocasta's present ἀπορία,
or dead-end situation. Indeed, she wishes the god to find a way to send her
a solution precisely because she feels at one level that Oedipus, who is eminently human in his failure to understand the present situation, is already
gone from her, since she herself is less and less capable of denying what she
may have suspected at some level for a very long time, that is, the gods' truth.

Thus we may interpret in a similar way the conjunction of words which
open Jocasta's invocation to Apollo quoted above, "δόξα μοι παρεστάθη,"
"an idea stood beside me," and Oedipus' own movement toward the gods
and away from the human domain. Both speak of the *para-doxa*, the paradoxical nature of the relation of the human to the divine. Oedipus' paradox, like
Jocasta's here, resides in the fact that his proximity to the gods' truth, his
being "beside" them, requires a distancing from the human realm for which
that truth seemed to have been written. Perhaps, in the end, the peril of such
a *para-doxa* is in language itself, or in thought ("opinion" is a more common
translation of "δόξα," but the noun is related to a verb, δοκέω, meaning "to
think or believe or seem"); since indeed thought is itself always beside (παρά)

its conceiver, and can seem to him a soothing escape from the chaos of his existence precisely because it is itself dangerously distant from the domain which it is meant to allow him to conceive.

vii. *Vitae Parallelae*

For Oedipus' paradox is the paradox of the truth, that which lies beyond human expression but the expression of which humans spend their lives pursuing. The paradox of the truth that Oedipus discovers at the end of the play is that it is always nothing more than what it is: within the confusion which it fosters in those attempting to understand it and coming up at various moments with variant interpretations of it, it never changes in itself but remains ever the same, a pillar of stability amidst the chaos which the pursuit of it wreaks around it. And those who, like Jocasta and Oedipus, discover the truth, the *whole* truth, must follow its model and let their lives come to a halt, because once they see themselves as a man, as one being, they can no longer live within the framework of human temporality, they can no longer change. If they move at all, it is in lines parallel to the lines of human existence, lines which will never converge with the human but will always be tantalizingly close to it, in sight but out of reach, beside (παρά) it but always other (ἄλλος). Like the gods, they have reached the status of paradigm.

It is precisely this ("παράδειγμα"[43]) that the chorus calls Oedipus once his story has all become clear.[44] But, like the knowledge of which he has become an unmovable paradigm, Oedipus is himself now irremediably distanced from human contact. The ἐξάγγελος describes the scene of Oedipus' frenetic search for Jocasta just before the self-blinding in terms which clearly show the king's separate status:

> λυσσῶντι δ' αὐτῷ δαιμόνων δείκνυσί τις ·
> οὐδεὶς γὰρ ἀνδρῶν οἳ παρῆμεν ἐγγύθεν.

But one of the divinities shows him what he's looking for [Jocasta's room and
                                                                                his spear];
for none of us men who were *nearby beside him* did.[45]

It is now the divinity which is assumed to show Oedipus the way and to separate him from the humans who are at his side; even though he is not yet blind, what he is in search of only the divinity can show him, since he has already glimpsed his relation to the divine and seen the nature of all of his previous human contacts.

Indeed, the words of the ἐξάγγελος describing the chorus's absence from the scene of the suicide and obliquely prefiguring the announcement of the self-blinding, "ἡ γὰρ ὄψις οὐ πάρα" ("Your sight *was not nearby*"[46]), depicts the mutual separation of Oedipus from the human and of the human from Oedipus. The end of Oedipus' story is one that must be stored and retained, both kept away from an immediate and unmediated perception and guarded against the dangers of a potential ultimate oblivion, for Oedipus' story is one that no one should relive *as such* and yet that no one ought to be allowed to forget. The king's unique concern will now be in finding a place to be stored, a literal stop not only to match his spiritual stop, but also to install in others the lessons which he has lost—and found—his life in learning.

For all one learns through the distances covered by a conventional symbolic system, one by which units move across a page and lives move from house to house, all in search of a meaning to keep them going and which only the search for meaning keeps going, is that the stability and the absolute nature of the god-like can be learned only by our distance to them and can only be learned by our distance to them. That only a stop—a refusal to run after a meaning which will be no closer or clearer after ten thousand words or after ten thousand lives than it was after one word or one life—can re-explore the conventional relations of any symbolic system, that any re-evaluation of such a system—any attempt to make it correspond to, and not simply point to, an underlying, unchanging meaning or value which it is not—requires a closing off from the system, or at least from its conventions, a kind of hermeticism, a wandering alone.

If, at the end of the *Oedipus at Colonus,* the king does not die so much as he disappears from life,[47] it is that he is no longer really alive once his life has been recognized as an exploration of the value of human existence. His disappearance into the earth corresponds to his perpetual storage as other than his individual identity, and yet as the only final and ultimate realization of human individuality insofar as he is the paradigm by which every human life is to be measured. Oedipus' disappearance as a simple self—and indeed, his story seems to indicate the impossibility of any simple identity for mortal creatures who cannot persist across time in themselves—is matched by the possibility of a perpetuation, a remembrance, a representation, the very memory which alone binds the moments of human existence together. Representation alone enables the minds of men to conceive of and to retain models in their search for a meaning which brings them close to the divine all the while it keeps them from ever reaching it. Its endless attempt to find meaning, like Oedipus' long run away from and toward the gods, is the finest of all lost causes.

Chapter Six: The Earthly Home and the Celestial Home

"Quand l'ombre menaça de la fatale loi"

The Azure is then that which presents itself beyond its absence, that which affirms itself beyond that which denies it, that which exists beyond that which does not exist. It is a presence, but at a distance.

Georges Poulet
The Interior Distance
Tr. Elliott Coleman

Quand l'ombre menaça de la fatale loi
Tel vieux Rêve, désir et mal de mes vertèbres,
Affligé de périr sous les plafonds funèbres
Il a ployé son aile indubitable en moi.

Luxe, ô salle d'ébène où, pour séduire un roi
Se tordent dans leur mort des guirlandes célèbres,
Vous n'êtes qu'un orgueil menti par les ténèbres
Aux yeux du solitaire ébloui de sa foi.

Oui, je sais qu'au lointain de cette nuit, la Terre
Jette d'un grand éclat l'insolite mystère,
Sous les siècles hideux qui l'obscurcissent moins.

L'espace à soi pareil qu'il s'accroisse ou se nie
Roule dans cet ennui des feux vils pour témoins
Que s'est d'un astre en fête allumé le génie.

"Je veux me donner ce spectacle de la matière, ayant conscience d'être, et cependant, s'élançant forcenément dans le rêve qu'elle sait n'être pas."[1] Mallarmé's much-quoted letter to Henri Cazalis expresses the paradox of movement and non-movement implicit in the sonnet which begins "Quand l'ombre menaça de la fatale loi" as well as in much of the poet's other work. The communicating medium is here represented by "la matière"; related to Latin *mater*, it designates the matter through which meaning is transmitted, the corporal entity which gives birth in substance to insubstantial ideas. The "élancement" of matter is indeed reminiscent of the movement of the mutually identifying halves of the *symbolon*, which are "thrown" away from themselves and toward each other precisely because they contain sense not in themselves, but only as complements of one another. The communicating medium is thus the means ("la matière") to an end ("rêve") which will require a journey of mediation, a middle time which measures the distance between the dream of being thoroughly proximate to the dream and the impossibility of being more than approximate to it.

The movement of proximation to and approximation of meaning is circumscribed by the poet's own control of the process, his god-like observation of a world whose workings he himself seems to have created: "Je veux me donner ce spectacle de la matière." It is as if the poet, an unseen god who refused to make an appearance on any visible *machina*, stood in the wings as the material substance of the words the man has chosen chased after his dream. It is in this process of giving himself a performance to observe that the poet considers himself both as human and as other than human, for the possibility of watching substantial words re-enact the human chase for divine, insubstantial meaning that he has set in motion requires his withdrawal from the chase itself, since he is the one who attempts to provide the transmitting medium, the correct words which only he can discover. And yet his is also the dream to be reached; it is only his very humanity which assures that the dream is only and always a dream, a paradox which Georges Poulet, in speaking of Mallarmé, succinctly characterizes: "How does one attain through dream that of which dream has precisely the need in order to be dreamed? How does one find a starting point?"[2]

The relation of dreamer to dreamed is thus not simply one of parent to offspring, it is rather one which functions as a kind of symbiosis: the dreamer takes his source of energy from the dream, which is dead—or not alive—to him insofar as it can never be reached, whereas the dream is given birth only if the dreamer goes beyond his human status and creates a perfect work to house the dream—one which says that a search for other words is unnecessary —and dies to the world of movement through which he has been forced to search for his dream but only away from which he can ever find it. "Mallarmé declared," so states James Lawler, "that it is by his own agony and ultimate death that the poet himself achieves beauty."[3] Even though mortals must die as themselves, just as they were born as the products of others, they can live through—by means of as well as across—their death as one-half of a symbolic relationship, one which links dreamer and dream such that if both cannot be present at the same time, since the dream must be at a distance from the dreamer in order to assure the forward movement of the latter toward it, both cannot be absent. If the dreamer must perish, his dream, his ability as a mortal to conceive of the immortal, will take his place and represent him where he is not present, reconstitute home in another way where home was never to be found as long as he was alive.

The tension in "Le Tombeau d'Edgar Poe" between attribute, or quality existing across time and therefore renewable or non-renewable, and epithet, or the process of naming which must be accomplished once and for all, takes the form in this sonnet of a tension between mortal life with its necessity for regeneration when old age comes ("Tel *vieux* Rêve . . . Affligé de *périr*") and the dream of existence as an unchanging, stable paradigm requiring no syntactical combination with other lives in order to persist. If the poet seems at first to have given birth to the Dream ("désir et mal *de mes vertèbres*"), that birth is not a simple centrifugal movement of procreation, self "pushing forward" (*pro-*) a life which was originally pushed forward onto it, but rather a reversible, ultimately reflexive motion; even though the poet appears to be the source of the dream, he is also its potential refuge as it faces death. The poet is placed in the position of being asked to protect from annihilation and obscurity the very dream which he himself generated because of his own mortality, a dream which aspires to the very state (immortality) the lack of which "engendered" it in the head of a mortal, and the reaching of which would make its progenitor other than what he is.

In the antagonism between the dream's ambition to definitive existence and all that is threatening that ambition, the poet, or the "moi" of the poem, is implicated, and this in the etymological sense of the word: for when the dream "a *ployé* son aile indubitable *en* moi," it has also "em-*ployé*" the poet, or *implicated* him[4] in its search for a transcendence of its condition.

The dream thus calls into question the normative birth process, or any possibility of a simple, unidirectional link between parent and offspring, since the action which links it with its potential shelter, the "moi" of the poem, is a sort of inverted birth. The "Rêve" is "vieux" and not "jeune"; it is about to die and not about to be born; even though the poet is ultimately its source, it here goes into him and does not come out of him; and the law by which it feels threatened is "fatale," or having to do with death, rather than "natale," having to do with birth, the latter echo suggested not only by the rhyme, but also by the replication in the poem's second line of the double movement of desire and pain ("désir et mal")—the seed going in and the child coming out—which constitutes the twofold process of human procreation.

Here again, as in "Le Tombeau d'Edgar Poe," the domains of mortal existence and artistic creation are placed in opposition such that the latter is seen as a possible, indeed a necessary transcendence of the former, a symbolic immortality which fills the gap left by its departed counterpart, the other half of the *symbolon*, the mortal body which conceived the dream of reproducing itself where it was not. Once again we are in the domain of the paradox, the impossibility for the living of becoming fully proximate (παρά, or "beside") to immortal, motionless paradigms and for the ephemeral to be fully expressed by the permanent. The "fatale loi" is not only deadly, it is also the law of speaking: *fatal*, from Latin *fatum*, "what the god has *said*,"[5] is deadly only to the extent that every existing poem is partially a dead poem, one that has had to kill the living beings it has had to immortalize. The ambition of thoroughly joining the permanence of the stable half of the *symbolon* to its unstable half forms the basis of the attempt to create a non-conventional Symbolism by which one's rebirth as other, as a being transcending the perishability of the mortal state, would not require a relegation of one's human identity.

The sonnet begins with a temporal conjunction, "Quand," which is indicative of the transitory nature of human existence, as Jean-Pierre Richard comments: "Le premier mot nous plonge dans le noir, et les quatre premiers vers confirment le caractère apparemment irrémédiable de cette plongée."[6] "L'ombre," the approach of death, is inextricably associated with human existence: not only does the word "ombre" constitute a paradigmatic approximation of the word *man* because of its closeness to *hombre*, the Spanish cognate of the French word *homme*, the very creature which the "ombre" limits and quantifies; but the word is also proximate in the poem to a syllable which forms the English word *men*, the beginning of "menaça." The latter word, the poem's first verb, expressive of the hostile nature of death, also suggests, by its approximate homonym *mène à ça*, death's inevitability, the ultimate goal of all of our human movements, one which limits our striving toward any absolute.

Indeed, the inexorable objectivity of the use of a *passé simple*, "menaça," the only one of the poem, and one the emphatic nature of which may be deduced from its unorthodox pairing with a *passé composé* ("a ployé"), introduces the problem of unity and duality in the poem: it pits the simple ("menaça"), unmitigated fact that death will always exist against the necessarily composite ("a ployé") nature of immortal human dreams which must "fold themselves" into mortal bodies just as those bodies must reproduce themselves through other bodies which are not they. Indeed, "l'ombre" may also suggest, as does the replacement of the "Maître" in the "Coup de dés," characterized as "celui son ombre puérile,"[7] the necessity for men of considering their own existence as doubled by that of the generation which precedes them as well as by that which follows them. Furthermore, the existence of the shadow implies that of an external energy source, which in the sonnet is represented by the earth's dependence upon the sun and also by the mortal need for birth from another. This play of unity (simpleness) and duality (compositeness) reflects the opposition between birth from two, normative human procreation and normative syntax in language, each of which produces "meaning" through a conventional conjoinment of distinct units, and birth from one, the heroic dream of self-creation and the dream of fusing signifier and signified in order to produce absolute meaning once and for all.

The "Rêve" is in apposition to an expression which, if its terms are reversed, suggests the well-known explanation, that given at the beginning of the Old Testament,[8] of the original need for procreation: the dream of absolute existence or of absolute meaning is a "désir et mal de mes vertèbres," as opposed to her, "Eve" and not "Rêve," who is created from the "vertèbres d'un mâle." This Old Testament echo, while it may not be intentional, is certainly appropriate in a poem the first line of which has all the uncompromising authority of an Old Testament pronouncement and indeed contains a reference to the *law,* one of the major concerns of that book. It is certainly the case that the story of Genesis itself places a bound on the limits of human aspirations and dreams: the fall from the house of Eden and the god-like stability it offers is a fall to an earthly domain built upon a separation of dream from fulfillment, the double process of "désir et mal," the striving to attain one's wishes and the pain which that striving entails.

It is the fall from perpetual life, from a life of non-time, that is hostile to the heroic dream of oneness: when the "Rêve" folds its "aile indubitable en moi," it is also folding up its "elle,"[9] or its feminine counterpart, its double. The needed second term in the conjugal process is thereby "undoubled" by the dream which is hostile to it: "indubitable" indicates not only what is beyond a doubt, but also what is no longer double or split.[10] The "Rêve," itself desiring ("désir") to escape the constraints of its own mortality, can exist beyond the shadow ("ombre") of a doubt ("indubitable"), can be winged ("aile") like the "ange" of "Le Tombeau d'Edgar Poe," only by ridding itself of its own shadow ("ombre"), simultaneously its death, the shade it is about

to become, and its need for regeneration, "elle"/"Eve" as opposed to "aile"/
"Rêve," the "shadow" or reflection of Adam as well as the original cause of
his need for procreation.

Thus the poet holds a paradoxical position as both mortal source or parent
of the dream and potential means of eternal birth through the relegation of
a conventional symbolism—by whose terms perishable ideas are simply replaced
by imperishable forms which have no ambition of re-placing them, placing
them again in the realm of the living—and the creation of a non-conventional
Symbolism in which the stability of immutable forms takes the place of
perishable ideas, but solely in the hope that the latter will take place within
the shelter of those forms. For the poet, in his search for a place for his dream,
wishes that, unlike the situation described at the end of "Un coup de dés,"[11]
more than the place itself will have taken place.

The poet's equivocal stance, split between his role as a mortal procreator
anxious about his homeless, aging offspring and his aspiration to an immortal
creation which would eternally house and protect that offspring, is emphasized
by the end rhymes of the first quatrain. The "fatale loi," itself a potential
tool of destruction ("menaça de"[12]), one which says that the end of each
mortal life (or idea) can neither be revoked nor postponed, is rhymed with
"moi," the poet considered as a potential tool ("ployé en" / "employé") of
definitive survival, if he can fully exploit, or fold out the potential of the
dream which has folded itself into him. The "fatale loi" is thus in apposition
(by rhyme) and in opposition (by sense) to the "moi": its uncompromising
presence beside (παρά) the "moi" is a constant reminder of the ultimate
absenting of all mortal forms which cannot attain the permanence of divine
paradigms without relegating their mortal status. Georges Poulet admirably
states the paradoxical relation in Mallarmé's work of presence and absence
in this way: "to the simultaneous presence of two spatial worlds, one made
of azure, the other of matter, and separated by a void, there corresponded
the presence at a distance of two mutually exclusive durations, the one of
pure Eternity, the other the perpetuity of a lack and the *permanence of an
absence.*"[13]

Analogously, the two inner lines of the quatrain, with their rhyme
"vertèbres"/"funèbres," set forth the same implicit confrontation between
the perishable, which lives and dies in cyclical time, and the imperishable,
depicted as a straight, static boundary beyond which all that is mortal and
cyclical dies either altogether or at least as itself. The word "vertèbres," from
the Latin *vertebrae,* related to the verb *vertere,* "to turn" (as in "revert,"
"convert"), implies a circular movement, as the vertebrae not only are round
themselves and "turnable" as pivotal points of the spine, but also serve as
articulations between the spinal column and the ribs, that is, as mediations
between what is *straight* and *erect* in man and aspires to the heavenly,[14] and

what is horizontal, parallel to the Earth's surface, indeed, the very rib from which woman was created so that she might subsequently bring on the *need* for human procreation by listening to a creature which moves only along the Earth's surface.[15] The "vertèbres" as structuring units of the human organism are thus not unlike the house as an organizing structure in that the latter works between, on the one hand, the earthbound cycles of human existence which move only horizontally along (or around) the Earth's surface and offer no capacity for commemoration, no resistance to or differentiation from the oblivion of a state of nature, and, on the other hand, the attempt to "erect" god-like permanence for its inhabitants by providing the continuity of a stable family name.

Indeed, if the vertebrae are round within the cross-section of the spinal column, and are points on larger circles, the arcs formed by the ribs, they are in contrast, by rhyme and by sense, to the "plafonds funèbres," or the celestial vault darkened by night. The "désir et mal de mes vertèbres" is indicative of all that is "upright" in man—who is, after all, a "vertebrate"—all that strives for divine meaning and strikes the "plafonds funèbres," the sky's reminder that the human house is not homologous to the divine house. The funerary ceilings are seen not as arched,[16] but rather as flat, "plafond" being composed of *plat* and *fond,* with the *fond-* element suggesting the finitude of an unmovable boundary, whether it be above, as here, or below, as in the idea of a *fondation,* the original earthbound and weight-supporting part of the house doubling its sky-reaching upper limits.

The sky-earth dualities implicit in the rhymed pair "vertèbres"/"funèbres" are reinforced by the aural opposition of the words' unlike elements, *vert-* and *fun-,* which are virtual antonyms: *vert-* suggests the circularity of the cycles of growing things, which are green (*verts*) for a time and then eventually turn (*vertere,* this being a genuine etymological relation) to dust, revert to their original condition ("dust to dust"), whereas *fun-* (Latin *funus,* related to French *fumée*) evokes a purely linear movement, the darkness brought on by death, and the inevitable decline of all mortal things.

Indeed, the opposition *vert-/fun-* recapitulates the tension between the metaphoric and metonymic aspects of symbolism, the joining of which is to be associated with the dream of a non-conventional Symbolism. The perpetual "turning" implied by the "vertèbres" as well as its parallelism to the Earth's surface is indicative of a metaphoric refusal to create and accumulate stable structures in space or across time. If man comes from dust and returns to dust, as the post-Edenic God tells the erring and hereafter errant couple in Genesis, he is always essentially the same, but with a sameness resisting the stability of any persistent identity, a sameness which is the "permanence of an absence." It is a sameness with which metaphor concurs, for metaphor attempts to destroy the difference presumed by the "barrier resisting signification,"[17] the difference between man-made, "stable" signifier and fundamentally unstable signified. It refuses the conventional structuring of meaning, for it recognizes the impossibility for mortals of reaching "meaning" through any kind of a stop.

It is precisely because metaphorical association is a constant process of becoming[18] that it never comes to an end, that it never arrives anywhere, since it says that meaning has nowhere to go, is always and everywhere open to question and attack, that it is not simply equal to itself because it has no stable limiting self to be equal to. The funerary ceilings, as opposed to the perpetually turning "vertèbres," place a metonymic limit on human life and human aspirations to god-like meaning: it is only thanks to the house and its limiting outlines that man thinks himself eternally upright, that he seems able to see at the same time his two *fonds,* or "ends," his beginning, or *fondation (fond* as "origin"), and his end, or "plafonds funèbres" *(fond* as "goal"), and that he believes he can put the parts of his life together to form a whole (the very process of metonymy). And it is when he tries to put the two aspects of symbolism together that he conceives of a superhuman Symbolism, of imitating what Mallarmé called "la Divinité, qui jamais n'est que Soi,"[19] simultaneously a perpetual turning into or becoming (metaphor) and an eternal identity by which one is equal to oneself as a whole at any given moment (metonymy), both a movement of endless potential (metaphor) and a total self-proximity (the homogeneity of outside and inside claimed by metonymy).

It is thus with the approaching necessity of "going across"—"périr," from the Latin *per-ire,* "to go completely or through"—of stepping over the boundary separating the cycles of life from the linearity of non-life, that the dream is afflicted. Here the internal rhyme at the *hémistiche* of the two inner lines of the quatrain, "désir" and "périr," reinforces the opposition established by the two pairs of end rhymes between the mortal poet's striving for the immortal ("désir," "moi," "vertèbres") and the mortality of that very dream of immortality ("périr," "loi," "funèbres"). The switch from the opening *passé simple* ("menaça") to the *passé composé* ("a ployé") which leads the way to the impending series of present tense verbs that will stretch all the way to the poem's last line is indicative of the heightened immediacy of the dream's appeal for mediation.

But the "moi" is not only the potential mediator between the appealer ("Rêve") and the annihilation ("fatale loi") threatening it; he is also the actual cause of the need for that appeal, since it is the poet's own mortality which cannot escape the law of fate. The illusory nature of the protection offered the dream by the "moi" continues to characterize the relationship between the mortal and the immortal in the second quatrain: the heavens are represented by the ostentatious spectacle of the night sky, false ("menti") not because it is transitory, as has been claimed by several critics,[20] but rather because it is *not* transitory in the human sense of the word. The constellations may be called "guirlandes," may seem to move in circles or cycles ("se tordent," from Latin *torquere*, "to turn or twist"), but they always come back to "life" with the coming of night. Their "death" is a present tense death ("se tordent," as opposed to "menaça") precisely because the stars "die" not once and for all but rather every morning, which proves that they do not die at all. For it is not the sky but rather the earth that is in transit; it is the spectator, the gullible king "seduced" by the star show, who is "turning" ever closer to his own death all the while he looks to the sky for transcendence.

Thus the house of night ("salle d'ébène," a development of the metaphor of the "plafonds funèbres") is, properly speaking, a celestial house, one which is humanized only by those who, in considering the sky as a metaphor for their own earthly home, hope to effect a kind of chiasmus between the two houses: if the celestial home is given the attributes of life and death which properly belong only to humanity, then perhaps the earthly home will be able to borrow immortality in return. This hope is, of course, in itself a lie, a "divertissement" in the Pascalian sense of the word, a turning away (again, *vertere*) from the inevitable and painful sight of one's own mortality: "La seule chose qui nous console de nos misères est le divertissement, et cependant c'est la plus grande de nos misères, car c'est cela qui nous empêche principalement de songer à nous et qui nous fait perdre insensiblement."[21] Indeed, Mallarmé himself comments on the aural disparity of the words "ombre" and "ténèbres," the two synonyms implicitly opposed here: "A côté d'*ombre*, opaque, *ténèbres* se fonce peu."[22] The intransigent honesty of the "ombre," the shadow of the law of fate, is precisely what the king is turning away from (*di-vertere*) as his attention is led aside (*se-ducere*) toward the "ténèbres," the darkness which is in itself a kind of lie, since it apparently "se fonce peu" even though it is in reality as dark as its "opaque" synonym.

The house of night, in its status as virtual oxymoron ("luxe" and its Latin source, *lux,* "light," as opposed to "ébène"), is yet another product of the dream of non-conventional Symbolism; it wishes to attain the unchanging stability of the stars (*lux*), which have no shadow ("ombre") and carry their own energy source with them as they travel, and to retain the beauty of the ephemeral, the constantly regenerating mortality implied by the "salle d'ébène" in its non-figurative meaning, ebony being in its first sense a tree. Indeed, the botanical meaning of the word "ébène," like that of the stars figured as "guirlandes," emphasizes the reaching up of the earthly domain toward the sky, in the case of the ebony a movement reinforced by the tree's upright position and its rootedness in the Earth, striving to join Earth and sky. The celestialization of the ebony (night sky) and the garlands (constellations[23]) thus provides a figurative link between the heavenly and the earthly domains through metaphor: the earthly house, like the ebony and the garlands, is thus rooted in the ground but reaching up, literally and figuratively, toward the immutability of the divine.

The figure of the king may be seen as a kind of mediator between his two rhymed counterparts in the first quatrain, "loi" and "moi," and is also to be associated with the poet: Robert Greer Cohn aptly recalls Mallarmé's characterization of artists as members of the new aristocracy,[24] one which links the "roi" here to the "moi" of the first quatrain by something more than rhyme. But perhaps the best descriptions of the mediating position of the king, one which likens him to a tragic figure, are provided by Jean-Pierre Richard and by Mallarmé himself. The former speaks of "l'homme, 'roi' de ce monde vide, maître de sa propre solitude,"[25] a description not unlike that which Mallarmé himself gives of man placed in the setting of Tragedy, the goal of which, Mallarmé says, is "de produire *en un milieu nul* ou à près *les grandes poses humaines* et comme notre plastique morale. Statuaire égale à l'interne opération par exemple de Descartes."[26] It is the ultimate nothingness of mortal existence, represented in the sonnet by the "fatale loi" and in Mallarmé's comments about Tragedy by the fleeting reference to Descartes and the universal doubt which that reference implies, out of which the king, " 'roi' de ce monde vide," attempts to forge a self-identity, a "moi" consisting of a new law of the self which counters the threat of the celestial with the mediation of a non-conventional Symbolism aiming to fuse the objectivity of the "fatale loi" and its impersonal *passé simple* with the subjectivity of the very self, "moi," which that law threatens.

As "mensonges," the "luxe" and the "salle d'ébène" are not only to be associated with the apparently, though falsely, reassuring cyclical nature of the night sky; they are also the "orgueils" of the poet who, in his striving for a kind of heroism straddling the human and the divine, is closely linked both to the king considering his own self as the ultimate guiding force of his universe—and for whom the poet may also be seen as a potential provider of "divertissement"—and to the night sky, which indeed offers the king the very spectacle which takes his mind off of his own mortality and makes him believe himself equal to a star (cf. "le Roi Soleil"). And if we recall Mallarmé's expressed goal, "Je veux me donner ce spectacle de la matière, ayant conscience d'être, et cependant, s'élançant forcenément dans le rêve qu'elle sait n'être pas," the "moi" of the poem becomes both spectator and stager, giving to himself ("moi") the spectacle which in the sonnet the king ("roi") is observing: it is as if the "moi" were divided between the divine law ("la fatale loi") which threatens its own mortality, and the earthly law ("roi") which falls prey to its divine counterpart precisely because it takes it as a model but cannot be it.

The last line of the second quatrain, with its completion of the rhymed series "loi"/"moi"/"roi"/"foi," and also with the introduction of the "solitaire," punctuates the conflicts of the two quatrains between things mortal ("moi"/"roi") and immortal ("loi"/"foi"). The "solitaire ébloui" is like the "moi" anxious to house his mortal dream of immortality and like the king diverted from his own mortality in that he, too, aspires to an absolute. Indeed, he also resembles the "moi" insofar as he is dazzled by something which has its ultimate source in him: "ébloui *de sa foi*," like "Tel vieux Rêve, désir et mal *de mes vertèbres*," presents the paradox of the faith's acting upon the very agent—"solitaire," like the "moi" of the first quatrain—which is its emitting source by asking that source to transform it into an autonomous external structure, a definitive edifice which will stand by itself without any need for rebuilding or regeneration and will thus surpass its mortal builders.

The conflict between earthly source and heavenly goal is present in the two constituent parts of the word "solitaire." The first element, *sol-*, has at least four possible meanings: "seul," as in Latin *solus*, or indeed, as in "solitaire"; "whole," as in Greek ὅλος, which is in fact related to Latin *solus*, whence "solitaire"; "sun," as in Latin *sol*, or French *soleil*; and "earth," as in French *sol*, or English *soil*. Each of the four meanings is reinforced by the visual image of the *o* in the center of the syllable, evoking the negation implicit in the state of solitude (*o* as zero), the inviolability of wholeness (*o* as unbroken boundary), and the physical form of both sun and earth. The second element, *-taire*, suggests not only its homonym, "terre," a word which appears in the very next line of the poem, but also the verb meaning "to be silent," the aural transposition of Mallarmé's famous ideal of the "page blanche." Indeed, the association "solitaire"/"taire" underlies a passage of "Quant au livre": "un *solitaire tacite* concert se donne, par la lecture, à l'esprit qui regagne, sur une sonorité moindre, la signification."[27] The modification of "concert" by both "solitaire" and a word which is etymologically related to "taire," "tacite," links the two words as much as the coveted silence—a silence more meaningful than conventional speech—which indeed seems to be the luxury of the "solitaire."

To be "solitaire" is, in fact, to go beyond convention, to reach a state of hermeticism. It is to dream of remaining alone (*solus*) and yet whole or complete (ὅλος), of not doubling oneself ("elle"/"aile indubitable") in order to reproduce oneself, not using a doubled conventional system to produce meaning. It is to dream of uniting sun (Latin *sol*) and earth (French *sol*) in order to merge celestial idea with earthly substance ("Du *sol* et de la *nue* hostiles, ô grief!"). It is to recognize that one is of the Earth ("terre") and that one will eventually be silent ("taire") under that Earth, a fact which, paradoxically, necessitates speech as a possible tool of transcendence, just as the perfect epitaph for the dead Poe would make him come alive in all the splendor which only his death could make apparent. It is, finally, to aspire to the "page blanche," that is, to being able to do without letters dividing and therefore doubling the wholeness of the page, just as a symbolic system composed of distinct, distant halves of a *symbolon* divides the wholeness which is one of the goals of the interior of the house by saying that one can identify that interior only from the outside.

The "Oui" that opens the tercets, a word which, as Cohn observes, echoes the word "ébloui" of the preceding line,[28] expresses the poet's faith in the creation of a monument in his own domain to the inventiveness of the human house which can use the immutable divine as a paradigm in fabricating a human symbolic system. Jacques Gengoux points out the "coïncidence plus que verbale" between the first line of the sonnet's first tercet ("Oui, je sais qu'au lointain de cette nuit . . .") and a passage from Mallarmé's letter to Cazalis cited at the beginning of this chapter: "Oui, *je le sais,* nous ne sommes que de vaines formes de la matière, mais bien sublimes pour avoir inventé Dieu et notre âme."[29] It is precisely the possibility of considering the Earth as other, as seen from the same distance from which its residents must view the celestial sphere, which forms the basis of the affirmation ("Oui") of the earthly which occupies the two tercets. Indeed, when seen from a distance, the Earth can provide the "ressemblance immortelle" of which Mallarmé speaks in his essay on Hamlet,[30] the legacy of an actor posing the question of mortal existence ("To be or not to be") as if it were a question, even though in fact the "ressemblance" is not a relation of equality but is formed of reflected light: "Oui, je sais qu'au *lointain* de cette nuit la Terre / Jette d'un grand éclat l'insolite mystère."

This turnabout of perspective is reflected by the reversal of the poem's observation point: it is now the stars, "des feux vils pour témoins," who are mere observers of the Earth which has taken them as a model. The symbolic birth of the Earth corresponds to the symbolic death of the stars, with the echo of "defunct" in "*feux* vils," the latter phrase being translatable as either "lowly fires" or "deceased lowly (ones)." It is in accepting the necessity of working within a symbolic system—even if it does not fully accept the conventions of that system—that the Earth, and the poet whose struggle for an absolute is parallel to that of his planet, re-enact the absolute nature of the stars symbolically, at the same time re-enacting their own birth as other (and more) than themselves and the death of their models as only themselves, as celestial beings untouched (and "unvilified") by the human observers which are taking them as a paradigm. The Earth's (and the poet's) celebration through symbolic forms makes it not only an "astre en fête," but also an "astre en fait": the act of celebration, perhaps related to the "insolite mystère," a reminder of the ancient Mysteries, is to be associated with the "guirlandes célèbres," themselves both perishable flowers and congratulatory wreaths for imperishable works of art, and results in the affirmation of the Earth's desire to transcend its own purported relativity by looking at itself from afar. For in throwing off "l'insolite mystère," the Earth becomes no longer hidden by the "siècles hideux," the secular as opposed to the spiritual, representing all that is hidden (here the echo of the English *hide* is almost certainly appropriate, especially with its proximity to "obscurcissent") by the passage of time as well as by any relegation to palpable form, because that act of throwing off holds within itself "un grand éclat" that rivals even as it mimics the brilliance of the distant lights of the night sky.

In the first tercet the Earth thus assumes the paradoxical role of the "solitaire ébloui de sa foi," and of the "moi" that is the source of the dream which wishes to transcend its author, for the Earth, too, is attempting to reach a state of non-contingency through a distancing from itself, through knowing itself from afar in a way it could never know itself from its own vantage point. In its search for itself it takes the paradigm of the stars as its own even as it reflects upon its own status as a reflector of their light, an identification by double reflection which confuses any simple notion of model and imitator.

The link between the Earth and the "solitaire" is felt at the level of sound by the rhyme "solitaire"/"Terre," as well as by the *sol-* element in the former word, and its repetition in the adjective "insolite" modifying "Terre." The dazzling source of light constituted by the faith of the "solitaire" is paralleled by the great outburst with which the Earth secretes its previously hidden secrets. Whether the expression "d'un grand éclat" is taken as a nominal complement to the phrase "l'insolite mystère,"[31] or as the adverbial complement to the verb "Jette,"[32] the emission of the "insolite mystère" becomes a sort of birth, a birth of what the Earth has up to now kept inside of itself ("hideux"/"hide"/"obscurcissent," as well as the Greek μύω, meaning "hide," in "mystère"), that is, its heroic ambition to send forth life not simply in the cyclical processes involved in all mortal existence, subjected and subjugated to the "siècles hideux" as well as "under" ("Sous") them, but, like the artist, with one fell swoop, with a symbolic conjoinment of divine stability and mortal mutability and change. Here we must not overlook the importance of Mallarmé's "Un coup de dés jamais n'abolira le hasard," suggested by the verb "Jette," the very action which initiates any roll of the dice, and by the presence of "Roule" in precisely the same position of the second tercet which "Jette" occupies in the first tercet, for the later poem is yet another emblem of the ambition of conquering the passage of time by abolishing once and for all the constant unattainability—akin to Poulet's "permanence of an absènce"[33]—of chance, by reaching the non-contingent state of chance itself.

The "mystère" which the Earth throws is therefore "insolite" not only in that it is "not habitual," the original meaning of the adjective,[34] and therefore represents an attempt to transgress the conventions separating the human and the divine habitats, but also in that it tries to deny, simultaneously, earthly procreation ("in-sol-ite," "denying the soil") and solar intervention in things earthly ("in-sol-ite," "denying the sun as a requisite source of energy"), precisely because it wishes to transcend the very distinction between heaven and earth upon which the Earth's reaching for heaven depends. Thus, even as the Earth and the poet ("Terre"/"solitaire") found a symbolic system constituted by two halves of a *symbolon*, they wish to join those two halves, to be both other, the stable half of the *symbolon* (like the heavens), and self, the mortal, changing half which the stable half only "represents" (like the Earth).

At the end of the poem, "L'espace à *soi* pareil" is in opposition to the "moi" of the first quatrain, for it is *only* itself; its unchanging stability is a kind of death as much as it is a perpetual life, a non-life more than a non-death. The revalorization through Symbolism of the human domain which can use the perspective of the divine as a paradigm is reflected by the reversal of the linear and the cyclical which the end of the poem provides: it is now the ever-recurrent stability of the divine which is exposed in all of the circularity ("Roule dans cet ennui"[35]) of its self-equality, as opposed to the necessarily self-regenerating cycles of mortal existence ("désir et mal de mes vertèbres"), an exchange of perspective which is emphasized by the aural association "nuit"/"ennui," the former still retaining the reputation of stability which the observation of the night sky has built up for it in the two quatrains, whereas the latter term points out the potential redundancy of the divine for any mortal follower of, or after it. The repetitive nature of the divine—and indeed, even if "L'espace à soi pareil" is not explicitly linked with the divine or even with the night sky in the poem, it is certainly analogous to "la Divinité, qui jamais n'est que Soi" of which Mallarmé speaks—is re-enacted by the first line of the second tercet as well, with its tripled as syllable, "L'esp*ace à s*oi pareil qu'il s'acc*roisse* ou se nie," perhaps a divine response to the Earth's "throw" of the previous tercet insofar as the divine hand holds nothing but *as*, or "aces"—the very reason for which it has nothing to aspire to in a game with human hands—and can no more grow than it can shrink: "L'espace à soi pareil qu'il s'accroisse ou se nie."[36]

Indeed, it is now the "feux vils," or the stars, who are "témoins" or observers of the Earth, as opposed to the earthly king who earlier had watched their spectacle, a reversal which seems to bring out the *moins* element of "témoins," the former term in fact constituting the rhymed counterpart of "témoins" in the first tercet. The Earth's (and the poet's) throwing off of a great burst of light ("Jette d'un grand éclat"), which *lessens* the obscurity threatening it by the passage of the never-changing centuries ("Sous les siècles hideux qui l'obscurcissent *moins*"), leads in a sense to a lessening of the latter's prestige and that of the unchanging stars which observe the Earth's revolution, not a simple turning but a symbolic rebirth as something other than itself. For if the heavens can never really be less than themselves, the Earth can at least lessen its distance to them by learning their lessons, a lesson which the Mock Turtle's story in *Alice in Wonderland* teaches us: " 'That's the reason they're called lessons,' the Gryphon remarked: 'because they lessen from day to day,' "[37] an explanation that makes far more sense than it appears to (and perhaps is meant to) if one considers that effective lessons do away with the learner's need for them as time goes on.

The ambiguous construction of the poem's final line is remarked upon by Davies; the phrase "d'un astre en fête" may be construed as a genitive taken with "génie" ("the genius of a celebrating star"), or adverbially with "s'est allumé" ("that genius has been lit up with, or by a celebrating star"[38]), an ambiguity closely resembling that of the second line of the first tercet ("Jette *d'un grand éclat* l'insolite mystère"). The double reading in both cases allows us to consider the source of energy of the Earth's final gesture ("d'un grand *éclat,*" "d'un astre *en fête*") as being either simply in the Earth itself ("l'insolite mystère d'un grand éclat," "le génie d'un astre en fête"), the Earth in that case seen as somehow having taken possession of a non-earthly source of energy and appropriated it as if it were its own, or in the Earth's imitation of its heavenly counterparts: "Jette d'un grand éclat," "le génie s'est allumé d'un astre en fête," the adverbial phrases indicative of the Earth's acting upon a divine model, as if it were a star but still attempting to retain its earthly identity.

Thus, the reciprocation between heaven and Earth is not an additive one, but rather a paradoxical one, not one by which two fully distinct entities act upon each other but one which confuses the very boundaries between identities upon which the idea of a reciprocation depends. The sky watches the Earth watching the sky and the Earth tries to assert its *proper* identity by acting in a way proper to the stars. The Earth's attempt to reaffirm its own identity and existence, indicated by the "Oui" which opens the tercets, is doubled by the final "gé-nie" of the poem, not only *rhymed* with a "nie" indicative of the sky's threat of a thoroughgoing *denial* of human existence—since the sky alone can offer itself the luxury of saying *either* yes or no to the question of existence without existing any more or less for the answer it gives—but also incorporating the perpetual sameness of the divine ("Qu'il s'accroisse ou se nie") into its own complex response to that existential question. For the last word of the poem embodies both the necessary death involved in any relegation to stable, unchanging form and the necessary birth as other than simply oneself which the creation of any symbolic system entails. It accepts the earthly house as a *pis-aller,* as one which holds none of the "aces" to match those of the celestial house, but it says that the kind of birth proper to the earthly house is a process of constant becoming—"génie" being related not only to Greek γένος, "birth," but also to the verb γίγνομαι, "to be born or to become"—of turning ("vertèbres"/"vertere") away from a simple fixation on our own mortality by generating new beings and new meanings to take the place of those who are gone, or of the part of us which is lost by any housing in stable form; but that it is also a process of returning ultimately to the place from which we have come ("fondation" to "plafond," or dust to dust). Indeed, it is precisely because the human house can fully possess neither the perpetual regeneration from moment to moment of mortal existence, a refusal to create and respect any stable structures, nor the perpetual stability of the divine which comes into being once and for all, because it can hold neither one in a simple way ("génie" as "J'ai ni"), that that human house discovers—or at least goes in search of—the dream of a non-conventional Symbolism that tries to hold both, the very genius that its mortality and its relativity send it off never to find, but somehow to found.

Chapter Seven: The Earthly Home and the Celestial Home

"La chevelure vol d'une flamme à l'extrême"

*Le choc sert à créer un contre-choc, et le principe se découvre
à travers un enchaînement d'opérations secondes. Une fois de
plus nous vérifions qu'en Mallarmé l'immédiat s'atteint par la
médiation, et que la proximité en soi se crée en une distance.*

J.-P. Richard
L'Univers imaginaire de Mallarmé

La chevelure vol d'une flamme à l'extrême
Occident de désirs pour la tout déployer
Se pose (je dirais mourir un diadème)
Vers le front couronné son ancien foyer

Mais sans or soupirer que cette vive nue
L'ignition du feu toujours intérieur
Originellement la seule continue
Dans le joyau de l'œil véridique ou rieur

Une nudité de héros tendre diffame
Celle qui ne mouvant astre ni feux au doigt
Rien qu'à simplifier avec gloire la femme
Accomplit par son chef fulgurante l'exploit

De semer de rubis le doute qu'elle écorche
Ainsi qu'une joyeuse et tutélaire torche.

The poet in "La chevelure vol d'une flamme à l'extrême" seems to take his inspiration not simply from his relationship to the *femme-spectacle*[1] whose hair opens the poem, but also from that of woman to sun, a relation which is itself emblematic of the link between the human and the divine which the poem explores. This almost triangular relation of poet, woman, and sun is one which resembles that of several other poems already discussed, and which is at the heart of the Mallarméan paradox: like the poet in "Sur les bois oubliés" who tries to be a go-between for the lovers separated by the threshold of death, and like the ambiguously named (and unnamed) "Poëte" of "Le Tombeau d'Edgar Poe" who is simultaneously dead and living poet, the poet-onlooker in "La chevelure" is in a kind of hinge position between the human and the non-human, represented in the sonnet, respectively, by the woman and the setting sun with which her flaming hair is in competition.

Despite the necessary confusion of the opening lines of the poem, a confusion which is as much a result of the poet's refusal to choose any simple scenario as it is that of the critic's often perverse desire to find one, several points support the possibility that the action alluded to in them is that of a woman who, at sunset, lets down her hair, shakes it briefly to loosen it from its arrangement on top of her head, and then allows it to hang down at full length, unbound. This interpretation resolves the difficulty of making the word "vol" refer either to a purely imaginary flight or to nothing more than a momentary gleam reflected in the hair, and instead gives to the word "vol" its full mobility as the released hair seems to be taking flight. The hair, leaping up from what appeared to be its source (that is, its roots above the forehead, from which it seemed to spring and also around which it was wrapped), now seems to be attempting to escape from that source as the woman shakes her hair free. Both hair and flame are thus simultaneously "unwound," the hair's flight away from its "foyer" recalling the mobility of a flame dancing about its "hearth," its own energy source.

The poem thus begins with a movement which is important in several ways: first, because it transforms what was circular (the bound-up hair coiled around the woman's head) into what is now linear (the hanging hair); second, because it gives an illusion of escape and flight where in fact no escape is possible, since the "chevelure" must, of course, remain attached to the woman's head; and finally, because it changes an artificial arrangement of the woman's hair into a natural one. And each of these features is important in the metaphor which terminates the first quatrain, one which relates the woman's head to a sort of home and which makes explicit the importance not only of celestial and earthly fire in the sonnet, but also of home: "le front couronné son ancien *foyer.*"

If the woman's hair in the sonnet is in competition with the setting sun for the poem's source of light which seems to be coming from everywhere and nowhere, it is that the human hearth of which she is a metaphor, by installing a god-like source of energy in the human realm, seems to transform into the unchanging constancy of a linearity what would otherwise be caught in the cycles of appearance, disappearance, and return. The house provides a sort of hinge for the cyclical and the linear elements of human existence: it transforms what would otherwise be an unmarked, neutral cycle of seasonal tasks into what seems to be the linear progression of a secure household and thus provides a heroic certainty against the fluctuations of mortal existence.

And indeed, the sonnet contains in its opening line a veiled allusion to a heroic figure whose importance might well be capital in a poem which features not only a heroic struggle for a source of energy, but also so many various kinds of fire: Prometheus. For the "vol d'une flamme" is not merely a flight but also a theft of the fire without which no "foyer," no concept of home, is possible. Fire in the Prometheus story is to be associated with all of the acquired crafts that distinguish culture from nature, artifice and artifact from an undifferentiated natural state. That Mallarmé was aware of the Prometheus story—even though it is quite possible that he intended no allusion to it here— is apparent from his translation of Cox's mythology manual, entitled in the French "Les Dieux antiques," in which Mallarmé not only speaks of Prometheus, but also uses several terms which are particularly interesting for this sonnet: "Quant à l'histoire de Prométhée, elle se rapporte à la *flamme* apportée du ciel, tandis que le *feu* allumé par Hermès est l'*ignition* produite dans les forêts par le frottement, au grand vent, de leurs branches."[2] Thus the flame is used to refer to the celestial fire stolen by Prometheus, as opposed to the spontaneous, natural fire which is beyond men's control, described by the words "feu" and "ignition" which are also present in the sonnet (although their meaning in it seems to bear no close relation to the Prometheus/Hermes passage).

Clearly, the "vol d'une flamme" is in some sense the attempted domestication of a divine fire, whether it be that stolen by Prometheus, that reflected by the woman's hair and "stolen" from the setting sun to which it belongs, or that of the poet who wishes to "steal" the fire of absolute meaning and rekindle it inside every word that he uses. The poet is thus like the tragic hero—himself emblematic of the paradoxical nature of home—who, in order to function as an individual away from his home, to be its representative on the road in his interactions with other homes through a conventional matching of *symbolon* to *symbolon,* must have the illusion, like the woman's "chevelure" which seems to be flying away from its "source," its former hearth, of escaping from his house and of functioning as a self-motivated, fully mobile individual who does not depend upon his house for his energy source but rather can persist as himself and in himself. The hero thus desires to be pure motion, "vol" in the sense that Mallarmé often uses the word, that is, as an evocation of a constant escape from convention—an escape which is as much a theft as a flight—and of an unlimited potential for the perpetual regeneration of meaning which is kept constantly in motion and is never fully or permanently housed within the stability of a fixed syntax.

The result of the domestication of divine fire—were such a domestication possible—would be to link artifice with nature, like the woman's hair to move between the bound and the unbound, since it would both bring the house closer to the power of a divine or natural state, the fire of the hearth re-enacting from afar celestial fire, and also bring nature into the house and thus "steal" it by making its fire available to the artificial state which the existence of the house presupposes. Indeed, the poet wishes to return to words a meaning which they as mere artifices cannot "deploy," both in the sense of "unfold," that is, re-enact and make manifest (which conventional language cannot do), and in the sense of "mobilize and utilize militarily." Mallarméan meaning can be had, if at all, only after a fight; perhaps, indeed, it is the fight itself.

It is perhaps the word "vol" with its double meaning which most closely characterizes the effect of the syntactical chaos of the poem's first lines, a chaos which also seems to move between the bound and the unbound, since it simultaneously glorifies the enormous possibilities of poetic syntax and its ambiguities by refusing to "bind" the words of the poem to any one meaning and strains at the limitations that any syntax must impose. Thus, not only do the words, read syntagmatically, seem to be flying across the page at a rate far too rapid to be made sense of, if only because most of them appear to belong in several places at once, but in addition the tremendous syntactical compression of the poem's opening, which provides several possible grammatical functions to a number of words, results in a scramble to "steal" the primary meaning of the lines, which, of course, cannot in reality be ascertained.

If the word "vol" is taken as "flight," then the poem's first syntactical ambiguities, dealing with the use of the prepositions "de" and "à," create a confusion between point of origin, destination, and moving agent. The preposition "de" here can have either of its principal meanings of "of" or "from": in the first case, the hair is a flame's flight, in the second it is a flight from a flame (perhaps the initial spark of desire in the poet-onlooker) to the

extreme Occident of desires (the culmination and satisfaction of desire?).
Thus, the expression "vol d'une flamme à l'extrême / Occident de désirs"
may be taken to evoke either a physical trajectory (a flame's flight) or a
temporal span (a flight from the inception of desire to its highest point).

Similarly, the meaning of the preposition "à" is unclear: is the extreme
Occident a geographical expression, the hair in that case flying *toward* the
West or perhaps being compared to a flame which is situated *in* the West
("une flamme à l'extrême / Occident," i.e., the setting sun)? Or is it temporal,
the hair being let down *at the moment* of the sun's final descent in the West,
or perhaps at the instant when desire, having reached its peak, must be satisfied and thus "fall off" ("Occident" from the Latin *ob-caedere*, "to fall
away")? The human drama and the geographical setting of the drama seem to
be in competition for the primary meaning of the sonnet's first lines as the
poet refuses to select either the human or the non-human element as
primordial.

The phrase "de désirs" also occurs at the juncture of two difficult expres-
sions and thus forms a complicated network of possible grammatical functions.
The phrase seems to be a complement to "Occident," to which it might also
be joined by the etymology which Littré gives as probable for the verb *désirer*,
from *desidera*, "from the stars," the *de-* element recalling perhaps the *ob-* of
"Occident," and the star component reminiscent of the setting sun. It is
also possible, however, to put "de désirs" in apposition to "d'une flamme,"
a pairing which is facilitated at any rate by the traditional metaphorical use of
"flamme" so frequent in Racine and Corneille, the phrase "à l'extrême Occident" then becoming autonomous and taking either its geographical (to or at
the far West) or its temporal (at the last moment before sunset) meaning,
and the opening lines being construed like this: "The hair flight of a flame
toward the far West, [flight] of desires to unfold it [flame or hair] completely."

Thus, the phrase "de désirs" may well serve the function not only of continuing thoughts preceding it ("d'une flamme," or "Occident"), but also of
leading into the grammatically ambiguous phrase "pour la tout déployer"
which, like "de désirs," is a sort of syntactical crossroads, since it may be
construed either with the expression following it ("Se pose"), or with the
expression preceding it ("de désirs"). If "pour la tout déployer" is taken with
"Se pose," independently of "de désirs," then the "la" must refer not to
"chevelure" but rather to "flamme," since the subject of "Se pose" is undoubtedly "chevelure," and if the subject is acting upon itself ("The hair sets itself
down to unfold *itself* completely"), its direct object pronoun must be "se" and
not "la." Thus the further confusion as to the antecedent of "la": either the
word refers to the hair, thus suggesting that the flame/desires take flight
("vol d'une flamme," "[vol] de désirs") in order to unfold the hair completely,
or the word refers to the flame, thus having the hair come to rest ("Se pose")
in order to unfold the flame. The fight for the reference of the "la" reinforces

the metaphor *chevelure/flamme* suggested by the initial "vol" shared by both hair and flame.

If the word "vol" is taken as "theft," we have further complications. Since the verb *voler* can take an indirect complement (i.e., one constructed with *à*) of the person or thing from which one has stolen, the phrase "à l'extrême / Occident" (with or without "de désirs") may well be construed as the complement of "vol": "The hair a flame's theft from the far West." Here again, the phrases "d'une flamme" and "de désirs" are in competition because of their identical grammatical form (*de* plus indefinite article—non-existent in the plural—plus noun), so that the sentence could read: "The hair theft by a flame [the light reflected on the hair's surface] of desires [*de-sidera*, light from the setting star?] from the far West," or even: "The hair theft of a flame by desires [the poet-onlooker's desire which is kindled by sunset and the nighttime ritual it both suggests and signals] from the far West."

If we have gone to what may seem to be excessive lengths to point out some of the grammatical ambiguities of the first two lines of the sonnet, it is in order to emphasize the extent to which Mallarmé prevents the reader or the listener from *stopping* at any point before the words "Se pose," that is to say, from feeling with certainty that he has reached the safety of the completion of a block of meaning. The poet is playing with the limitations imposed upon him by the Alexandrine line, and in so doing he himself, like the woman undoing her wrapped-up hair, attempts to make the cyclical linear, to efface the notion of return to a beginning at the start of a new line, since the reader may not take the "rest" that he expects at the end of each line until the hair itself takes a rest ("Se pose" with its suggestion of "pause" as well, both in contrast to the original frenetic "vol").

Indeed, the *rejet* that links the first and second lines of the sonnet is a kind of transgression of boundaries itself in that it oversteps the barrier of the dodecasyllabic line. The sentence is thus a kind of re-enactment of the extreme nature of the hair's flight/theft and of the human aspirations that the Occident, the land of "newness" and of the unknown for centuries, here evokes, since the sentence falls off the edge of the line just as those who pushed the limits of the known world ever westward were thought to be in danger of falling off the surface of the earth. This geographical element of the poem's opening—which Davies points out as well by mentioning the "réminiscence amusée d''extrême Orient'"[3] in "extrême Occident"—the overstepping of bounds linking the hair attempting to escape its "foyer," the fire trying to leap from its source, the capturing of divine fire by Prometheus and by the poet in search of a meaning which he can control and rekindle at any moment, and the explorer attempting to stretch the limits of the charted regions of the world, is reinforced by the placement of the word "Occident" which, if the physical arrangement of the sonnet on the page—a matter of great concern to Mallarmé —is considered as a kind of map, finds itself at the extreme West of the poem, having fallen off the extreme eastern edge of the first line. The poet thus emphasizes his desire, like that of the tragic hero, to move ever forward without feeling the constraints of what has gone before him, even those of his own earlier actions and creations; in short, his wish to reject the cyclic insofar as it implies a constant return and to embrace the transitivity of a linear progression.

Thus the opening metaphor of the sonnet matches the woman's hair not only to the flame which it at the same time reflects and resembles, but also to the poet's ambition to "straighten" language, to deploy words as though their full power had never been used before and not as if they represented nothing more than a return to accumulated past meanings, a recycling of the same linguistic elements, a straightening which we may also compare to Plato's discussion of the "straightness" of words in the *Cratylus*.[4] The recycling of past meanings would preclude the reaching of the destination of absolute meaning, of words which fully "contain" their meaning and are thus capable of carrying that meaning along with them without referring either to a past or to a future—an anti-destination in that its reaching would eliminate the necessity of a further linguistic output to "fill the gap" that relative meaning always leaves. The very image of circularity which plays such an important role in the hair's release implies a definition of location by two points, since any point on a circle exists both in its own location and as a function of another point, that is, at a fixed distance from the center of the circle, which may be seen in a sense as the circle's *source*. The geometry of the cyclical is indeed suggested by the word "foyer" itself, derived ultimately from the Latin *focus*, "center." The poet here is attempting to refuse the limitations imposed upon him by the consideration of language as being grounded in a past, in an "ancien foyer" from which it cannot escape and which always partially defines it.

This is not to say that Mallarmé systematically devalorizes the linguistic past, since he often uses words in their etymological sense precisely in order to give the impression that their roots descend deep into a mythical time which is one of the keys to their essential meaning. Indeed, the poet shared the attitude of many of his contemporaries toward Sanskrit, thought to be a mysterious, perfect language by linguists of the nineteenth century.[5] What Mallarmé does do battle with is the sullying of words by their accumulated past utilizations, which are often non-artistic or belong to the domain of unsatisfactory art, and which tend to limit the poetic potential which the poet wishes to activate as a presence within each word.

Thus the poet, like the "chevelure," wishes to "accomplish the exploit" of building inside of the human realm a fire which is not a mere reflection of the divine but rather which contains its source within itself, like Prometheus —whose name means "foreknowledge"—to give humans the possibility not only of conceiving the need for a civilizing fire, but also of knowing that it will always be at their disposal once they, like the gods, know its secrets. Similarly, the hair's own stealing of fire is partially an attempt to take hold of the veritable source of light in the sonnet, which is in doubt throughout the poem. It is impossible to ascertain whether the sonnet's moving force is the sun which by its descent signals the end of the day, evoking both the limitations of human life and the need for desire and procreation, and thus kindles the desires which unwind the hair, or whether the desire itself takes precedence and draws the "Occident" into it in a metaphorical transformation, the intensity of the sun in its cycles being compared to the rising and falling of human desire.

The almost constant calling into question of the actual source of energy in the sonnet, a procedure typical of Mallarmé, creates confusion as to the location of meaning in the poem, as it is impossible to determine if a given element is being compared to something else or if something else is being compared to it. Thus the poem is a "vol," a flight and a theft, in that since nothing in it has a stable, isolated identity, everything is metaphorical: every interpretation of the poem steals a meaning away from an inextricable network of meanings, so that one could satisfactorily read the poem only if one were able both to move forward syntagmatically and to remain stationary in order to examine the different possible paradigms into which each word of the sonnet might fit, to enjoy simultaneously an absolute potential for displacement and a total mobilization of poetic possibility within each word eliminating the need for a displacement from word to word, each word being fully deployed in itself and not depending upon its neighbor for meaning.

And indeed, at the first point of the sonnet which furnishes even a momentary stop, the appearance of the first finite verb which is put off until the third line even though its subject opens the poem, the impression of flight at least momentarily seems to die: "je dirais mourir un diadème." Once again the referent is unclear: is it the hair whose shine is obscured by its immobility, or is the dying diadem brought to mind by the unwinding of the now released and unfolded hair ("diadème," from the Greek *dia*, "around," and *deō*, "to tie or bind")? Or, a third possibility, is the "diadème" the glowing forehead of the woman which "dies" because the released hair comes to rest upon it and therefore obscures it? In any case, the source of the metaphorical diadem's death is the movement from circularity to linearity, or, if the word is taken in its etymological sense, from boundedness to unboundedness. Here again a veiled allusion to Prometheus may be present—although Mallarmé's use of the word "diadème" with its Greek origins probably was meant to make no more specific allusion to things Greek than to create a vague impression of Hellenism (as, to a lesser extent, in the word "héros" in the third quatrain) appropriate to the theatrical and dramatic nature of the scene—in that

Prometheus' punishment for his "vol d'une flamme" was indeed to be "tied up."[6]

The diadem's death may well also be a signal of the at least momentary end of the hair's "deployment," of its struggle with an immortal force for the apparent source of power and light, all the more so as the diadem is itself a symbol of power. The dying diadem punctuates the movement of the sonnet's first lines: the hair's unwinding may then be seen as a sort of defense against the sun's disappearance, an attempt on the part of human desire—which, like the sun, moves toward the *couchant* in order to be "achevé" or brought to a head ("chef"/"chevelure")—to capture the source of vital power that is about to disappear and upon which it does not wish to be contingent in its own finitude. That finitude is evoked not only by the necessary termination of the hair's flight, but also by the hint of "L'achève" in "La chevelure," emphasized furthermore by the synonym of the verb "Achève" in parallel position to "La chevelure" at the end of the third quatrain: "Accomplit par son chef," the latter word recalling "chevelure" as well.

The death of the "diadème" is thus the death of the boundedness implied by the contingency of the human upon the divine for its source of energy and life, since the three essential features of the diadem, its reflective brilliance, its circularity, and its use as an emblem of power, are all called into question by the hair's "competition" with the setting sun. The hair itself seems to have its own light source, even if it is a stolen one; it unwinds itself, moves from a circular to a linear disposition as a preliminary step toward the satisfaction of desire through which new life will be created just as the sun's linear progression (i.e., its disappearance) recalls the limits of individual human lives; and by these actions, it attacks the sun's ultimate power over the human, an attack suggested not only by the ambiguous and potentially hostile words "vol" and "déployer," but also by the word-play on "la tout," which can be aurally construed as "l'atout."

For humanity in its weakness and vulnerability does hold a few trump cards, a fact which the Prometheus myth vividly recalls. If humanity is contingent upon an energy source outside of itself, Prometheus himself serves to moderate that contingency by enabling men to build their own home, a "foyer" against the vagaries of nature, which is itself in competition with the home of the gods, the original source of fire (Zeus' lightning bolt). As Mallarmé himself says of Prometheus, again translating Cox: "Qu'était-ce que Prométhée? L'être puissant qui aida Zeus dans sa guerre contre Cronos et qui enseigna aux hommes à bâtir des maisons et à obéir à la loi, puis leur rapporta du ciel le feu."[7] Even though Prometheus' theft of fire is not here directly related to his teaching man to build houses, the fact that he is seen as a figure representing those two civilizing elements is not surprising. For indeed, the essential result of building a fire is that one can "create" (or have the impression of creating) a source of life within one's own property rather than going out in search of it elsewhere; the former searcher loses his identity as a searcher once he has installed divine fire in his own hearth, an action which gives him the impression of having reached the stability of a permanent, autonomous home.

The end of the "vol" which takes place in the sonnet's breathless first two lines and is punctuated by the verb "Se pose" is followed not only by a figurative death, that of a certain kind of power (diadem and its associations) the absolute nature of which is being challenged at the same time as it is being confiscated, but also by a figurative birth, that of a certain kind of potential. If the first lines of the poem depict a movement away, an attempt to escape and a stretching of limits (e.g., "extrême"), the transition to the second quatrain describes a movement toward ("Vers"). The status of the forehead/hearth is a double one: it is first of all a point of origin, the site in which the hair is rooted and which holds it back in its flight. But it is also the destination of the released hair, the site of its "pose" and of its "pause." The adjective "ancien" here seems to take on the sense of "former" rather than "ancient," particularly as it precedes the noun: the "front" is no longer the hair's hearth, the source of fuel and strength for the metaphorical flame which dances above it, but is now covered by the hair which takes precedence over it and which thus wishes to transcend the home fires which have fueled its motion.

The "front"/"foyer" is thus in a sense the source of continuity for the hair, since it defines both the starting and the finishing points of the hair's trajectory, a continuity which is emphasized by the ambiguous use of the adjective "couronné," which seems to straddle two time periods: the forehead was "crowned" by the hair coiled above it before its release, and is perhaps now "crowned" by the glow of the fringe of hair which covers it. The "front couronné" is thus the internal counterpart of the dying diadem of the preceding line, first because the latter may refer to the disappearance of the shining forehead beneath the settled hair, in which case the reappearance of a shining "crown" formed by the hair's fringe would be a sort of rebirth of what seemed to have died when the hair settled; and second because of the -né element in "couronné" ("couronne née"), which both responds to and effaces the diadem's death described in the adjacent line across the *hémistiche* from it. The disappearance of an external source of power (sunset / hair settling) gives way to the appearance of a potential internal one (creation of new life by the "feu toujours intérieur").

If the first quatrain depicts a struggle for the source of energy between the human and its habitat—the hair representing both the individual who cannot fully fly away from his hearth, his own heritage and initial source of life, and the human species which can never completely separate itself from its non-human energy source and yet which fights with the house of nature which it has done nothing to construct[8]—the second quatrain bespeaks the creative and procreative potential of a generative force which the human individual uses to build his own house and which the poet uses to create an edifice in language using words in a way particular to him, as if they were his own creation. While the first quatrain features a sort of syntactical struggle of phrases which fight it out for the various meanings which each grammatical rendering of the text would provide, the second quatrain is composed mainly of phrases which complement and continue one another. Whereas the units of meaning in the first quatrain demand to be defined and redefined constantly, one unit overlapping onto another from which it attempts to "steal" the shared element, in the second quatrain the units of meaning slide into each other and are so ill-defined as to seem practically non-existent, since the entire quatrain appears virtually to be formed by a series of loose appositions, perhaps linked by a finite verb ("continue," which also may be construed as an adjective) which itself is evocative of the process of apposition, a process by which one thought is *continued* and stretched out rather than moving forward to another one and allowing the sentence to advance. Nothing in this verse is really "complete": even if the word "continue" is taken as a finite verb, the only possible one of the stanza, the lines still remain subordinated to the opening infinitive ("soupirer") which, despite the several syntactical possibilities it offers, at least partially serves the function of removing the entire quatrain from any fixed temporal domain, a particularly appropriate use of the infinitive since the quatrain deals with infinite, non-manifest potential, with unidentified, nascent power.

That the second quatrain deals with potential power and represents both an internal conflict and a potential birth is evident in the verse's end rhymes. Each of the two pairs of rhymes includes one word which is fully contained in the other: "nue" in "continue," "rieur" in "intérieur." Furthermore, both of the larger words may be used to describe the very process by which they "swallow" their rhymed counterpart: "rieur" is included in the interior of "intérieur," and "continue" not only continues "nue" by prolonging what the shorter word had only begun (or rather finished), it also *contains* the earlier word, "contenu" and "continu" both being derived ultimately from a common Latin source meaning "to hold together." Finally, the first member of the second quatrain's masculine rhyme, "intérieur," echoes the first member of the first quatrain's feminine rhyme, "extrême," in that the latter is derived from a superlative form of the word meaning "exterior."

And indeed, the second quatrain describes the containment and the continuation of the external fire of the first quatrain, its housing in the human domain of perishable form and procreation as opposed to immortal form and creation. The quatrain is introduced by a "Mais" which is indicative of a break with what has gone before: now we are "sans or," without the gold of the sun that has now set.[9] "Or" here also contains a hint of its temporal meaning, "now,"[10] since the energy source of the sun is absent: its promise of a perpetual presence, of an ever-renewed return day after day, while it comprises much of the sun's value in human terms, is also to be tempered by the sun's unfailing daily disappearance, against which humans must plan by taking shelter at nightfall, and the figurative significance of which they must counter by answering the sun's immortality with their own form of immortality, the continuation of the chain of human existence, not by prolonging their own *presence* (*or*-ness) indefinitely, which they cannot do, but rather by substituting for it the symbolic *value* ("or," "gold") of other lives coming from theirs. The rhetorical meaning of "or," which can serve to indicate a further step in a logical series moving toward a conclusion, reinforces the cause-and-effect nature of its two other principal meanings, the present ("sans, or, soupirer") absence of gold ("sans or soupirer") leading to the need to replace the sun's treasured presence by a human fire. If the "chevelure" was in competition with the sun in the first quatrain, it is faced in the second with the task of housing and making manifest an internal source of energy in the absence of an eternal, external one which it can reflect.

Thus the "chevelure" is described as "cette vive nue," the last word of the expression being simultaneously noun and adjective,[11] "cloud" (the mist-like released hair) recalling the absence of the sun and "naked" emphasizing the vulnerability as well as the desirability of the woman and the natural state of her unarranged hair. So that the "vive nue" is in opposition to the "or" of the beginning of the line, because it is both "cloudy"—an appropriate image for perishable, human form—and unadorned by the glint of a diadem or a golden crown once the sun and the hair have both set and the former gives off no light to be reflected or "stolen" by the latter.

This opposition is reinforced by the possible if unconventional rendering of "cette vive nue" as the direct object of the infinitive "soupirer," which would yield a prose translation something like that given by Jean-Pierre Richard: "Sans soupirer d'autre or que son vivant nuage."[12] In that case, "vive nue" would be in virtual apposition to "or," all the while falling short of it, the implied meaning of the line being: But without having any more convincing "gold" to give off than this living, human matter (hair/woman). The subject of "soupirer" might in that case be "L'ignition du feu toujours intérieur," the finite verb of which, "continue," would be definitely without a direct object. Or, as another possibility, the entire second quatrain might be seen as "continuing" the first, in which case the first sentence of the poem would extend over eight lines: "La chevelure . . . / Se pose . . . / Sans or soupirer que cette vive nue . . . ," the rest of the second quatrain being in apposition to "cette vive nue" and "continue" being adjectival and not verbal. The possibility of taking the second quatrain as a continuation of the first is appropriate as a reflection of the hair's attempt to "continue" the function of creating an energy source left unfilled by the disappearing sun.

While this rendering of the text is certainly possible, it is equally conceivable to take the infinitive as governing the entire second quatrain, as setting the tone for it as a virtual synonym for *dommage que,* with an introductory pronoun and the verb "to be" implied (*"C'est* dommage que," *"Il est à* soupirer que").[13] One advantage to this interpretation is that it surreptitiously introduces the thus far unnamed "héros" into the poem without any explicit reference to him, for he is at least one potential subject of the infinitive "soupirer" as well as being conceivably evoked by the difficult-to-identify "œil véridique ou rieur" of the quatrain's last line.[14] Furthermore, allowing the infinitive to govern the rest of the quatrain creates a meaningful confusion between appositional phrases and direct objects in the subsequent lines: "cette vive nue," the subject of the subjunctive form "continue," may well have no direct object, but rather stand in apposition to the line following it ("L'ignition du feu toujours intérieur")—the cloud/nude being identified as the ignition of desire because it/she is seen as the perishable energy source through which the always internal fire of desire externalizes itself—or else the line might be the direct object of the verb "continue," in which case the "vive nue" would be the agent through which the internal fire reached the eye, perhaps simply because as a manifestation in palpable form of the object of desire it or she creates an image which the eye can hold. The appropriateness of the confusion resides in the fact that like the rather vague use of the infinitive "soupirer," it creates an atmosphere of non-differentiation and of non-identity which is particularly fitting in this quatrain which features a sort of birth and precedes the poet's utterance of a name ("diffame" / "dit femme") which will fix in immutable form what is still inchoate.

The impression of impending birth which the second quatrain creates is reinforced by the continuation of a series begun in the first quatrain: to "mourir" and the *-né* element of "couronné" in the last two lines of the first quatrain correspond in the first two lines of the second quatrain "vive" and "feu": just as the death of the sun's power must be answered by the birth of a properly human power, the externalization in living form of an everlasting fire (unquenchable desire as well as the insatiable quest for meaning) means exposing that fire to the possibility of a death and the necessity of a perpetual renewal, the very stuff of human survival. The fire without fuel, the preliminary desire which precedes a birth into perishable form, may well be eternal (not only "toujours intérieur," but also simply "toujours," "everlasting"), but it is also not fully alive ("feu" as "defunct," certainly not the primary sense here but suggested by the proximity of other birth and death words) until it has been given mortal life.

Similarly, as an answer to the setting sun ("Occident de désirs") we find the rising of the "vive nue" that is "originellement la seule" (the latter phrase referring by its ambiguous placement both to "vive nue" and to "ignition"), the adverb here recalling "Orient" not only by its parallel position to the noun "Occident" but also by its relatedness to the root of "Orient": Latin *oriri*, "to rise" (in "origine," the sense is "arise"), and its aural proximity to "or," suggesting a false etymology: "originellement," having to do with the birth (*gen-*) of gold (*or-*, present as well in the quatrain's first line), or the rising sun. It is only the sun's setting which "sets off" the woman's rising, the start of a new human life implied by the rising of desire, a rising which comes in response to the disappearance of an immortal source of life the power of which can never be captured permanently by the human species.

And indeed, just as human life must take physical form, and as fire must be housed in a human hearth if men are to use it to their own advantage, the poet must have recourse to the word in his housing of meaning. The term "véridique" (from Latin *verum-dicere*, "truthtelling"), while it modifies either "joyau" or "œil" or both, is suggestive of the poet's task of "saying," the *-dique* element also serving as a transition to the following line, in which the hero is first mentioned amidst a flurry of *dit-* elements: "nu-*dit*-é," "diffame" / "*dit* femme."

Furthermore, in "Originellement" we have an anticipatory doubt as to the value to attribute to the external vision of the woman, a doubt recalled by the eye which is "véridique ou rieur" presumably depending on the veracity of what it is reflecting: the *elle ment* element of "Originellement" may also be suggested by the possible echo of Genesis given off by the word "Originelle-ment" ("péché *originel*") and also by the possible reversal of the story of the creation of Eve, since the hero in this poem seems in a sense to take life from the woman whom he is observing. On the other hand, it is he as well as she who is the source of her "glory," since it is he who will ultimately name her "woman" ("dit femme"), a naming which is as unfortunate ("diffame") in its limited potential to celebrate the woman's "fame" and thus make "famous" the essence of her womanhood (her *femme*-ness) as it is necessary if she is to be born as a stable, perceptible entity into the poem which she inhabits.

Thus, while the first quatrain is essentially metaphorical, dealing as it does with two forms, the sun and the woman's hair, which fight it out for the possession of meaning (the source of energy and light) the location of which they seem to possess in common but which is indefinitely defined, the second quatrain is basically metonymical: it says that the always interior fire is "con-tinued" in the jewel of the eye, either that of the observer or that of the woman herself. In either case, the fire of the first quatrain is no longer situated between two external forms (hair/sun), rather it straddles inside and outside, the internal source of desire being made manifest by the external form of the woman, whether by her own eye or by her entire form projected onto the eye of the observer and, implicitly, by the description of that form which he is in the process of writing.

The necessary metonymic aspect of normative, stable language—in which the external form of words is "taken" for the meaning they contain, as opposed to the non-normative, shifting metaphorical quality of language which the poet attempts to mobilize by confronting two external forms and forcing them to "open themselves up" in order to produce the meaning which they possess only as a couple—is indeed a source of disappointment for the poet, perhaps the cause of his sigh. Indeed, what holds for language and its attempt to generate meaning holds also for other forms of generation: the satisfaction of a desire which is ongoing and never really satisfied can be only intermittently and imperfectly "housed," that is, given a physical expression which is necessarily insufficient, if only because temporary and imperfect and thus inferior to the continuous impulse which it is attempting to express. Whence the possibility of interpreting "continue" as an adjective: the ignition of the always interior fire is originally the only *continuous* one in the poet's eye, since the perpetual nature of desire precedes the establishment of an institution, the home or the poem, which houses and regulates desire by giving it form.

The poet's necessarily unsatisfied aspiration to generate meaning continuously by always activating the metaphorical potential of language and never allowing himself to become fully reconciled to its metonymical limitations is analogous to the observer's sigh that the fire of desire must result in a concrete birth into perishable form, whether that birth be of a new human being himself as contingent as his parents or of a poem as limited as the words and the human agent that compose it. The birth hinted at by the biblical echo of "original sin," both the cause and the agent of human procreation, and by the ambiguous syntax of the second quatrain, which confuses direct objects with phrases in apposition and thus renders unclear the relationship between units of meaning, so that one phrase seems simultaneously to be equated with the next and to "produce" it as the object of a transitive action, is also suggested by the quatrain's last line, partially by the idea of continuing one thing "in" another, a possible definition of birth, and also by the ambiguous use of the preposition "de": "le joyau de l'œil" may mean the jewel that the eye is (subjective genitive) or the jewel belonging to the eye (objective genitive), that is, a part of the eye (the pupil, the part that "glitters"?). The eye thus seems to give birth to the jewel which neither fully is it nor entirely belongs to it but is somewhere in between the two, another fitting description of the bond linking parent and child.

Furthermore, the two adjectives which follow the phrase "le joyau de l'œil" may well "belong" to "joyau," in which case the image is equally apt. Just as the eye—whether it be the woman's or the observer's—may be truthful or playful, depending on whether or not the image it creates (in the case of the woman) or sees and describes (in the case of the poet-onlooker) is true to the internal desire which it "continues" by feeding it with a palpable form, so the jewel of the eye—whether that jewel be a metonymical subset of the eye or a metaphorical transformation of it—may be of true value (here the resonance of real and false jewelry makes itself heard), that is, like a successful poem an everlasting *ornament* of basic worth, or simply a kind of plaything, a possibility reinforced by the derivation of the word "joyau," related to the word *jeu*.

The two poles thus defined by the doubt suggested by the line, a doubt that is continued into the final couplet of the sonnet ("le doute qu'elle écorche"), are the very ones which are recalled in the poem's last line in a kind of chiasmus: "joyeuse et tutélaire" echo, in reverse order, "véridique ou rieur," and also possibly "joyau" and "œil," the former by a phonic resemblance ("joyau"/"joyeuse," perhaps meant to create a false impression of etymological relation), the latter by its traditional status as seat of knowledge and learning, reflected by the relation in a number of languages between the verbs *to see* and *to know*.[15] The importance of the game in the sonnet is its relation to the idea of metaphorical association which, as is clear in the first quatrain, sets up a competition between the words which participate in the "game" of capturing meaning, a game by the terms of which neither member can win absolutely but which both must play. The initial presupposition of the game of metaphorical association is the acceptance of an untruth: human hair is neither a flight nor a flame's flight nor a setting sun, but its relation to those things can be explored poetically only by the admission of a pretense which says that hair is and is not a flight, that the two do and do not belong together. Thus the game, the playful element of the "joyau"/"œil," is a source of poetic vision—the saying (*dicere*) of a truth (*verum*)—and also of an "ornamentation" in the Mallarméan sense of the word.[16] If the poet is successful in *his* creation, the two aspects of his external product—its "truthfulness" to an internal source of inspiration and to an interior desire to express absolute meaning, to reach the stability of an end point and a destination, a definitive home that is beyond question and attack, and its own inventiveness, its treatment of the world as a potential locus for the unending series of "lies" which make up metaphorical language, its willingness to be constantly in motion and to "fight" for meaning like Prometheus by "playing with fire," competing with the immortal realm which contains that fire—will not be mutually exclusive ("véridique *ou* rieur"), but rather mutually supportive ("Ainsi qu'une joyeuse *et* tutélaire torche").

The figurative birth which takes place in the second quatrain, in addition to "continuing" the life extinguished by the figurative death of the sun, also serves to introduce the "héros" who appears explicitly at the start of the third quatrain, having perhaps been alluded to in the form of the unnamed subject of the infinitive "soupirer" and the unspecified possessor of the "œil véridique ou rieur." It seems almost as if he takes life from the eye which sees the woman, as if she herself, by one of the possible appositions of the second quatrain "Originellement la seule" ("vive nue"), were now "continued" by her observer. The poem thus moves from a combat between human and non-human forces (first quatrain) toward the formation of a human couple who, even if they are not meant to be figurations of the first couple in Genesis, seem nonetheless as naked and as vulnerable as the biblical pair. The hero's "nudité," which subsumes his identity by acting for him ("Une nudité de héros," the closest he comes to being present in the sonnet, is the subject of the verb "diffame"), matches that of the woman suggested by the ambiguous "nue" of the second quatrain, by the unclear "Celle" of the third quatrain, which may refer either to the woman's own "nudité" or to the woman herself, and by the description of the "Celle": "ne mouvant astre ni feux au doigt," "Rien qu'à simplifier avec gloire la femme," the woman's unadorned fingers and her halo-like, unarranged hair evoking at least a form of bareness, partially a response to the gold of the setting sun.

The naming of the "héros," if discreetly masked by an almost depersonalizing rhetorical transformation ("Une nudité de héros," possibly a substitution for "Un héros nu," the nominalization of the adjective being a process typical of Mallarmé), brings with it an even more direct naming of his partner: the homonym "diffame" / "dit femme" is supported not only by the rhymed counterpart to the verb, "femme," but also by the equal grammatical coherence of both interpretations, perhaps even greater for the one not printed: "A tender hero's nudity [or a nude, tender hero] calls 'woman' / Her who . . . (etc.)." The "héros" is thus also a "héraut" whose message, the utterance of a name with all the biblical overtones it bears, may come from a source as superhuman as that from which the woman's hair originally "stole" fire, a fire which itself now takes on a religious aura by being named "gloire," reminiscent of the Latin *gloria*, "the glow surrounding the body of Christ."

The poet's naming of the woman, if it is successful (and the text as it stands makes explicit his doubt in the matter, his consideration of the naming of the woman as at least potentially or at least partially a "diffamation"), would thus "simplify" her in the same sense that she herself, or perhaps her own nudity, "simplifies" her (or possibly simplifies "woman," to be taken here generically and not particularly): that is, in the "nudity" of that naming, its ability to make manifest the woman that it names and not to cover her up. This interpretation is supported by Littré's discussion of the origin of the word "simple," in which he refers to the Latin grammarians' own theories on the matter: that *simplex* came from *sine-plica*, "without a fold," a state suggestive of nakedness. The woman's nudity is thus at the same time a mark of her being revealed in her essence by poetic language which activates and makes perceptible her hidden qualities and also an indication of her potential as a vessel of the generation of metaphorical meaning through association, since metaphor can work only if words are not understood simply by their outer wrappings but are "undressed" and explored, unveiled in all of their power.

So that if the woman seems in a sense to give birth to the "héros," it is through his utterance of her name, his activation of a linguistic potential which recalls all of the power of the prelapsarian word, that she becomes "femme," a named human being, the occurrence of that word in the third quatrain coming after two full stanzas which feature the woman without coming close to naming her. And indeed, it is at this point that the woman reveals the quintessentially human form of power, the one which enabled Prometheus to steal fire from Zeus: that of "le chef," here representing not only the hair, but also the mind, the very word which forms the kernel of Prometheus' name ("forethought"). The woman need not deploy celestial fire like Zeus ("ne mouvant astre ni feux au doigt"), she can simply mobilize her own capacity for thought—the most compelling foundation of any human home—by which she too is "fulgurante," a word which indeed recalls Zeus' thunderbolt (Latin *fulgur,* French *foudre*), the source of divine fire. The action of the woman's "chef" thus modifies her entire being, so that it "stands for" her such that she becomes defined and identified by its action: the adjective "fulgurante," which must modify "Celle," the subject of "Accomplit," actually refers to the lightning-like glow ("avec gloire") of the woman's hair. And yet it agrees with and thus calls to mind the entire woman, not simply her head: she thus becomes virtually assimilated to the "chef" which defines her human power.

Thus, the "exploit" which the woman's head accomplishes is the counterpart to the "deployment" of her hair in the first quatrain, the earlier action being revealed as a mere attempt whereas the later one results in a genuine accomplishment. The link between the words "déployer" and "exploit" is reinforced by the aural echo of the feminine rhymes of the first quatrains ("extrême"/"diadème") suggested by "semer," the occurrence of which at the beginning of the poem's next-to-last line reflects also the placement of "extrême" at the end of its first line and tempts one to generate the series "flamme à l'extrême" / "mourir un diadème" / "sème de rubis," particularly since the first two phrases deal with a dying light (*in extremis*) and the last with a potential birth of light. The woman's "exploit" is to "fold out" her hair not beyond its limits ("à l'extrême"), in direct competition with a sun against which she will always lose, but only to the extent of its "simple" human potential, the properly human counterpart to the sun's own energy and power. The ancients' theories about the derivation of *simplex* may also link the verb "simplifier" to "déployer" and "exploit" for Mallarmé: to "simplify woman with glory" is to reveal her not in relation to an entity (sun) which can always deploy a greater force than she, but rather in her own beauty, unfolded ("déployée" and "exploitée") and revealed in itself (*sine-plica*) and not as a reflection of something else.

So that the light which the woman's hair sows in the sonnet's closing couplet is not one stolen from any immortal source, rather it appears amidst a host of words which suggest the acceptance of the duality and the relativity of human life. The couplet, the two-line composition of which also creates a dual element, not only is the only stanza which "joins" with another one by the *rejet* which begins it,[17] but also abounds with two's: the sowing of rubies unites the external and internal fires of earlier lines, the "flamme à l'extrême" and the "feu toujours intérieur," in that it is both external and internal: the verb might seem to imply a burying of the seed of light in a dark place where it might take root, a mixed metaphor at best, but here it appears to take on its more general meaning of "strew" or "scatter," as one does seed which will eventually be covered by a thin layer of earth. Thus the "sowing" of the rubies (or the ruby, since the number of the word "rubis" is unclear) either places a potential light in darkness or strews darkness with a glittering light, depending on whether the word "doute" is assumed to suggest the darkness of the air or a more solid, substantial one, that of the earth (whence Noulet's interpretation, "le bloc dur du doute"[18]).

The "doute" that the woman (or her nudity) "scrapes" or "skins" is another major element of duality in the couplet: derived from the Latin verb *dubitare,* from the root *dub,* "double," the word indicates a division of mind. Here its very doubleness is emphasized by the verb *écorcher,* which presupposes an outside and an inside, since it partially removes the former and thereby exposes the latter. The action of the verb "écorche" thus recalls that of "semer": both work to join outside and inside all the while recognizing the existence of both, "semer" implying a conjoinment of two distinct quantities, a creation through difference, and "écorche" indicative of the necessarily double nature of the world of appearance, in which any exterior form may be exposed as covering an essence which it cannot fully express (whence "le *doute* qu'elle écorche," doubt being a by-product of the doubleness of things). Both "semer" and "écorche" are opposed to "extrême," which attempts to push exteriority to its limits in an attempt to match the impulse to immortality with an undying external form, like the gods to be always oneself and always one, and to the "feu toujours intérieur," which is a perpetual refusal of exteriority, an infinite potential which precedes a "sowing" into the external world and a participation in a conventional symbolic system by which a mortal creature must "sow" outside of himself his potential for creating new life only because he does not contain eternal life within himself.

As for the actual reference of the word "doute," it is itself doubtful at best. Since any interpretation requiring the presence of a crowd—e.g., Richard's "les doutes d'un public"[19]—draws upon the context of "La déclaration foraine" which the sonnet itself does not replicate, the "doute" may simply refer to the series of doubts created by the woman herself and her competition with superhuman elements (the sun, and perhaps immortality, the role of Eve in Genesis possibly being hinted at here). The question posed implicitly by the first quatrain as to the source of the light and energy which permeate it, as well as that of the second quatrain concerning the value of the vision ("véridique ou rieur") which survives the sunset, are both answered by the actions of the two verbs of the couplet, both of which have the word "doute" as a direct object, the "doubling" of verbs acting upon "doute" indeed adding another dual element. The "scraping away" of the darkness by the woman's hair, while it cannot erase the "doute," the doubleness of human existence by which life (light, or perishable form) must imply death (darkness, or the disappearance of form), can mobilize a certain fertility ("semer"), a joining of forces that can create a human source of energy which, while it is not independent and self-perpetuating like the sun's but rather needs continual renewal, is at the real hearth of a human and not a divine home, the institution which brings together a couple in order to effect that renewal.[20] Thus the woman who had been alone ("Originellement la seule," with its unclear syntactical function possibly referring to the "vive nue," living cloud or Eve figure) is now joined by the "héros tendre," as a hero himself straddling the human and the superhuman, who builds a house for her in mortal words ("dit 'femme' ") and watches her sow its garden ("semer"), not a self-perpetuating one like the Garden of Eden precisely because the challenge upon immortality has been mounted and has failed.

For it is within the very doubleness of the mortal state and of the conventional symbolic systems of which it conceives in order to transcend its mortality but which do nothing more than measure it that the poet attempts himself to sow rubies—the *bis-* element of which may be seen as indicating both the necessary doubleness which his enterprise bespeaks and the applause for his at least potential success—that he desires, in the absence of absolute, always-present value ("sans or," "without gold-now") by which things human could always be only themselves and have no need for generating other things which are extensions of themselves, to create an ornament which is the measure of the very doubt which produced it, the division in the poet's mind between the aspiration to perpetual, divine fire (absolute meaning, expressed once and for all) and the necessity to house human fire within a perishable form, one which cannot do without renewal and regeneration.

It is perhaps in the light of the poet's acceptance of limitations after having transgressed them in order to test them out that we may interpret the final line of the sonnet as the rendering explicit of the poet's presence with the apparatus of figurative language that had previously been hidden: "*Ainsi qu'*une joyeuse et tutélaire torche," the comparison that ends the sonnet, completes a series of figurative structures which terminate each of the sonnet's four stanzas, but is the only one that announces its presence explicitly. Thus, the "front couronné son ancien foyer," the metaphor of the first quatrain, gives way to the "joyau de l'œil," straddling the domains of metaphor and metonymy (jewel from or standing for the eye / jewel that the eye is), and to the essentially metonymic "fulgurante" of the third quatrain, which implies that the entire woman is to be identified with her head which alone is "fulgurant." But even though the figures seem to become increasingly metonymical as the poem proceeds, which already implies a certain recognition of the limitations of language in that it creates a stabilization by saying that one term "stands for" another rather than "standing against" it in a fight for meaning, none of the three phrases announces its figurative nature in the way that the last line of the sonnet does.

The poem ends with a kind of solidification, with its own grounding in a self-awareness. If the woman's presence in the poem seems to perform a didactic function for the onlooker, he appears to learn from her the lesson that she herself has learned in her own struggle with the absolute (the sun): that she can and must be "simplement femme," that by attempting to compete with an absolute which she cannot conquer she is revealing her own relativity, her own status as a reflection of that absolute. Only by *re-enacting* on a human level what cannot be otherwise accomplished by mortals, by lighting the fire in the hearth as a human substitute—the mortal half of the *symbolon* the divine half of which the mortal can never truly join, and the divine home of which the mortal traveler can visit only as a guest—for the truly divine, perpetual fire whose presence can neither be controlled nor reproduced but can be experienced only *symbolically,* can human beings define humanity, a definition which affirms the symbolic as properly and essentially human.

The final realization that the woman exemplifies is emblematic of the poet's acceptance of the dual nature of human thought and human language, which are not only symbolic but are also aware of their symbolic nature, and thus of their own limitations. The self-consciously poetic language of the last figure of the poem unites the domain of pretense and competition for meaning on the one hand ("joyeuse"/"joyau"/"rieur") and that of essential meaning and the reaching of the stability of an end point, of a lesson, on the other ("tutélaire"/"œil"/"véridique"), the realms of *mimic* as a human effort to ape the divine—as pretense in the sense of play and in the sense of that which precedes (and precludes) a stable notion of tense and temporality— on the one hand, and of imitation as the recognition of the necessity of models on the other.

Indeed, the two domains which are joined at the end of the sonnet bear some resemblance to the two kinds of *mimesis* which Jacques Derrida brings up in his long essay on Mallarmé's short piece "Mimique":

S'annonce ainsi une division intérieure de la *mimesis,* une autoduplication de la répétition même. . . . Peut-être y a-t-il donc toujours plus qu'une seule *mimesis*; et peut-être est-ce dans l'étrange miroir qui réfléchit, mais aussi déplace et déforme une *mimesis* dans l'autre, comme si elle avait pour dessin de se mimer, de se masquer elle-même, que se loge l'histoire—de la littérature—comme la totalité de son interprétation. Tout s'y jouerait dans les paradoxes du double supplémentaire: de ce qui s'ajoutant au simple et à l'un, les remplace et les mime, à la fois ressemblant et différent, différent parce que—en tant que—ressemblant.[21]

Perhaps the story of "La chevelure vol d'une flamme à l'extrême" is "lodged," too, in the fold between two sorts of relations between the human and the divine which the poem explores. Insofar as the "chevelure" is a metaphoric transformation of the sun and the sun a metaphoric transformation of it—for the very notion of metaphor precludes any priority of model over modeler, or even any strict identification of the two roles—it "mimics" the sun; it challenges the power of the superhuman precisely by staking its claim to equality on the basis of an appearance ("flamme") which does seem to equate human and divine lights, but only to the extent that appearance covers no essential underlying identity or essence, as a sort of "game" by which the characteristic of the moment, in this case, brilliance, places the bearers of that trait in a common category. But insofar as the hair becomes an emblem, itself a kind of paradigm of what human knowledge can (and cannot) be based on, it is a metonymic, stabilizing entity, one which says that the part (appearance) must be taken for the whole (essence), but must never try to do away with it, that any syntactical displacement (and metonymy is indeed a displacement) works toward a goal of truth which it may never reach but which it nonetheless does not seriously challenge or replace.

At the end of the poem, the self-conscious language of the final figure follows the model of the woman whose hair is no longer a flame flying away from a source, attempting to deny its reflective (and perhaps reflexive) nature, but is rather a "torche," derived from the Latin *torquere*, "to twist," and therefore meaning a cloth "twisted about" itself and then lighted. The poet, like the woman, does not take light from elsewhere but uses his own interior light, his aspiration to the divinity and the immortality of the perfect poem, to illuminate his own hearth, like Prometheus to allow men to build a human home lighted not by uncapturable divine fire—the very intangibility of which is the point of departure for the need of a human house—but by the quest for that fire which in itself has undying value.

Chapter Eight: The Earthly Home and the Celestial Home

"Ses purs ongles très haut dédiant leur onyx"

Avant et derrière la voix *et la* graphie *il y a l'*anaphore: *le geste qui* indique, *instaure des* relations *et élimine les entités.*

Julia Kristeva
Σημειωτικ ή: *Recherches pour une sémanalyse*

Ses purs ongles très haut dédiant leur onyx,
L'Angoisse, ce minuit, soutient, lampadophore,
Maint rêve vespéral brûlé par le Phénix
Que ne recueille pas de cinéraire amphore

Sur les crédences, au salon vide: nul ptyx,
Aboli bibelot d'inanité sonore,
(Car le Maître est allé puiser des pleurs au Styx
Avec ce seul objet dont le Néant s'honore).

Mais proche la croisée au nord vacante, un or
Agonise selon peut-être le décor
Des licornes ruant du feu contre une nixe,

Elle, défunte nue en le miroir, encor
Que, dans l'oubli fermé par le cadre, se fixe
De scintillations sitôt le septuor.

The sonnet which begins "Ses purs ongles très haut dédiant leur onyx" is perhaps the single sonnet of Mallarmé which best deals with the double nature of tragic and Symbolist language. Language in the poem is simultaneously an earthly tool pointing with admiration to something which it is not, *indicating*, as would a finger, phenomena which are outside of itself and distinguishable from it, and a celestial mirror, a reflexive locus of meaning *dedicating* and sacralizing the site of the linguistic utterance.

From the very outset of the poem, language points both outside of itself and to itself. The image of the fingers implied by the "ongles" element of the opening metaphor, by which the groupings of stars in the sky seem to be the fingernails of "L'Angoisse, ce minuit," is indeed suggestive of the process of indication, related to *index*, "that which points out or shows," particularly as the word "dédiant" (from Latin *dedicare*, related to *indicare* and thus to *index*) is used to describe the action of the fingernails. Mallarmé himself was likely to have been aware of the connection between *digitus* and *indicare/dedicare*, if only from a passage in Cox's *Mythology of Aryan Nations*, the main source of "Les Dieux antiques": "The connection of δάκτυλος and *digitus* with the root from which sprung the Greek δείκνυμι, the Latin *indico* and other words, is generally admitted."[1] At the same time as the opening lines of the poem point up to a realm which can be reached for (although not attained) only through language, they attempt to "ground" the words which compose them by demonstrating their relativity, their relatedness to the words of other times and other languages.

The onyx which is "dedicated" by the fingernails of Anguish sets up the first category of correspondences in the sonnet's first two lines, that of etymological association. Since "ongles" and "onyx" are, historically speaking, the same word, it is as if the poet were returning the present-day word with its Latinate root ("ongle," from Latin *ungula*) to a distant past in which it is buried (the Greek word ὄνυξ, like the Latin *ungula*, meaning "nail"; even if the Latin and Greek words are actually cognate and neither is derived from the other, the Greek is certainly seen as having priority in time for cultural reasons). This idea of translucence, of attempting to make a mystical past glow through the necessary opacity of fixed present forms, is reinforced as well by the choice of the words that are here paired: "onyx" is a translucent gem, named for the fingernail because it, too, is neither fully opaque nor fully transparent. Thus in a sense the word "ongles" dedicates the word "onyx" as much as the metaphorical fingernails of Anguish dedicate the jewels of the midnight sky: the more recent form is not allowed the full transitivity of an opaque, unmotivated sign, but rather retains some measure of self-awareness as a linguistic form pointing as much back to earlier forms, its linguistic predecessors (or at least to words considered as such for cultural reasons), as to a present concept which it is meant to "indicate" with every use of it.

Further support for this interpretation of the two words "ongles" and "onyx" comes from the much earlier version of the sonnet that Mallarmé wrote in 1868.[2] In that version the play on "ongles" and "onyx" is already present in the form of the phrase "les onyx / De ses ongles," and the last line of the first quatrain includes another example of the same device: "le vespéral Phénix / De qui la cendre n'a de cinéraire amphore." The words "cendre" and "cinéraire" come from the same word, Latin *cinis, cineris,* meaning "ash," the essential difference between the words being that the noun form is more fully gallicized (note the introduction of the *d* to make the transition between the two liquids *n* and *r,* as well as the nasalization of the first vowel) than the adjective, which consists more or less of the stem of the Latin noun (*ciner-*) plus an adjectival suffix. If the "cendre" has no "cinéraire amphore," it is that the more recent word seems to have lost its attachment to the past (note also the Hellenic "amphore"). In its neutrality it has become fully opaque; it is the poet's ambition to "burn" it just as the Phoenix is burned, and thus to regenerate the potential energy the word contains.

That the effect of verbal bantering of the opening lines is a reflection of the necessarily self-referential nature of human language which, insofar as it can never give enough information about its "antecedents" (both syntactical and etymological) at a time, cannot provide the quantification of a *simple* indication, is hinted at by the very important *langue-* element of the subject of the opening lines, "L'Angoisse." Whether the source of the rather ill defined and puzzling anguish, to which "ce minuit" may possibly be in apposition—otherwise it would be a temporal adverb modifying the verb "soutient"—is the absence of sunlight at midnight or the distance and the unreachability of the celestial state represented by the stars, that anguish is essentially caused by isolation from a non-human energy source upon which the human must depend and to which it may reach out through language but which it cannot reach through language. And that anguish is shared by language itself, which feels its own sources (its etymology) to be outside of itself.

And indeed, the pairs "ongles"/"onyx" and "cendre"/"cinéraire" resemble each other also by the fact that each of the pairs describes the process by which linguistic transformation takes place across time: the fingernails are important not only because of their translucence, recent linguistic forms "letting through" the light of older forms which they resemble and at the same time partially obscuring those forms by replacing them, but also because they are hard and seem to be utterly fixed and unchanging, and yet are capable of, even require, growth and transformation. The ashes of the Phoenix and the dream which its pyre presumably also consumes, on the other hand, are emblematic not only of the need of language to regenerate itself periodically, to destroy its inherited forms and allow new ones to rise from the ashes, but also of the very process of regeneration, since a "burnt" form leaves meaning unhoused (the lack of a "cinéraire amphore") and free to search for a recipient to replace the one which has been destroyed.

Indeed, we may compare the Phoenix' burning of the evening dream to the "vol d'une flamme," the theft of divine fire by the human hearth in "La chevelure vol d'une flamme à l'extrême"[3]: it is the domain of *metaphor,* the potentially metaphorical quality of all human language once the belief in the existence of an attainable, stable absolute is given up, which makes both possible and necessary the chase for meaning in "La chevelure vol d'une flamme" and the search to house unhoused meaning in "Ses purs ongles." To this extent the poem's three past participles, "brûlé," "Aboli," and "fermé," the first and last of which occur in identical constructions (noun phrase–"Maint rêve vespéral"/"l'oubli"–participle–"brûlé"/"fermé"–preposition–"par"–and agent–"le Phénix"/"le cadre") and all three of which seem to speak of a *loss,* perhaps that of an absolute, carry as well the sense of a *potential.* The seeming destruction which the first two participles describe and the seeming construction of the last one ("fermé," with its variant "formé" in the 1899 edition of Mallarmé's *Poésies*[4]) actually cross over in terms of their value in the poem, since the destruction is to be seen largely as positive and the need for stable, firm form, for a *closure,* as negative.

The opening lines of the sonnet expose the "relativity" not only of words that are etymologically related, but also of synonyms belonging to different languages. This translation effect is blatantly apparent only in the use of the word "lampadophore," which serves the function of stating what is happening in a far clearer way in gallicized Greek than all of the preceding words have stated it in French: "lampadophore," or "torch bearing," which describes both of the Anguish's actions ("Ses purs ongles très haut dédiant leur onyx" and "soutient . . . / Maint rêve vespéral"), each of which seems to suggest the holding up of some sort of celestial light, includes a near translation of the French word immediately preceding it, "soutenir," which could be loosely construed as "bear" (cognate, in fact, with Greek φέρω) in the double sense of both words, that is, "to carry and to withstand." That the most readily comprehensible description of the opening scene is offered by a word which is so clearly a foreign import helps to accentuate the impression that meaning resides at an unreachable distance, be it geographical, historical, or astronomical.

Two other words in the first two lines of the poem may have been chosen partially for their proximity to Greek words the translations of which are also very important in the sonnet: "purs" and "onyx," suggesting, respectively, the Greek πῦρ ("fire") and, in addition to ὄνυξ ("nail"), the Greek word νύξ ("night"). Both concepts, fire and night, occur in the sonnet's first quatrain: "Maint rêve vespéral brûlé par le Phénix"; "L'Angoisse, ce minuit." That Mallarmé was aware of the two Greek words may be assumed from passages in "Les Mots anglais" in which he gives the Greek cognates for both words in English: under the letter F, we find "FIRE, feu. PEAT, tourbe, (Gr. πῦρ)."[5] Similarly, under the letter N: "NIGHT, nuit, Lat. nox (Gr. νύξ, νυκτός)."[6]

Moreover, the correspondences set up by the two pairings are not without interest: "pur" and "fire" go together by the association of fire with all sorts of purifying processes, and in this case they link the burning of the Phoenix to a sort of religious purification one of the conditions of which may well be a relegation of substantial form. The association ὄνυξ/νύξ/"night" can be easily integrated into the poem: the "onyx" is night-colored first of all, and thus forms a counterweight to both the "purs ongles," which are certainly not black and contain a suggestion of fiery brightness, and the Phoenix, which, while it rhymes with "onyx," does not contain the νύξ element (Greek Φοῖνιξ, with ι and not υ) and is itself the cause of a burning ("brûlé par le Phénix"). The onyx may well be associated with the obscurity of night precisely because it partakes of a linguistic past and as such is covered over by the manifestation of more recent forms.

The pairs "purs"/πῦρ and "onyx"/νύξ can be seen as thematizing not only linguistic relativity, since no one form can be perfectly suited to its content if the same form carries different meanings in different languages, but also another form of human relativity, that by which humans must depend upon the non-human (sun, stars, precious stones) for the sense of permanence they themselves cannot supply. The "purs ongles" thus "dedicate" the night with fires, human mutations of celestial fires which as imitations cannot reach a state of non-contingency like the stars but can only reveal themselves as reflections of immortal lights. The anguish caused the "purs ongles" as human constructs by their own relativity (the necessity of dying and the mourning which death implies suggested by the echo of funeral "pyre" in "pur" and the well-documented use, in Greek Tragedy, of fingernails as instruments of self-inflicted pain) furnishes them in turn with the basis for a consecration of that relativity, a consecration which is supported by the transformation of the covert fire element of the first line into the grandly processional fire of the second ("lampadophore") and by the now explicit recourse to Greek terminology, which necessarily bespeaks a relation to the past.

Furthermore, the importance of the onyx as a mineral transformation of the fingernails emphasizes the human attempt to infuse the immortal (stone) with human value or, conversely, to house mortal value in an immortal setting. As Mircea Eliade puts it: "Among countless stones, one stone becomes sacred—and hence instantly becomes saturated with being. . . . incompressible, invulnerable, it is that which man is not. It resists time; its reality is coupled with perenniality."[7] So that the value attributed to a precious stone becomes the analogue to the meaning borne by an unchanging linguistic form: both sets of forms are in themselves capable of a duration impossible for an individual human being, and yet retain their importance only insofar as they are consecrated again and again by human values.

Thus, if the sonnet's first two lines simultaneously point up to the heavens which they can never reach, even through language, but can only indicate, and down to the poem's grounding in a consecrated foundation which dedicates the necessarily unsuccessful, earthly attempt to reach the celestial, they prefigure the occurrence in the third line of "Maint rêve vespéral brûlé par le Phénix," the unspecified dream which seems to resemble that of "Quand l'ombre menaça de la fatale loi" ("Tel vieux Rêve, désir et mal de mes vertèbres") to the extent that both dreams are afflicted by the passage of time ("vieux," "vespéral"), and seem, indeed, to be in direct contradiction to the limitations imposed upon human beings by their own mortality. The onset of the evening in both poems not only signals the moment at which mortals begin to dream, but also elicits the first mention of a domestic object ("Affligé de périr sous des *plafonds* funèbres"; "Que ne recueille pas de cinéraire *amphore*," the verb "recueille" and the closely related "accueille" also suggesting the function of a hearth).

For the home is, indeed, caught between a mortal, necessarily symbolic grounding, one which recognizes the limitations of human existence and attempts to consecrate the time and the space within those limitations, and an immortal yearning for an absolute which the house, and particularly the hearth, at least partially imitate by establishing the illusion of a permanence. Mallarmé himself speaks in "Les Dieux antiques" of the imitative nature of the individual hearth: "Voyons encore jusqu'où s'élargit la fonction de Hestia, qui n'est point limitée aux âtres de la maison et à la cité, ni même aux bornes de la patrie, car on supposait qu'au centre de la terre il existe un foyer répondant au foyer placé au centre de l'univers total."[8] Mallarmé considers the individual hearth and the universal hearth as responding to each other, so that the individual hearth imitates and perhaps even replaces the universal one. Once again, the implicit goal of Symbolism is expressible as the contradictory aim of what wishes to be single—as a thoroughgoing replacement of the divine and the absolute, a replacement which might partake of their ability to exist simply as one, as only themselves, without the doubling of any conventional symbolic system—even as it must be double insofar as it needs to delegate paradigms based upon the stability of an absolute.

The adjective "vespéral" continues several currents which are already present in the sonnet's first two lines: it is, first of all, a term deriving from the Greek ($\dot{\epsilon}\sigma\pi\dot{\epsilon}\rho\alpha$,[9] "the evening hour," Latin *vespera*) and as such resembles "onyx" and "lampadophore," and prefigures "Phénix" as well. In addition to retaining at least a suggestion of foreignness, the word continues, and makes more explicit, the geographical motif introduced by the pointing to the stars that takes place in the first line: $\dot{\epsilon}\sigma\pi\dot{\epsilon}\rho\alpha$, like the French *couchant* ("le soleil se couche") and the German *Abendland,* determines a geographical region of the earth through the position of the sun in the sky at a given time and thus defines the earth as contingent upon the heavens, since man must "orient" himself with reference to something which he can always point to, something not only external to himself but also outside of the planet which he inhabits. That he must look for a sense of permanence to something "accidental" (as well as "occidental"), something not necessary in terms of his *own* domain and thus infringing upon the priority of that domain, is yet another source of anguish. Finally, the adjective "vespéral" continues the series of religious terms begun by "purs," "dédiant," and "lampadophore" in that it is reminiscent of the evening service, *vêpres,* a service which both points up to the non-human realm and turns back upon itself as a reflection of the human capacity for symbolic process.

The "rêve vespéral," particularly given its proximity to the Phoenix, is also important in the establishment of the two geographical axes which play a central role in the sonnet: East-West and North-South. The "rêve vespéral" might in this context be compared to the "Occident de désirs" in "La chevelure vol d'une flamme" in that both of them evoke the aspiration to something new, to the establishment of a new order by which the sun, moving always from east to west, might find a symbolic substitute, a human counterpart which both imitates it and replaces it in its life-supporting capacity. That counterpart—which in "La chevelure" is represented by the woman along with the desire and the procreation associated with her, as well as her hair which kindles that desire and also appears to be the source of its own light—is in "Ses purs ongles" the house (or at least the room of a house) which fills the sonnet's last lines. The house faces not along the East-West axis of the solar and stellar movement that marks the passage of time, but rather toward the North, not away from but rather perpendicular to the Earth's daily cycles. As such the house, which seems as much responsible for the poem's final glow as the stars ("selon peut-être le décor"), appears to be emblematic of the symbolic function by which humans create their own habitat. For if that habitat cannot beat the cycles of nature on their own terms, it is at least capable of creating a properly human domain (the mythmaking function represented also by the appearance of Ursa Major in the North) which is complementary to them in that while it cannot run their race ("lampado-phore" is, according to Littré, a synonym of *lampadiste,* "celui qui s'exer-çait à la course des flambeaux"), it can at least be stationed at right angles along their path and observe—both watch and commemorate—their passage.

The East-West axis, which dominates the first quatrain, is set in place by the opposition of the "rêve vespéral" and the "Phénix," since the latter word in both of its mythological meanings evokes the East: it is first of all the fabulous bird from Egypt (an import from even further east, Arabia) which is periodically cremated and reborn of its own ashes, and is to be asso-ciated with the East because of its origins. But as important here as the term's relation to Middle Eastern mythology is the link with the East provided by its association in Greek myth with Phoenicia, presumably named after *Phoenix,* the brother of Cadmus who, like him, set off in search of their sister Europe, born, interestingly enough, in Phoenicia, at least according to Mallarmé's "Les Dieux antiques": "Europe, selon l'histoire connue, est la fille d'Agénor et de Téléphassa, et la sœur de Cadmos (le Cadmus latin) et de Phœnix. Née en Phénicie . . ."[10] The link—whether or not it is spurious—between the legendary Egyptian bird and the eponymous Phoenix is made explicitly by Cox: "the connection of the purple hue with the birth and early life of the sun is seen not only in the myth of the bird known as the Phénix, but in Phoinix, the teacher and guide of Achilleus in his childhood."[11] The latter, son of Amyntor, Cox (and Mallarmé after him) mistakenly confuses with the other Phoenix, the brother of Europe and the son of Agenor. As Mallarmé has it:

La Phénicie, où est née Europe, est la terre de pourpre du matin. . . . Phœnix, frère de l'héroïne est le maître du grand héros Achille, amant de Briséis; et Téléphassa (celle qui brille de loin), est, comme Télèphe et Télémaque, un nom de la lumière de l'aurore, qui, éclatant à travers le ciel, meurt dans l'Ouest.[12]

The tension between East and West consists not only of that between the rising sun and the setting sun, but also of the association of past (East) and present or future (West) attributed to the two compass points, the East being seen as prior as much for historical reasons as because of the sun's path, which always takes it from East to West. To this extent, "Maint rêve vespéral brûlé par le Phénix" is emblematic of the undeniable link between the present and the past, seen in part as a hindrance in the eyes of one who wishes above all to evoke a presence. The "rêve vespéral," the dream of a totally *new* order (like the flight to the far West) cannot escape being at least partially fueled by the old order.

That there is a need for the establishment of a new home is made apparent by the first quatrain's last line, which speaks in terms of an absence of form to house the remains of the Phoenix and/or the evening dream, the relative pronoun "Que" referring potentially to both. Whence the curiously contra-dictory nature of the last term of the first quatrain, "cinéraire amphore": apparently meant to denote a sort of funeral urn, the expression nonetheless is a hybrid in that the noun, "amphore," is normally used of an object function-ing as an everyday domestic implement, a two-handled jug (ἀμφί-φορος, liter-ally, "carried by both," conflated to αμφορεύς, whence "amphore") used to transport wine or oil. This domestic aspect of the dream/Phoenix' potential resting-place adds to the impression that more than a repository for dead ashes, what the dream and the Phoenix are in search of is a recipient to *house* them, in the case of the dream a hearth or a lamp which at evening might replace the disappearing fire of the sun, in the case of the Phoenix a new nest in which it might set up house.

The word "amphore" is in itself interesting in that it may well be meant to suggest the rhetorical term *anaphore,* particularly because it is perfectly possible in Greek poetry to find the contraction ἀμφέρω for ἀναφέρω (whence "anaphora"). The appropriateness of the term here is triple: it refers, first of all, to the rhetorical device by which the first word of a sentence is repeated several times for effect, and may here suggest the repetition of historically related words ("ongles"/"onyx," and in the poem's first version, which also boasts an "amphore," "cendre"/"cinéraire").

Secondly, the term indicates the reference (in fact, a Latin translation of the Greek term ἀναφέρω, *referō,* "to carry back") of one thing to something else considered as a sort of standard. In the context of the sonnet this is very much in keeping with the questioning of the relation between present and past (i.e., does the present need to *refer* to a past?), as well as with the chal-lenge upon the non-human which the human seems to need to refer to in spite of itself in its search for a standard going beyond its own limitations. Language wishes to be "anaphorical" in a positive sense, that is, wishes to carry its users up (ἀναφέρω) to something other than itself, to some kind of transcendental standard; but it is in fact anaphorical in a negative sense, to the extent that once it is willing to take something other than itself as a destination, it becomes a conventional symbolic system moving toward a goal.

Indeed, the notion of a standard to which one is linked is also at the basis of the final meaning of anaphora which is temptingly appropriate here: to bring back from exile (going *up* or *back* being seen as returning home), home at least partially fulfilling the function of creating a standard for its inhabi-tants. Mallarmé thus may be speaking of his own attempt to bring language back "home," to return it to its foundations, be they historical (i.e., etymo-logical) or of his own creation (e.g., the pictorial value he attributes to indi-vidual letters). But bringing language "home" in a genuine way, putting together and fusing the two halves of the *symbolon,* leads to destroying the home language has led (and been led) to. Indeed, the play metaphor/anaphora is not without interest: if there is no "cinéraire amphore" to house the dream/ Phoenix, it is that at one level, all language for Mallarmé should be metaphorical rather than anaphorical, since one of the poet's goals is to activate the metaphorical possibilities of words, and to do so, he must loosen them from their purely referential function, must free them from their traditional housing, their attachment to an earthly standard. But doing this involves giving up the hope, however faint it might be, of ever reaching a divine standard, for the activation of metaphor, the perpetual enemy of *reference,* destroys the very notion of a standard.

Furthermore, the word "amphore" recalls the duality both of the human house and of human language; the *amphi-* element of the word defines the duality of the household, the need for domestic objects to be borne by two and not by one, as well as the necessity for human beings to be born of two and not of one. The human generational process is here to be contrasted to that of the Phoenix in that the latter can "reproduce" only himself—rather than producing any new being—so long as the process by which he is renewed depends only upon himself and not upon another as well.

As for language, it too is two-handled (or perhaps too handled) in that it must serve a perfectly neutral, everyday function as well as that of a consecrating tool; it must serve as a vessel of communication and thus of commonality, be borne by at least two people, a speaker and a listener or a writer and a reader, a fact which is hostile to the poet's ambition of creating a hermetic home for himself and for individual words to which he is attempting to delegate a personal mythology, an ambition parallel to that of the "rêve vespéral" and the "Phénix" in that each of them dreams of being its own origin and its own energy source, its cause and its effect.

The importance of the "amphore" as indicative of a duality is substantiated by the occurrence in parallel position in the next line of the word "ptyx" about which a great deal has been written by various commentators of the poem, but which, whatever else it may mean (if anything), certainly seems related to the Greek word meaning "fold," another term implying a duality. Moreover, the word "ptyx" is a commentary on the arbitrariness of forms, since Mallarmé claims to have invented it "par la magie de la rime"[13] and thus implies that a word can be created on formal grounds without carrying any other meaning.

And indeed, the entire second quatrain can be seen, by contrast to the first, as dealing with the arbitrariness of forms. If the first quatrain goes to great pains to attempt to ground language in a dedicated foundation, at the same time expressing its anguish at not being able to reach the absolute nature of the immortal and the non-human, the second quatrain speaks of the absence of a house connecting the two necessary functions of any symbolic system, that is, the function of a transitive indication assured by a syntax, a movement toward meaning, and that of a dedication which establishes the unseen ground-work for the delegation of meaning. Perhaps more than the absence of the *form* of a house, the second quatrain deals with the absence of a *Master* within the house who might give the house meaning, the emptiness of human forms corresponding on the level of language to the almost constant attention drawn in the second quatrain to the nothingness of words, to linguistic forms taken as meaningless shells, pure exteriors devoid of substance or content.

Thus the term which brings the first quatrain to a close, "cinéraire amphore," the only undeniably domestic object of the quatrain even though it is in fact absent,[14] leads into the proliferation of terms describing absent or useless domestic entities in the second quatrain, including outmoded pieces of furni-ture ("crédences"), an empty living room ("salon vide"), an abolished knick-knack, and, most important of all, a departed Master. Indeed, it is perhaps because the forms of the house which are mentioned here have not been grounded in a consecrated foundation that the Master goes on the quest which is spoken of at the end of the quatrain.

That quest, not unlike that of Prometheus suggested by "La chevelure vol d'une flamme," may be distantly alluded to by the word "bibelot" which, while unrelated etymologically to "Bible," might well evoke by the formal similarity of the two words and the nearby association of "crédences" to "croyances" the holy book of Western religions, and which furthermore suggests the story of the Tower of Babel as well, itself emblematic of a chal-lenge to immortality. The entire line ("Aboli bibelot d'inanité sonore") not only sounds like babble, it also describes babble ("inanité sonore"). Indeed, the opacity of human language which Mallarmé deals with in the introduction to "Les Dieux antiques" seems in the poet's eyes (reflecting, of course, Cox's view of things) to be due to a dispersion of peoples which exactly reverses the terms of the Babel story:

Les légendes de toutes ces nations ont une seule source commune. . . . Les mots et les phrases usités par les anciennes tribus pour parler de ce qu'elles voyaient, entendaient ou sentaient dans le monde situé autour d'elles. . . . Comme le temps marcha, et que les peuples se séparèrent, le vieux sens s'oblitéra, totalement ou partiellement.[15]

Whereas the theory espoused by Cox/Mallarmé makes the separation of peoples precede the development of distinct linguistic forms, the Babel story pairs the same two phenomena, but in the opposite order, linguistic differentiation coming before the dispersion and undoubtedly providing one of its principal causes. It is in the very challenge upon the absolute raised by the builders of the Tower of Babel and by the would-be visitor of the river of invulnera-bility, "le Maître"—the latter also representative both of the poet who is raising his own challenge upon the limits of conventional language and of the words he uses which try to reach the heavens they are pointing to—that the limits of gravity, of mortality, and of linguistic convention become salient. It is the arbitrariness of human forms that sends the "Maître" down to confront "le Néant," for it is precisely their lack of grounding in a symbolic system of beliefs which makes them representatives of "le Néant," that is, of non-identity (from Latin *nec-entem*, "non-being"). Thus the tears which the Master is in search of and the cause of which is not explicitly given may well point back to the sense of loss brought on by the burning of the "rêve vespéral" in the first quatrain along with its ambition which cannot be forgotten as the sonnet moves from out of doors (first quatrain) to indoors (second quatrain).

The importance of the water element of the tears, emphasized by the earlier version of the poem which has "Car le Maître est allé puiser l'eau du Styx," may reside in its reflective capacity, one by which the water may be seen as a transition between ungrounded symbolic forms—that is, disbelief in their efficacy—and the acceptance of the need for symbolic systems as a counter to the mortal state. Even though the Master is searching for *tears* in the River Styx, we must not overlook the fact that immersion in its waters was thought to render the immersed invulnerable (as in the story of Achilles and his mother Thetis), so that the river itself carries a doubled but coherent identity as the river both of immortality and of mortality. Indeed, it is only insofar as the human dies *as itself* and becomes other than simply human that it can survive through the symbolic systems it creates. And to the extent that water, unlike fire, works to create a mirrored image, its appearance here, especially by contrast to the earlier domination of fire in the first quatrain, may well announce a movement toward an identification of symbolic process as the only possible tool for a human immortality, such as it is. The water/tears of the Styx prefigure the "nixe" named in the first tercet, herself a water sprite, in that she too is a reflection of a mortal being ("Elle, défunte nue en le miroir"), one which once again joins the ideas of mortality and symbolic process as reflection, that is, as a recognition and an extension of the limits of mortality.

Indeed, the implement with which the Master attempts to dip tears from the River of the Dead may well bear a resemblance to an element of an established symbolic system, that is, the very Dipper which is suggested by the final grouping of metaphorical stars of the sonnet's first lines into the constellation alluded to in the poem's final words: although the appellation "Big Dipper" is not applied in French to the constellation Ursa Major, the fact that the latter is recognizable as a household implement is apparent in the article describing the constellation in the *Grand Larousse Encyclopédique,* in which Ursa Major is said to form "le profil d'une casserole armée de sa queue."[16] It is the very illusion that the human can get a *handle* on the immortal (cf. the handle of the

Dipper, its *manche,* from Latin *manicum,* "little hand") which takes the "Maître" to the realm of those who have crossed the boundary of death and who know secrets hidden from the living. In this context the "Maint rêve" takes on the full value of a "Main-rêve," the dream of laying hands on what is constantly in the process of disappearing (the sun and the stars and the immortal state they represent) and the distance to which means that one can reach it only symbolically, as other than what it is in itself.

Thus the second quatrain features a journey *down* for what has been reached *up* for, but not reached: a link between mortal forms and the immortal foundations they aspire to. The house which the "Maître" leaves behind has no history, it exists only from moment to moment: "Ce minuit" contains (or is) anguish precisely because the house has no capacity to *replace* what the sun's setting seems to have taken away. The house cannot refer itself to a past, it cannot recollect ("ne *recueille* pas," from Latin *recollegere,* "to gather together again") and thus has no memory, no possibility of restoring a lost source of energy or of storing the resources necessary for survival, since the act of storing presumes an external form which can be used as a container, one which is not empty ("pas de . . ."; "vide"; "nul"; "aboli"; "inanité"). If Hades was thought of by the Greeks as a storehouse of wealth (*Pluto,* from Greek πλοῦτον, "wealth") partly because of its underground mineral riches and partly because those that came to it stayed permanently, so that its "population" could only increase, the house above ground which the Master presumably leaves is devoid of value. If the jewels ("onyx") which the fingernails of Anguish stretch out for in the first quatrain are not to be found in the treasure chest of the house, among the empty forms of the living, they must be searched for below ground, among the dead, or perhaps in a past which present forms as they are cannot recall.

It is in the light of the Master's search for what has been lost or perhaps never yet been discovered that the poem's evocation of a human home, like its treatment of anguished language in the first quatrain, can be seen as operating between the poles of indication, of attempting to *take the place of* something which is irrevocably lost or cannot be reached, and dedication, *taking place* within the very lack of a possible transcendence of the human. If the first quatrain functions on the East-West axis in that it laments the passage of time and the incapacity of human forms either to reach the intemporal or to replace what cannot be reached and held onto, the tercets move out of the temporal domain, into the North-South axis, which is far less affected by the daily movement of the sun across the sky. Thus the "croisée au nord vacante" of the first line of the tercets is not "vide" like the "salon" of the second quatrain, "vide" coming from the Latin *vacuus,* "empty"; rather it is opened, vacant in the sense that its emptiness points to a potential future filling, the participle *vacans* (whence "vacant") implying a process and not an irrevocable state (as in *vacances,* certainly not a permanent idleness). As a structure which closes off a window without preventing light from coming through from outside, the "croisée" may be seen as analogous to the translucent "ongles" of the sonnet's first line—both terms representing an attempt to relate human forms ("ongles" and the inside of the room) genuinely to the immortal ("onyx" and the light issuing from outside) all the while leaving them identifiable as human, that is, with a certain opacity of their own—but whereas the fingernails leave tracks of anguished grieving at the sun's departure and the unreachability of the stars, the casement is close at hand: "proche la croisée," while its first meaning is probably "near *to* a casement," suggests by the suppression of the preposition "a casement nearby." For by refusing to look out onto the path of the sun and the stars (East to West), the casement provides the sonnet with a ninety-degree turn, so that its field of vision is not competing with the course of celestial bodies but is self-admittedly human and symbolic, one which reflects the human need for mythologizing, for dwelling in a world peopled by symbolic forms.

The sonnet's rotation about itself, representative of the acceptance of the human nature of symbolic forms which cannot compete with the apparent East-West movement of celestial bodies but can step out of the domain of temporal progression and create their own mythologies, is reinforced by several elements of the poem. The "oubli fermé par le cadre" relates the number four ("cadre"/"quatre," a genuine etymological relation) to the creation of a frame of reference, the mirror reflecting the light of the constellation just as human geography must reflect the celestial bodies' movements. The term "croisée" can also mean a crossroad (*croisée* or *croisement de chemins*), which forms four quarters resembling the compass points, and may be associated as well with the "crédences" of the first line of the second quatrain, partly by the formal resemblance of the two words (the shared *cr-*), but even more importantly by the undertone of "belief" in "croisée," similar in form to the verb *croire* and related etymologically to one of the most important of the symbolic forms of the Church, the cross (*croisée/croix,* both from Latin *crux*).

Indeed, the word "croisée" can also be used as an ecclesiastical term meaning the point at which the nave and the transept of a church cross—once again forming a kind of compass—a point which itself is meant to reproduce the holy cross on which Christ was crucified. The suggestion of the cross here may also hint at one of the roles of the *x* rhymes of the sonnet, each of which features a visual representation of the cross, and of the poem's rhyme scheme, which is composed uniquely of *rimes croisées* except, perhaps ironically, for the couplet in which the word "croisée" is to be found.

The occurrence of the "croisée" at the juncture between quatrains and tercets, moreover following a "Mais" indicative of a change, is located at a crucial point in the sonnet, at a kind of crossroads, so that the sonnet's "turn" is to be here taken literally (or perhaps geographically) as well as figuratively. From the highly Hellenic vocabulary of the quatrains, including all four of the -yx (-ix) rhymes and two of the -ore rhymes as well, we move now to a more localized vocabulary—the only word with a fairly close relation to the Greek being "agonise" (from ἀγών, "a contest"), the gallicized form of which does not bring special attention to its Greek origins—and, more importantly, to a rather more *Nordic* mythology. The two main mythological beings inhabiting the tercets, the "licornes" and the "nixe," even though only the latter is undeniably Northern (from German *Nixe*, "a water sprite"), are both to be contrasted to the mythological terms of the quatrain (at least the "Phénix" and the "Styx") to the extent that they are more readily associated with medieval legends than with even older tales, and as such represent a movement not only northward from the Mediterranean, but also one from more ancient to more recent.[17] Indeed, the word "nixe" may well suggest the common dialectical form of the German word *nichts, nix,* or "nothing," perhaps a Germanic translation of the earlier "Néant."[18] Furthermore, the "licornes" form a kind of North-South axis with the unnamed Ursa Major of the poem's last line, since, as the Littré so dear to Mallarmé indicates under the entry "licorne," the latter is a "constellation méridionale" as opposed to the northern constellation of Ursa Major which we must assume to be visible from the "croisée au nord vacante."

The poem thus moves from a reaching upward ("très haut") to a reaching downward ("Styx") to a relative localization on the surface of the earth, whether on land or at sea ("licornes"/"nixe"), a localization, furthermore, which for the first time puts some emphasis on a human house and not merely on the world of nature (first quatrain) or on what is missing from a potential house (second quatrain). It is interesting to note that that localization replicates the fire/water duality represented by the celestial and infernal domains in the first two quatrains, since the "licornes" which in themselves are not especially associated with fire are figured as kicking fire against the water nymph in the "décor" which is "perhaps" the source of the dying light of the first tercet.

The "nixe," as the Australian poet Christopher Brennan observed, may well be identified with the nymph Callistô, who is said to have been changed into a she-bear by Artemis or Hera and then metamorphosed into the very constellation (Ursa Major, the Great Bear) which is evoked at the end of the sonnet.[19] She thus appears to be doubly a reflection, first of all one in the mirror ("Elle, défunte nue en le miroir," supported as well by the "encor" which goes with the following line but provides an appropriate commentary on the status of the reflection), and second of all that of an earlier Hellenic myth of which she is the Teutonic transformation. Callistô's unnamed presence in the poem is supported by a passage in "Les Dieux antiques" that speaks of the nymph,[20] one which furthermore links her to the region of Arcadia—a name supposedly related to Arcas, Callistô's father—the very place where the Styx was thought to be located.[21] The reference to Callistô may be closer to being explicit in the original version of the sonnet, in which the first tercet includes "un dieu que croit emporter une nixe," an inversion of the action by which Zeus usually carries off unwilling mortal maidens. The reversal of roles linking the "nixe" and the unnamed god may well be an allusion to Callistô's ultimate transformation from a lowly nymph into something nearly as eternal as Zeus himself, either a star or a story, a transformation by which Callistô, like Prometheus, "l'emporte sur" the god or at least, like human participants in a symbolic system, might believe that she has.

If the mythological elements of the first tercet, unlike those of the quatrains, are housed in a human framework, the gold which comprises the first end rhyme of the tercets corresponds to the "onyx" which forms the first end rhyme of the quatrains, a correspondence created not only by their shared characteristic as precious metals, but also by the almost cabalistic link between the words following them: "Agonise" is nothing more than "Angoisse" with its letters rearranged—less an extra s which could even be provided by the first letter following "Agonise." Indeed, like the unicorns as opposed to the "ongles," the gold inverts the action of the earlier term: whereas in the first quatrain the human ("ongles") dedicates the non-human ("onyx"), which is seen as having an overriding value (priority of the word in time; value of the precious gem), in the first tercet the non-human ("or") goes through a human action ("Agonise," that is, is in the throes of death) *according to* a human "décor," perhaps the scenario of mortality as much as the mirror's framework.

For in fact, the very state of mortality which is properly and unavoidably human is depicted by the reflective nature of the mirror: if the anguish of language is that it can never reach the immortality of absolute meaning, that it can never capture the value of the stars, then the value ("or") of mortality ("Agonise") resides precisely in its relativity, in the limits placed upon human existence by its anchoring in time, limits which can be used to define units of meaning in any of a number of symbolic systems. Thus the unicorns answer the dilemma posed by the "crédences" of the second quatrain, since the word was used in the Middle Ages of the table upon which dishes were placed in order to be tested for poison, and the unicorn's horn was thought to be a universal antidote to any poison (Littré notes this fact under the entry "licorne"): their presence celebrates and "cures" on a mythological level the limitations ("Agonise") which no mortal can otherwise escape. Similarly, the "or" carries simultaneously the sense of a presence ("or" in its adverbial meaning)—and the value which the present can bear for beings who are not eternal—and that of a reflection, a meaning suggested by the gold's action "selon" a human decor ("selon" here also recalling and correcting the empty "salon," void and not vacant, which itself had no decor), and also re-enacted

by the echo effect "au *nor*d vacante u*n or*," the gold appearing to repeat the
north-facing window just as the scene on or in the mirror seems both to reflect
and to call forth the northern constellation that the mirror and the window are
facing.

The poem can thus be seen as moving between an attempt to ground the
human in the immortal or in a mystical past ("ongles"/"onyx") and the final
grounding of the immortal in the human through the mediation of a symbolic
system. The proliferation of terms denoting or suggesting death ("Agonise";
"défunte"; "oubli"; "fermé") represents not a complaint (as in the beginning
of "Sur les bois oubliés") but rather an awareness of the limitations of symbolic forms. The vacillation in the poem's next-to-last line between "fermé"
and "formé" is in itself a commentary on the nature of human forms which,
as soon as they are formulated, are to a large extent *closed,* fixed. But it is
only through a fixing that a human home can be created: the sonnet's last
finite verb, "se fixe," can indeed be used of a person who is setting down roots
and the use of the preposition "dans" ("dans l'oubli fermé par le cadre, se
fixe . . . le septuor") gives the impression that the Big Dipper is going to be
settling down in the mirror. Everything in the poem's last lines seems to
be approaching a *limit*: the gold of the stars and the mirror is dying perhaps
with the gradual onset of morning or perhaps merely insofar as it reflects
the mortal world; the nixie is vulnerable both in her nakedness ("nue" as
cloud is certainly possible as well and may be related to the nixie's connection
to water) and in her mortality ("défunte"); and the reflecting surface of the
mirror must necessarily be "fermé" by its external framework just as the house
itself is closed off from the outside world, while remaining open to let in its light.

Indeed, the poem's final "fixing," its stabilization, points up the fact that
unlike "La chevelure vol d'une flamme," this sonnet is essentially a static
one, one which "goes" nowhere. The absence of the syntactical chaos so
essential to "La chevelure vol d'une flamme" and many other of Mallarmé's
poems is matched by the general lack of movement in the verbs: "dédiant"
as opposed to its unnamed partner "indiquant" indicates (or dedicates) a
non-indication, a lack of transitivity; "soutient," "recueille," "Agonise,"
and "se fixe" all speak of an essentially stative action,[22] thereby contributing
to the very marked plasticity of the sonnet, the statue-like impression it
creates. Indeed, only the "Maître" and the "licornes" seem to move ("est
allé"; "ruant"), and in both cases their freedom of movement may be seen
as at least potentially illusory: one wonders if the "Maître" will be able to
return from the Styx, the boatsman of which generally issues only one-way
tickets, and the unicorns' kicking up of fire is belied by their frieze-like capturing on a "décor," presumably that of the mirror frame.

The poem ends with a kind of foundation, with a fixing in symbolic forms.
Thus, unlike the "Néant" which closes the quatrains, and also perhaps unlike

the *o-* elements of the first line of the poem ("très *haut*"; "*onyx*"), the sonnet ends with a counting up (*cadre/scin-/si-/sept-*[23]). Although the resemblance of the poem to the "Coup de dés" has certainly been commented on, its very close correspondence to the last lines of the longer poem has not been sufficiently emphasized: for the sonnet ends up doing what the longer poem talks about. The last Page of the poem consists of a kind of parenthesis indicating what is left after "toute réalité se dissout": "EXCEPTE à l'altitude PEUT-ETRE aussi loin qu'un endroit fusionne avec au-delà . . . UNE CONSTELLATION froide d'oubli et de désuétude pas tant qu'elle n'énumère sur quelque surface vacante et supérieure le heurt successif sidéralement d'un compte total en formation . . . avant de s'arrêter à quelque point dernier qui le sacre. . . ." The end of the longer poem recalls the final tableau of the sonnet: the *place* merging with (beyond) a constellation might well describe the room and the constellation which, as Mallarmé said in his description of the sonnet, "relie au ciel seul ce logis abandonné du monde."[24] The constellation of the "Coup de dés" which, as Davies points out, is also a northern one,[25] is furthermore described as "froide d'oubli et de désuétude," thus recalling the "oubli fermé par le cadre": it is "forgotten" to the extent that anything formulated in human terms is forgotten, that is, in the very finitude of any human formulation. The constellation is thus "désuet," not itself (*de-suetus,* "[fallen] off from itself"), in that like any signified quantified by a signifier, it becomes completely identified by its label. The fixation (if not asphyxiation) of the constellation is qualified, however ("pas tant qu'elle n'énumère"): like the seven stars of Ursa Major which "count themselves out" on the mirror insofar as their numerical labels are reflected in the last two lines of the poem, the constellation *enumerates* on a "surface vacante" (cf. "une croisée au nord vacante," like an empty sheet waiting to be written on) the "successive knock starwise of a total count in formation."

The last line of the sonnet thus takes the measure of human forms and says that even within the limits they cannot go beyond, those forms, unlike "le Néant," *count.* The poem ends up at a "point dernier qui le sacre," one which says that only symbolic human forms can join the tangibility of an index to the intangibility of a sacralization, even as it recognizes that the human impulse to reach for the divine will never allow for a thoroughgoing and constant acceptance of the limitations of conventional symbolic systems. For it is in the very effort to hold the unholdable, to make forms correspond to the unformable, to travel the road to a dreamed-of home the reaching of which would preclude the need for travel and which the need for travel prevents one from ever reaching, that the human can dedicate the foundations of its symbolic institutions, can fix its imprint in the *attempt* to find a properly human home.

Postface

i. A paradise never abolished a pair o' dice

> *The whole household suffered from it. They all felt that there was*
> *no sense in their living together, and that any group of people who*
> *had met together by chance at an inn would have had more in*
> *common than they.*

Leo Tolstoy
Anna Karenina
tr. Maude

Whatever else it is and is not, home is the enemy of chance. As a structuring unit it attempts to eliminate any random element within it. That members of a household feel as if they are kept together only by chance is a sure indication that their household is on the point of collapse, that it is becoming a house without a hold.

And yet the need for home derives from the dominion of chance in its absence and outside of its doorstep. Were home to abolish chance, it would abolish its very *raison d'être* and put itself out of business. To say that no institution of home can put an end to the need for home is perhaps no more than saying that no home can quite furnish what it aims to furnish, that is, a thoroughgoing elimination of chance, a perfect order; it is to say that so long as humans are humans (whatever else humans may be taken to be), they will need homes, and that a man's home may be his castle, but that it will never be his paradise. And finally, that if he attempts to make a paradise of his home, he may be loading the dice, but he will never do away with them.

It is not only home which fights perpetually with the random; it is also language, for language is rooted in the same sense of the intelligibility of things as home. Martin Heidegger draws an explicit parallel between home and language:

> Language is the precinct (*templum*), that is, the house of Being. . . . It is because
> language is the house of Being, that we reach what is by constantly going through

this house. . . . All beings—objects of consciousness and things of the heart, men who impose themselves and men who are more daring—all beings, each in its own way, are *qua* beings in the precinct of language.[1]

Is home a metaphor for language? Is language a metaphor for home? Or are both home and language simply necessary preconditions for a certain kind of identity, an identity which cannot help itself from "imposing itself" and "daring," which endlessly flirts with the divine—just as home, insofar as it is upright, strives at times toward paradise—and yet which is at the very heart of what we call human?

Would it be going too far to say that home would not be home without trying to be *more* than home, without striving to reach a limit it can never equal? That language would not be language unless it wished to express more than it can? And finally, that human beings would not be themselves—indeed, would not be *any* selves—were they not to try to be more than themselves? It may be true that God created man in his own image; it may be true that man created God in his own image. But is it not equally possible that man created himself in God's image, having necessarily created God's image in the process of creating himself?

Home and language are two of the structural models of human civilization; perhaps it is not surprising that both of them define us partially by means of a refusal, by telling us where we dream of living and what we dream of expressing all the while they remind us, regretfully, of what dreams are. Perhaps it is inevitable, if the God in man created the conception of man that man inhabits, that built into that conception of man, intrinsically and inextricably, is something that is not-man.

ii. A pair o' docs never abolished a paradox

Tragedy and Symbolism are two reminders of that inevitability, two "no's." They are not simple "no's"; rather, they are recognitions that the conditional status of all we do (the French *si* which leaves open the possibility of a negative response) can be a tremendous affirmation (the French *si* which negates a negative response), and that the only true affirmations are those at a double remove, those that know "no" well enough to say it to itself.

Indeed, Tragedy and Symbolism are both predicated upon the need for struggle and resistance, upon the existence of a negating mechanism within the human spirit which can also be an affirmation of that spirit. Here is Plato's double definition of existence, "οὐσία":

That which we term οὐσία (being or existence or essence) is by some called ἐσία, and by others again ὠσία. Now that the essence of things should be called ἐστία

[hearth] . . . is rational enough. And there is reason in the Athenians calling that
ἑστία [hearth] which participates in οὐσία [being or essence]. . . . Those again
who read ὠσία [thrust or push or expulsion] seem to have inclined to the opinion
of Heracleitus, that all things flow and nothing stands; with them the pushing
principle (ὠθοῦν, [to push or banish]) is the cause and ruling power of all things,
and is therefore rightly called ὠσία [thrust or push].[2]

Plato's definition of existence as something which both *inhabits* and *travels*
is similar to the definition of home which the concept of the *symbolon*
provides: home exists both to receive and to send out, to produce and comfort
those who are born into it and to lead them outside, for home cannot provide
the needs of an entire life, and indeed must ultimately send its members
outside of itself if it is to provide anything at all.

Language, too, leads us to itself and away from itself: in Heidegger's terms
it provides us with the house of Being, that is, provides us with what *is*. But it
can also serve to question whether anything is, to question its own capacity
for storage and protection. Like Plato's definition of home, Heidegger's definition of language allows for the limiting outlines of what it is defining, for
it leaves us with the question: If we leave the domain of language, where are
we? And what still *is*? And just as those who are thrust out of home cannot
help but look for home elsewhere, *symbolically*, those who question what
persists outside of language do so in language, for language, like home, is the
model of their very being. It is in this sense that the questioning of language
by language and the necessary exile from home brought on by home itself
can be the ultimate assertion of the value of these two institutions, for it is
only in the movement away from them that we can take the full measure of
their value.

The tragedy of home and the tragedy of language cannot be better described
than by Aristotle's concepts of tragic recognition and tragic reversal,[3] so long
as we understand that in this case, recognition and reversal coincide. To look
at home from the outside and to look at language from the outside is to
understand at last what they were like from the inside, for only being outside
of them and reversing our perspective teaches us to recognize them for what
they are. It is in this light that we might finally understand Heidegger's sphinx-
like definition of man as "He who must show what he is." For in order to
define oneself, one must reverse one's normal perspective and look at oneself
as if one were another; and in the process of this reversal, one *becomes* another
self, the very self whose definition started the process of recognition rolling.

iii. The tragic roll, or the holy guest

A house without a hold may well be a house that is on the point of collapse;
but it may also be a house that is afraid of strangling its inhabitants and wants

to send them out for a stroll. It may be a house which, unlike the Sphinx named for her power of strangulation, recognizes that just as life can be paradoxical, some paradoxes can be life-giving and life-affirming, that some circles are not vicious, and that leaving and coming back can be better still than staying put. For the best of homes knows that the road itself may help any potential guest in his quest to find home.

Here is how Heidegger describes the relationship of home and homelessness:

> The real plight of dwelling is indeed older than the world wars with their destruction, older also than the increase of the earth's population and the condition of the industrial workers. The real dwelling plight lies in this, that mortals ever search anew for the nature of dwelling, that they *must ever learn to dwell.* What if man's homelessness consisted in this, that man still does not even think of the *real* plight of dwelling as *the* plight? Yet as soon as man *gives thought* to his homelessness, it is a misery no longer. Rightly considered and kept well in mind, it is the sole summons that *calls* mortals into their dwelling.[4]

Even as Tragedy calls us out of our homes and into the theater to view from a distance what we have been living close up, it sends us away again with a longing to see home once more, in a new way. By letting us experience our homelessness and dwell upon it, by pulling us out of our homes and ourselves, Tragedy infuses us with a new respect for the tenuousness of our link to home and to those it allows us to share our lives with, and strengthens our link to home by reminding us of its ultimate fragility.

For the strength of the *symbolon* itself, let us recognize it at last, in fact derives from being based on its own enemy, chance, since it can devise a security-insuring split only if chance provides it with a thoroughly irregular pattern dividing its two halves. The best the *symbolon* can do is to turn its random split into a kind of key, to use chance as a tool which, once its nature is *recognized* by the fitting together of two arbitrary but matching patterns, provides comfort and nurture—the prerogatives of the guest—against itself.

The circular path that Tragedy sends us on, from home to the theater to home, reminds us in the end that the *symbolon* is needed not only in order to enter the house of our host, but also to go back to our own, for as humans we will always be up against the terrifying powers of chance; we will always be exiles or strangers. Or, if we are lucky, and we can provide the right *symbolon,* guests.

Notes

Preface

1 George Steiner, *The Death of Tragedy* (1961; rpt. New York: Oxford University Press, 1980), p. xi.

2 Friedrich Nietzsche, *"The Birth of Tragedy" and "The Case of Wagner,"* tr. and comm. Walter Kaufmann (New York: Vintage Books–Random House, 1967), p. 104.

3 Lucien Goldmann, *Le dieu caché* (Paris: Gallimard, 1955), p. 58.

4 Blaise Pascal, *Pensées*, "Contrariétés," 130, in *Œuvres complètes*, ed. Louis Lafuma (Paris: Editions du Seuil, 1963), p. 514.

5 Paul Valéry, "Existence du Symbolisme" in *Œuvres*, ed. Jean Hytier, Bibliothèque de la Pléiade (Paris: Gallimard, 1957), I, 686-87.

Introduction: Tragedy and Symbolism

1 Jean Lallot, *"Xumbola kranai*: Réflexions sur la fonction du *sumbolon* dans l'*Agamemnon* d'Eschyle," *Cahiers Internationaux du Symbolisme*, 26 (1974), 39.

2 Sophocles, *Oedipus Tyrannus*, vv. 219-23, hereafter abbreviated as *OT*. All references to the play are taken from the text established and annotated by Sir Richard Jebb (1885; rpt. Cambridge: Cambridge University Press, 1975). All translations are mine unless otherwise noted.

3 *OT*, note to v. 220, pp. 31-32.

4 See Oedipus' catalytic role in the play's prologue: not only is he the one who sets the city aright (vv. 49-51), he also leads the suppliants gathered around him at the play's opening to stand up (v. 142: "stand up"; v. 147: "let us stand up"), appropriately just after Oedipus himself has mentioned the possibility that in the present crisis the city might fall (v. 146).

5 *OT*, v. 8.

[6] Bernard Knox, *Oedipus at Thebes* (New Haven: Yale University Press, 1957), p. 150.

[7] *Language as Symbolic Action* (Berkeley: University of California Press, 1966), p. 16.

[8] See Jean-Pierre Vernant, *Mythe et tragédie en Grèce Ancienne* (Paris: Librairie François Maspero, 1973), pp. 29 ff.

[9] *OT*, v. 1182.

[10] See *Cratylus*, e.g., 437d.

[11] Claude Lévi-Strauss, *Structural Anthropology*, tr. Claire Jacobson and Brooke Grundfest Schoepf (New York: Basic Books, 1963), p. 61.

[12] "Hestia-Hermes: The Religious Expression of Space and Movement among the Greeks," tr. H. Piat, *International Social Science Council*, 7, No. 4 (August 1969), 134.

[13] *OT*, v. 1080.

[14] Georges Poulet, *The Interior Distance*, tr. Elliott Coleman (Ann Arbor: University of Michigan Press, 1964), p. 241.

[15] Maurice Blanchot, *L'Espace littéraire* (Paris: Gallimard, 1955), pp. 33-34.

[16] Gérard Genette, *Figures I* (Paris: Editions du Seuil, 1966), pp. 91-100.

[17] Jean-Pierre Richard, *L'Univers imaginaire de Mallarmé* (Paris: Editions du Seuil, 1961), p. 601.

[18] A. J. Lehmann, *The Symbolist Aesthetic in France* (Oxford: Blackwell, 1950), p. 6.

[19] Lehmann, p. 14.

[20] Lehmann, p. 33.

[21] Marcel Raymond, *De Baudelaire au Surréalisme* (Paris: Corti, 1947), p. 30.

[22] Robert Greer Cohn, *Toward the Poems of Mallarmé* (Berkeley: University of California Press, 1965), p. 57.

[23] Cohn, p. 58.

[24] Cohn, p. 133.

[25] James Lawler, *The Language of French Symbolism* (Princeton: Princeton University Press, 1969), p. 13.

[26] Paul Valéry, "Stéphane Mallarmé," *Etudes littéraires*, in *Œuvres*, I, 622.

[27] Stéphane Mallarmé, "Crise de vers," *Œuvres complètes*, Bibliothèque de la Pléiade (Paris: Gallimard, 1945), p. 364.

28 Mallarmé, "Catholicisme," *Œuvres complètes*, p. 391.

29 Mallarmé, "Argument d'Igitur," *Œuvres complètes*, p. 434.

30 Quoted by Charles Chassé, *Les Clés de Mallarmé* (Paris: Editions Montaigne, 1954), p. 55.

31 Mallarmé, "Richard Wagner," *Œuvres complètes*, p. 544.

32 Gérard Genette, *Mimologiques: Voyage en Cratylie* (Paris: Editions du Seuil, 1976), p. 36.

33 Plato, *Cratylus*, 425d, in *The Dialogues of Plato*, tr. Benjamin Jowett (1892; rpt. New York: Random House, 1937), p. 214.

34 Mallarmé, "Richard Wagner," *Œuvres complètes*, pp. 544-45.

35 Lehmann, p. 62.

36 Mallarmé, "Crise de vers," *Œuvres complètes*, pp. 363-64.

37 Richard, p. 532.

38 Chassé, p. 22.

39 Mallarmé, *Œuvres complètes*, p. 1164.

40 Chassé, p. 24.

41 Nietzsche, p. 106.

42 Chassé, pp. 15-16.

43 Vernant, *Mythe et tragédie en Grèce Ancienne*, p. 21.

44 *Les Structures anthropologiques de l'imaginaire* (Paris: Bordas, 1969), p. 69.

45 Mallarmé, *Œuvres complètes*, p. 302.

46 Mallarmé, "Le Genre ou des Modernes," *Œuvres complètes*, p. 321.

47 Mallarmé, "Solennité," *Œuvres complètes*, p. 334.

48 Albert Thibaudet, *La Poésie de Stéphane Mallarmé* (Paris: Gallimard, 1926), p. 366.

49 Mallarmé, "Solennité," *Œuvres complètes*, pp. 330-31.

50 Thibaudet, p. 377.

51 Mallarmé, *Œuvres complètes*, p. 1440.

52 Mallarmé, *Œuvres complètes*, p. 1442.

[53] About *L'Après-midi d'un Faune,* Thibaudet remarks: "Rappelons cependant, qu'il a rêvé pour l'*Après-midi d'un Faune* quelque développement extérieur, l'a même réalisé d'abord sous cette forme . . ." (p. 366).

[54] Haskell Block, *Mallarmé and the Symbolist Drama* (Detroit: Wayne State University Press, 1963), p. 6.

[55] Block, p. 130.

[56] Thibaudet, p. 365.

[57] Mallarmé, "Solennité," *Œuvres complètes,* p. 335.

[58] Thibaudet, p. 367.

[59] Poulet, p. 281.

[60] Poulet, p. 283.

[61] "Divagations," cited by Thibaudet, p. 369.

[62] Richard, p. 405.

[63] Thibaudet, p. 369.

[64] Poulet, p. 283.

[65] Mallarmé, "Bucolique," *Œuvres complètes,* p. 405.

[66] Stéphane Mallarmé, *Propos sur la poésie,* ed. Henri Mondor (Monaco: Editions du Rocher, 1946), p. 174.

[67] Thibaudet, p. 378.

Interface

[1] Knox, p. 49.

[2] Poulet, p. 283.

[3] "Wer ist der Mensch? Jener, der zeugen muss, was er sei." Martin Heidegger, *Erläuterungen zu Hölderlins Dichtung* (Frankfurt am Main: Klostermann, 1951), p. 34 (translation mine).

Chapter One: Asymmetrical Equality in the *Oedipus Tyrannus*

[1] *OT,* vv. 31-32.

2 Knox, p. 159. The use of equality as an indicator of Oedipus' role as a political and mathematical measuring stick of Greek thought is very richly and fully developed in Knox's treatment of the concept of equality (pp. 147-59). Some of my discussion of equality in the play may indeed be close to what Knox has done, but of course his emphasis is entirely different, since he places the play in the larger intellectual context of fifth-century Athens.

3 *OT,* vv. 165-66.

4 *OT,* v. 53.

5 See the immediately preceding lines: "You held that luck beside us *then.*"

6 *OT,* vv. 33-34.

7 *OT,* vv. 59-64.

8 *OT,* vv. 93-94. For a discussion of Oedipus' status as a public figure, see Seth Benardete, "Sophocles' *Oedipus Tyrannus,*" in *Sophocles: A Collection of Critical Essays,* ed. Thomas Woodard (Englewood Cliffs, N. J.: Prentice-Hall, 1966), pp. 108 ff.

9 *OT,* note to v. 93, p. 17.

10 See Jean-Pierre Vernant, *Mythe et pensée chez les Grecs* (Paris: Librairie François Maspero, 1965).

11 *OT,* v. 569. The same sentiment is repeated almost word for word by Creon at v. 1520.

12 *OT,* v. 341.

13 *OT,* vv. 543-44.

14 *OT,* vv. 408-09.

15 *OT,* note to v. 408, p. 51.

16 Thomas Gould, tr. and comm., *Oedipus the King* (Englewood Cliffs, N. J.: Prentice-Hall, 1970), p. 30 (note).

17 *OT,* vv. 138-41.

18 *OT,* note to v. 138, p. 22.

19 *OT,* vv. 605-07.

20 *OT,* vv. 626-27.

21 *Metaphysics,* III, iv, tr. Tredennick.

22 *OT,* vv. 328-29.

[23] Roman Jakobson and Morris Halle, *Fundamentals of Language,* 2nd ed. (The Hague: Mouton, 1971), p. 74.

[24] Jakobson and Halle, p. 83.

[25] Jakobson and Halle, p. 80.

[26] Jakobson and Halle, pp. 80-81.

[27] Jakobson and Halle, p. 85.

[28] See Terence Turner, "Oedipus: Time and Structure in Narrative Form," *Proceedings of the American Ethnological Society* (1969), pp. 26-68.

[29] Lévi-Strauss, p. 215.

[30] The problem is posed in precisely the same terms in Aeschylus' *Seven against Thebes,* which deals with a period posterior to that of the *Oedipus,* and which pushes the doubled/ halved family relations of Oedipus' line into the next (or rather same) generation. For a discussion of doubles and halves in the *Seven,* see C. Froidefond, "La Double Fraternité d'Etéocle et de Polynice," *Revue des Etudes Grecques,* 90 (1977), 211-22.

[31] *OT,* vv. 810-12.

[32] *OT,* vv. 1016-21.

[33] Gould, p. 120 (note).

Chapter Two: The House of Life and the House of Death: "Le Tombeau d'Edgar Poe"

[1] Mallarmé, *Œuvres complètes,* p. 70. All reproduction and quotations of poems of Mallarmé, including variants, are taken from this edition.

[2] Mallarmé, "Villiers de l'Isle-Adam," *Œuvres complètes,* p. 481.

[3] *Mallarmé: Poésie et poétique* (Lausanne: Mermod, 1949), p. 144.

[4] Gardner Davies, *Les "Tombeaux" de Mallarmé: Essai d'exégèse raisonnée* (Paris: Corti, 1950), p. 112.

[5] Davies, p. 111.

[6] Richard, p. 201.

[7] Cohn, p. 154.

[8] *The Language of the Self: The Function of Language in Psychoanalysis,* tr. and comm. Anthony Wilden (New York: Dell, 1968), pp. 244-48.

9 Mallarmé himself translated "grief" as "struggle" in his English translation of the poem, as Davies reports in Les "Tombeaux" de Mallarmé, p. 90.

10 "The Angel means the above said poet," cited in Davies, Les "Tombeaux" de Mallarmé, p. 90.

11 Mallarmé, Propos sur la poésie, p. 164.

12 Mallarmé: L'Homme et l'œuvre (Paris: Hatier-Boivin, 1953), p. 100.

13 See Mallarmé's own English translation of the poem: "Of which Poe's dazzling tomb be adorned," cited by Davies in Les "Tombeaux" de Mallarmé, p. 90.

14 Grand Larousse Encyclopédique.

15 Mallarmé, Propos sur la poésie, p. 164.

16 In stanzas 11, 8; 11; 2 and 8 through 18; 10; and 16, respectively. See Œuvres complètes, pp. 190-93, for Mallarmé's translation of the poem.

17 My emphasis. In the original this passage in stanza 2 is as follows: "the rare and radiant maiden whom the Angels name Lenore– / Nameless here for evermore." English citations are taken from Edgar Allen Poe, Poems and Essays (New York: W. J. Widdleton, 1876).

18 "But whose velvet violet lining with the lamp-light floating o'er / She shall press, ah! nevermore!" stanza 13.

19 " 'Tell this soul with sorrow laden if, within the distant Aidenn, / It shall clasp a sainted maiden whom the angels name Lenore– . . .' / Quoth the Raven, 'Nevermore!' " stanza 16.

20 " 'Take thy beak from out my heart, and take thy form from off my door!' / Quoth the Raven, 'Nevermore!' " stanza 17.

21 Stanzas 1 and 15, respectively.

22 The Death of Stéphane Mallarmé (Cambridge: Cambridge University Press, 1982), p. 39.

23 Mallarmé's already frequent use of English homonyms in his poetry becomes even less surprising in a poem about an American poet. Furthermore, his characterization of the essential meaning of the letter b in Les Mots anglais as that of "production ou enfante-ment" (Œuvres complètes, p. 929) might be of some importance here as well in the echo of "born" underlying "borne."

Chapter Three: The House of Life and the House of Death: "Sur les bois oubliés"

1 Paul Valéry, Le Cimetière marin, ed. and tr. Graham Dunstan Martin (Austin: University of Texas Press, 1971), pp. 33-34.

2 To this extent the interpretation of this line of the poem by Gardner Davies, as well as by several other commentators, seems to have missed the point somewhat: "Car pour sortir du sépulcre le revenant est obligé de soulever la pierre d'une main certes bien engourdie," *Les "Tombeaux" de Mallarmé*, p. 124.

3 See the above discussion of "s'encombre" (p. 71), a "piling up" of nothingness.

4 Davies, *Les "Tombeaux" de Mallarmé*, p. 126.

Chapter Four: The House of Life and the House of Death
"Le vierge, le vivace et le bel aujourd'hui"

1 Mallarmé, "Conflit," *Œuvres complètes*, p. 357.

2 In both the sonnet and the essay we find "aujourd'hui," "hante," "autrefois," "région," and "lieu"; in the sonnet we find "déchirer," "magnifique," "resplendit," "espace," and "songe," and in the essay "déchirure," "magnifiée," "resplendirait," "spacieux," and "songer." See *Œuvres complètes*, pp. 67-68 and pp. 355-60.

3 Emilie Noulet, *L'Œuvre poétique de Stéphane Mallarmé* (Paris: Droz, 1940), p. 265.

4 Edward Bird, *L'Univers poétique de Stéphane Mallarmé* (Paris: Nizet, 1962), p. 129.

5 Noulet, p. 265.

6 Michaud, p. 117.

7 Thibaudet, p. 217.

8 Thibaudet, p. 217.

9 Ferdinand de Saussure, *Course in General Linguistics,* tr. and comm. Wade Baskin (New York: McGraw-Hill, 1966), p. 68.

10 Jacques Derrida, *Of Grammatology,* tr. Gayatri Chakravorty Spivak (Baltimore: The Johns Hopkins University Press, 1974), p. 47.

11 Emile Littré, *Dictionnaire de la langue française* (Paris: Hachette, 1962), IV, 403.

12 From the Greek ἀγών, "a contest between two adversaries."

13 Cf. the rhyme "nie"/"génie" in "Quand l'ombre menaça de la fatale loi," Chapter Six.

14 Cf. "Renouveau": "Le printemps maladif a chassé tristement / L'hiver . . . ," *Œuvres complètes,* p. 34.

15 Derrida, p. 50.

16 The echo of "livre" in "se délivre" is pointed out by Kristeva, who remarks on "la différentielle /livRə/ avec ses surdéterminations 'ivre,' 'délivre,' 'givre,' 'vivre'" in "Eventail," *La Révolution du langage poétique* (Paris: Editions du Seuil, 1974), p. 243.

17 In his discussion of the etymology of the word *éclater*, Littré makes a comment particularly appropriate to the juxtaposition "éclat"/"vivace" and the opposition "éclat"/ "vierge": "L'ancien français avait *esclate*, race, extraction; celui-là vient de l'ancien haut allemand *slahta*, race; allemand *Geschlecht*," III, 420.

Chapter Five: Proximity and Approximation in the *Oedipus Tyrannus*
παρά and the Search for Home

1 *OT*, vv. 6-7.

2 *OT*, note to v. 7, p. 6.

3 Knox, p. 48.

4 *OT*, v. 714.

5 *De Sophisticis Elenchis*, Ch. I, my translation and my emphasis.

6 Knox, p. 49.

7 *OT*, vv. 35-36 and vv. 51-53.

8 See Aeschylus' Προμηθεὺς Δεσμότης, *Prometheus Bound*.

9 *Odyssey*, Bks. 14-24.

10 *OT*, v. 935.

11 *OT*, v. 1039.

12 See *OT*, vv. 6-7.

13 "Does [the one surviving witness of Laius' murder] happen to be present in the house now?" (v. 757).

14 "ὡς πλεῖστον εἴη τοῦδ᾽ ἄποπτος ἄστεως," "so as to be as much as possible out of sight of this city," (v. 762).

15 *OT*, vv. 834-35.

16 *OT*, vv. 73-75.

17 "Won't someone turn this one's hands behind him immediately?" (v. 1154).

18 *OT*, vv. 765-66.

19 "ὡς παρόντα νόμιξε αὐτόν· οὕτως ἔχει εὐκόλως ἀφίξεσθαι," *Scholia Graeca in Sophoclem*, ed. Brunck (Oxford: Clarendon Press, 1801), p. 265.

20 *OT*, note to v. 766, p. 86.

21 *OT*, vv. 1128-30.

22 Gould, pp. 131-32.

23 *OT*, vv. 1178-79.

24 *OT*, vv. 1002-03 and v. 35, respectively.

25 *OT*, vv. 435-37.

26 *OT*, vv. 437-39.

27 *OT*, vv. 128-31.

28 *OT*, vv. 445-46.

29 *OT*, vv. 284-86.

30 J. C. Kamerbeek, *The Plays of Sophocles, Commentaries, Part IV The Oedipus Tyrannus* (Leiden: E. J. Brill, 1967), pp. 79-80.

31 "[The chorus] addresses Teiresias by the same name as the god, and says that he sees the same things as that one," *Scholia Graeca in Sophoclem*, ed. Brunck, p. 241 (translation mine).

32 *OT*, v. 95.

33 *OT*, vv. 711-25.

34 *OT*, vv. 726-27.

35 *OT*, note to v. 727, p. 82.

36 *OT*, vv. 971-74.

37 "εἴ τι μὴ τὠμῷ πόθῳ / κατέφθιθ'· οὕτω δ' ἂν θανὼν εἴη 'ξ εμοῦ," *OT*, vv. 969-70.

38 *OT*, vv. 918-21.

39 "The attempt to move the hero is described as 'advice' (παραινῶ) . . . so Jocasta tries, unsuccessfully, to 'advise' Oedipus (παραινοῦσ', v. 918)," Bernard Knox, *The Heroic Temper: Studies in Sophoclean Tragedy* (Berkeley: University of California Press, 1964), p. 12.

40 Kamerbeek is quite right in translating "τὰ θεῖα" as "religion" (*The Plays of Sophocles,* p. 181), that is, not simply "divine matters," but rather the very relation between the human and the divine which is forever shifting.

41 *OT*, vv. 911-12.

42 Gould, p. 112.

43 *OT*, v. 1193.

44 *OT*, v. 1182.

45 *OT*, vv. 1258-59.

46 *OT*, v. 1238.

47 *Oedipus at Colonus,* vv. 1656-65, in Sophocles, *Fabulae* (1924; rpt. Oxford: Oxford University Press, 1975), n. pag.

Chapter Six: The Earthly Home and the Celestial Home
"Quand l'ombre menaça de la fatale loi"

1 Mallarmé, *Propos sur la poésie,* p. 59.

2 Poulet, p. 237.

3 Lawler, p. 11.

4 The use of "ployé en" here may well be partially an etymological play either on *employer* or on *impliquer,* both of which ultimately come from Latin *in-plicare,* "to fold in."

5 From the past participle of *fari,* "to speak or say."

6 Richard, p. 180.

7 Page 5 of "Un coup de dés jamais n'abolira le hasard," Mallarmé, *Œuvres complètes,* p. 464.

8 Genesis, Ch. 2.

9 Cf. Mallarmé, "Eventail (de Madame Mallarmé)," *Œuvres complètes,* p. 57: "*Aile* tout bas la courrière," with its resonance "elle," the wing/woman/messenger ("Aile" can also be a verb here: "The future verse . . . Wings the woman messenger") creating an opposition between heaven and Earth.

10 See Littré's derivation of the verb *douter,* "du latin *dubitare,* d'un radical *dub* qui signifie double," III, 273.

11 "RIEN . . . N'AURA EU LIEU . . . QUE LE LIEU," Page 10 of "Un coup de dés,"
Œuvres complètes, pp. 474-75.

12 The "de" here may be taken instrumentally, which would give a translation like:
"When the shadow threatened such an old Dream with the law of Fate"; or it may be
taken as part of a subjective or objective genitive linking "ombre" and "loi": "When the
shadow of the law of fate threatened such an old Dream." But in either of the above cases,
the "fatale loi" is essentially to be seen as the potential tool threatening the dream.

13 Poulet, p. 247; my emphasis.

14 Cf. Ovid's *Metamorphoses,* Bk. 1, vv. 84-86: "Pronaque cum spectent animalia
cetera terram, / Os homini sublime dedit, caelumque videre / lussit et erectos ad sidera
tollere vultus," "And while the other animals look downcast at the earth, man has been
given an uplifted face, and he has been bidden to see the sky and, erect, to carry his
face uplifted to the stars" (translation mine), a passage to which Mallarmé might well
have been sent by Baudelaire's "Le Cygne": "Vers le ciel quelquefois comme l'homme
d'Ovide, / Vers le ciel ironique et cruellement bleu . . ."

15 Genesis, Ch. 3.

16 Which is, in fact, the case in the astronomical notion of the "celestial sphere."

17 Lacan's term. See Chapter Two, note 8.

18 Cf. the relation of *vert-* and *vertere* to German *werden,* "to become, turn into."

19 Mallarmé, "Catholicisme," *Œuvres complètes,* p. 391.

20 E.g., Cohn, p. 122: "menti: used as a synonym of *démenti,*" implying that the "luxe"
is ultimately disproven by the night sky and by the approaching death with which it is
associated.

21 *Pensées,* "Misère," 414, in Pascal, p. 549.

22 Mallarmé, "Crise de vers," *Œuvres complètes,* p. 364.

23 Various critics are divided on the physical identity of the "guirlandes," most
seeming to see in them constellations, but Gardner Davies insisting on their being "des
nuages qu'animent momentanément les derniers reflets du couchant" (*Mallarmé et le
drame solaire* [Paris: Corti, 1959], p. 52). While the latter is a possible interpretation,
it would seem to be contradicted by the "salle d'ébène," the blackness of which would
appear to indicate a fully darkened night sky.

24 Cohn, p. 122.

25 Richard, p. 181.

26 Mallarmé, "Le Genre ou des modernes," *Œuvres complètes,* p. 319.

27 Mallarmé, "Le Livre, instrument spirituel," *Œuvres complètes,* p. 380, my emphasis.

28 Cohn, p. 123.

29 *Le Symbolisme de Mallarmé* (Paris: Nizet, 1950), p. 59, Gengoux's emphasis.

30 Mallarmé, "Hamlet," *Œuvres complètes*, p. 302.

31 Cf. Cohn's translation, "Throws the unprecedented mystery of a great burst of light," *Toward the Poems of Mallarmé*, p. 122.

32 As Davies, following Noulet, seems to prefer, *Mallarmé et le drame solaire*, p. 59.

33 Poulet, p. 247.

34 Cf. Old French *soudre*, "to be in the habit of."

35 The phrase carries the same tautological implications whether it is intransitive here— "Rolls in that boredom of the lowly fires"—or transitive—"Rolls lowly fires in that boredom."

36 Cf. "La chevelure vol d'une flamme à l'extrême": "pour la tout [l'atout] déployer"; see Chapter Seven below.

37 Lewis Carroll, *Alice's Adventures in Wonderland* (New York: D. Appleton and Co., 1866), p. 145.

38 Davies, *Mallarmé et le drame solaire*, p. 65.

Chapter Seven: The Earthly Home and the Celestial Home
"La chevelure vol d'une flamme à l'extrême"

1 There has been considerable disagreement over the preliminary action of the poem, ranging between the two extremes represented by Emilie Noulet's interpretation of a woman unwinding and then rewinding her hair (*Dix poèmes de Stéphane Mallarmé* [Lille: Giard, 1948], p. 126) and by Davies' reading of a non-action, that is, of a purely fantasized undoing of the woman's hair (*Mallarmé et le drame solaire*, p. 187). A more fruitful analysis of the poem's first lines comes from Albert Thibaudet, who speaks of a confusion of external and internal action (*La Poésie de Stéphane Mallarmé*, p. 196). For a thorough discussion of the prose poem "La déclaration foraine," within which "La chevelure" originally appeared, see Ursula Franklin, *An Anatomy of Poesis* (Chapel Hill: North Carolina Studies in the Romance Languages and Literatures, 1976), pp. 119-35.

2 Mallarmé, *Œuvres complètes*, p. 1210.

3 Davies, *Mallarmé et le drame solaire*, p. 169.

4 See Introduction, p. 9.

5 See Introduction, pp. 18-19.

6 Aeschylus' play *Prometheus Bound* has as a Greek title Προμηθεὺς Δεσμότης, the latter word coming from δέω, the verb from which "diadème" is taken.

7 Mallarmé, *Œuvres complètes*, p. 1218.

8 Cf. Mallarmé's own description of nature in "La Musique et les lettres": "La Nature a lieu, on n'y ajoutera pas," *Œuvres complètes*, p. 647.

9 Noulet's claim that "sans or" refers to the absence of artificial lighting (*Dix poèmes de Stéphane Mallarmé*, p. 127) is another possibility; indeed, the double reference of "or" to sun and lamps would reinforce the metaphor "chevelure"/"flamme" which links hair to sun in the first quatrain.

10 Mallarmé's delight with the word "or" is apparent in the essay which carries that word as its title (*Œuvres complètes*, pp. 398-99) and contains no less than three (and probably more) words which rhyme with "or" and also "gloss" it: "dehors" ("or" being seen as an external manifestation); "alors" (as opposed to "now"); and "trésor" (cf. Valéry's "Stable trésor . . . Mais comble d'or" in stanza 3 of *Le Cimetière marin*, and Graham Dunstan Martin's comment: "'Trésor' seems even more golden in French than 'treasure' does in English; for its last syllable, '-or,' is the French for gold," p. 30).

11 As Robert Greer Cohn has remarked, "The *nue-nue* ambiguity is constant in Mallarmé," *Toward the Poems of Mallarmé*, p. 152, note 6.

12 Richard, p. 348. Both Richard and Cohn credit Antoine Adam with this interpretation.

13 Jacques Gengoux's reading of "soupirer" as a synonym of *souhaiter*, precisely the opposite of my reading, which would make it a synonym of *regretter*, is certainly possible, "soupirer" in that case being oriented more toward the future than toward the past (or the present). See *Le Symbolisme de Mallarmé*, p. 219.

14 Camille Soula and Kurt Wais agree that it is the woman's eye: *Gloses sur Mallarmé* (Paris: Editions Diderot, 1945), p. 145; *Mallarmé: Dichtung, Weisheit, Haltung* (Munich: C. H. Beck, 1952), p. 598. Jean-Pierre Richard speaks of "le regard multiple d'une foule," *L'Univers imaginaire de Mallarmé*, p. 348. Austin Gill, who hypothesizes the importance of Prometheus in the sonnet but does not make much use of his theory, speaks of "the lucid eye of the poet," *Mallarmé's Poem: La chevelure vol d'une flamme* (Glasgow: University of Glasgow, 1971), p. 22.

15 E.g., classical Greek οἶδα, "I know," the perfect of a verb meaning "to see," related to the second aorist εἶδον, "I saw." Also German *wissen* and English *wit*, which are related to the same verb, the present of which is thought to have been ϝείδω.*

16 See Chapter Two on "Le Tombeau d'Edgar Poe."

17 Austin Gill's interesting suggestion that the third quatrain actually continues the sentence begun in the first and continued in the second is certainly a possibility. Gill reconstructs the single "skeleton sentence" which he sees as comprising the entire sonnet in this way: "La chevelure . . . Se pose . . . Vers le front couronné . . . Mais sans or soupirer que cette vive nue . . . continue . . . Une nudité de héros tendre (direct object of 'continue'),

diffame (second verb of which 'cette vive nue' is the subject) Celle qui . . . accomplit par son chef l'exploit De semer . . . (etc.)" (*Mallarmé's Poem*, p. 9). In this case the first and second and the second and third quatrains would be closely linked grammatically, as well as the third quatrain and the couplet. Still, the close grammatical link between the quatrains and the couplet is the only irrefutable one between any two stanzas of the poem.

18 Noulet, *Dix poèmes de Stéphane Mallarmé*, p. 129.

19 Richard, p. 349.

20 Perhaps the mixed metaphor of flowers and jewels ("semer de rubis") may be partially explained by a comparison with the end of the "Scène" of *Hérodiade* (*Œuvres complètes*, p. 48), in which Hérodiade's lips are described as a "fleur nue" which sobs at the "separation" of the childhood dreams of "froides pierreries." In both poems we find the dream of conjoining the lasting (jewels) and the ephemeral (flower, sowing): the pain of Hérodiade is in realizing that she cannot have both of these things at the same time, and the exploit of the woman in "La chevelure" is in both realizing she cannot have them both and in trying to have them both anyway, symbolically.

21 "La double séance," in *La Dissémination* (Paris: Editions du Seuil, 1972), p. 217.

Chapter Eight: The Earthly Home and the Celestial Home
"Ses purs ongles très haut dédiant leur onyx"

1 George W. Cox, *The Mythology of Aryan Nations* (London: Longmans, Green, and Co., 1870), II, 314, note 2.

2 Here for future reference is the earlier version of the sonnet, entitled "Sonnet allégorique de lui-même" (*Œuvres complètes*, p. 1488).

La nuit approbatrice allume les onyx
De ses ongles au pur Crime lampadophore,
Du Soir aboli par le vespéral Phénix
De qui la cendre n'a de cinéraire amphore

Sur des consoles, en le noir Salon: nul ptyx,
Insolite vaisseau d'inanité sonore,
Car le Maître est allé puiser l'eau du Styx
Avec tous ses objets dont le rêve s'honore.

Et selon la croisée au nord vacante, un or
Néfaste incite pour son beau cadre une rixe
Faite d'un dieu que croit emporter une nixe

En l'obscurcissement de la glace, Décor
De l'absence, sinon que sur la glace encor
De scintillation le septuor se fixe.

[3] See Chapter Seven.

[4] Mallarmé, *Œuvres complètes,* p. 1489.

[5] Mallarmé, *Œuvres complètes,* p. 934.

[6] Mallarmé, *Œuvres complètes,* p. 962.

[7] *The Myth of the Eternal Return: Cosmos and History,* tr. Willard R. Trask, Bollingen Series XLVI (Princeton: Princeton University Press, 1954), p. 4.

[8] Mallarmé, *Œuvres complètes,* p. 1192.

[9] There is conceivably also a word-play here on *espérer,* which would certainly be supported by the action of dreaming.

[10] Mallarmé, *Œuvres complètes,* p. 1240.

[11] Cox, II, 23, note 3.

[12] Mallarmé, *Œuvres complètes,* p. 1241.

[13] Mallarmé, *Œuvres complètes,* p. 1488. It is nonetheless unclear whether Mallarmé was aware of the word's relation to the Greek πτύξ, in spite of his disclaimer.

[14] Thibaudet's suggestion that "L'Angoisse ici symbolisée était vraiment un bronze lampadophore" is ingenious, but the lamp would still seem as likely to be metaphorical as the Anguish; *La Poésie de Stéphane Mallarmé,* p. 47.

[15] Mallarmé, *Œuvres complètes,* p. 1164.

[16] *Grand Larousse Encyclopédique en dix volumes,* 1963 ed., VIII, 49.

[17] Cf. Villon's famous "Ballade des Dames du temps jadis,"which is largely organized around the same principle, ending with the naming of a figure roughly contemporaneous to the poet himself (Jehanne).

[18] I am indebted for this suggestion to Professor Victor Brombert.

[19] Davies cites Brennan's very interesting observation in a note (*Mallarmé et le drame solaire,* p. 136, note 19).

[20] Mallarmé, *Œuvres complètes,* p. 1243.

[21] H. J. Rose, *A Handbook of Greek Mythology* (New York: E. P. Dutton, 1959), p. 32.

[22] Even though several of the verbs are transitive, all of them—with the possible exception of "se fixe" with its modifier "sitôt"—have a stative rather than a punctual aspect.

[23] Robert Greer Cohn has pointed this out, *Toward the Poems of Mallarmé,* p. 144.

24 Mallarmé, in a letter to Cazalis of July 1868, quoted in *Œuvres complètes,* p. 1490.

25 Davies, *Mallarmé et le drame solaire,* p. 126.

Postface

1 Martin Heidegger, "What Are Poets For?" in *Poetry, Language, Thought,* tr. Albert Hofstadter (New York: Harper and Row, 1975), p. 132.

2 *Cratylus,* 401c-d, in *The Dialogues of Plato,* tr. Jowett, p. 191.

3 *Poetics,* 1452a.

4 Heidegger, "Building Dwelling Thinking," in *Poetry, Language, Thought,* p. 161.

Selected Bibliography

I. Works on the *Oedipus Tyrannus*

Benardete, Seth. "Sophocles' *Oedipus Tyrannus.*" In *Sophocles: A Collection of Critical Essays.* Ed. Thomas Woodard. Englewood Cliffs, N. J.: Prentice-Hall, 1966.

Dodds, E. R. "On Misunderstanding the *Oedipus Rex.*" In Sophocles, *Oedipus Tyrannus.* Tr. and ed. Luci Berkowitz and Theodore F. Brunner. New York: W. W. Norton and Co., 1970.

Gould, Thomas. "The Innocence of Oedipus." In Sophocles, *Oedipus Tyrannus.* Tr. and ed. Luci Berkowitz and Theodore F. Brunner. New York: W. W. Norton and Co., 1970.

Green, André. *Un Œil en trop: Le Complexe d'Œdipe dans la tragédie.* Paris: Editions de Minuit, 1969.

Kamerbeek, J. C. *The Plays of Sophocles, Commentaries, Part IV, The Oedipus Tyrannus.* Leiden: E. J. Brill, 1967.

Knox, Bernard. *The Heroic Temper: Studies in Sophoclean Tragedy.* Berkeley: University of California Press, 1964.

_____. *Oedipus at Thebes.* New Haven: Yale University Press, 1957.

Scholia Graeca in Sophoclem. Ed. Richard Brunck. Oxford: Clarendon Press, 1801.

Sophocle. *Œdipe-Roi.* Tr. Paul Masqueray. Paris: Les Belles Lettres, 1946, Vol. I.

Sophocles. *Fabulae.* Ed. A. C. Pearson. 1924; rpt. Oxford: Oxford University Press, 1975.

_____. *Oedipus the King.* Tr. and comm. Thomas Gould. Englewood Cliffs, N. J.: Prentice-Hall, 1970.

_____. *Oedipus the King.* Tr. David Grene. Chicago: University of Chicago Press, 1942.

_____. *Oedipus Tyrannus.* Ed. and comm. Sir Richard Jebb. 1885; rpt. Cambridge: Cambridge University Press, 1975.

Turner, Terence. "Oedipus: Time and Structure in Narrative Form." *Proceedings of the American Ethnological Society* (1969), pp. 26-68.

Vellacott, Philip. *Sophocles and Oedipus.* London: Macmillan, 1971.

II. Works on Mallarmé

Adam, Antoine. "Pour l'interprétation de Mallarmé." In *Mélanges d'histoire littéraire offerts à Daniel Mornet.* Paris: Nizet, 1951, pp. 221-26.

Beausire, Pierre. *Mallarmé: Poésie et poétique.* Lausanne: Mermod, 1949.

Bersani, Leo. *The Death of Stéphane Mallarmé.* Cambridge: Cambridge University Press, 1982.

Bird, Edward. *L'Univers poétique de Stéphane Mallarmé.* Paris: Nizet, 1962.

Block, Haskell. *Mallarmé and the Symbolist Drama.* Detroit: Wayne State University Press, 1963.

Cellier, Léon. *Mallarmé et la Morte qui parle.* Paris: Presses Universitaires de France, 1959.

Chassé, Charles. *Les Clés de Mallarmé.* Paris: Editions Montaigne. 1954.

Cohn, Robert Greer. *Toward the Poems of Mallarmé.* Berkeley: University of California Press, 1965.

Davies, Gardner. *Mallarmé et le drame solaire.* Paris: Corti, 1959.

_____. *Les "Tombeaux" de Mallarmé: Essai d'exégèse raisonnée.* Paris: Corti, 1950.

Derrida, Jacques. "La double séance." In *La Dissémination.* Paris: Editions du Seuil, 1972.

Franklin, Ursula. *An Anatomy of Poesis.* Chapel Hill: North Carolina Studies in the Romance Languages and Literatures, 1976.

Gengoux, Jacques. *Le Symbolisme de Mallarmé.* Paris: Nizet, 1950.

Gill, Austin. *Mallarmé's Poem: La chevelure vol d'une flamme.* Glasgow: University of Glasgow, 1971.

Kristeva, Julia. *La Révolution du langage poétique: L'Avant-garde à la fin du XIXe siècle: Lautréamont et Mallarmé.* Paris: Editions du Seuil, 1974.

Mallarmé, Stéphane. *Œuvres complètes.* Bibliothèque de la Pléiade. Paris: Gallimard, 1945.

Mallarmé, Stéphane. *Propos sur la poésie.* Ed. Henri Mondor. Monaco: Editions du Rocher, 1946.

_____. *Selected Prose Poems, Essays, and Letters.* Tr. Bradford Cook. Baltimore: The Johns Hopkins University Press, 1956.

Mauron, Charles. *Introduction à la Psychanalyse de Mallarmé.* 1950; rpt. Neuchâtel: A la Baconnière, 1968.

Michaud, Guy. *Mallarmé: L'Homme et l'œuvre.* Paris: Hatier-Boivin, 1953.

Mondor, Henri. *Vie de Mallarmé.* Paris: Gallimard, 1941.

Noulet, Emilie. *Dix poèmes de Stéphane Mallarmé.* Lille: Giard, 1948.

_____. *L'Œuvre poétique de Stéphane Mallarmé.* Paris: Droz, 1940.

Orliac, Antoine. *Mallarmé tel qu'en lui-même.* Paris: Mercure de France, 1948.

Richard, Jean-Pierre. *L'Univers imaginaire de Mallarmé.* Paris: Editions du Seuil, 1961.

Scherer, Jacques. *L'Expression littéraire dans l'œuvre de Mallarmé.* Paris: Droz, 1947.

Sonnenfeld, Albert. "Elaboration secondaire du grimoire: Mallarmé et le poète-critique." *Romanic Review,* 69 (January-March 1978), pp. 72-89.

Soula, Camille. *Gloses sur Mallarmé.* Paris: Editions Diderot, 1945.

Thibaudet, Albert. *La Poésie de Stéphane Mallarmé.* Paris: Gallimard, 1926.

Wais, Kurt. *Mallarmé: Dichtung, Weisheit, Haltung.* Munich: C. H. Beck, 1952.

III. Additional Works Consulted

Bachelard, Gaston. *La Poétique de l'espace.* Paris: Presses Universitaires de France, 1957.

Benveniste, Emile. *Problèmes de linguistique générale.* 2 vols. Paris: Gallimard, 1966, 1974.

Blanchot, Maurice. *L'Espace littéraire.* Paris: Gallimard, 1955.

Bourdieu, Pierre. *Esquisse d'une théorie de la pratique.* Genève: Droz, 1972.

Burke, Kenneth. *Language as Symbolic Action.* Berkeley: University of California Press, 1966.

Cox, George W. *The Mythology of Aryan Nations.* 2 vols. London: Longmans, Green, and Co., 1870.

De Man, Paul. "The Rhetoric of Temporality." In *Interpretation: Theory and Practice.* Ed. Charles Singleton. Baltimore: The Johns Hopkins University Press, 1969.

Derrida, Jacques. *Of Grammatology.* Tr. Gayatri Chakravorty Spivak. Baltimore: The Johns Hopkins University Press, 1974.

Detienne, Marcel. *Les Maîtres de vérité dans la Grèce antique.* Paris: Maspero, 1973.

Durand, Gilbert. *Les Structures anthropologiques de l'imaginaire.* Paris: Bordas, 1969.

Eliade, Mircea. *The Myth of the Eternal Return: Cosmos and History.* Tr. Willard R. Trask. Bollingen Series XLVI. Princeton: Princeton University Press, 1954.

Froidefond, C. "La Double Fraternité d'Etéocle et de Polynice." *Revue des Etudes Grecques,* 90 (1977), 211-22.

Genette, Gérard. *Figures I.* Paris: Editions du Seuil, 1966.

―――. *Figures III.* Paris: Editions du Seuil, 1972.

―――. *Mimologiques: Voyage en Cratylie.* Paris: Editions du Seuil, 1976.

Goldmann, Lucien. *Le dieu caché.* Paris: Gallimard, 1955.

Goujon, Francine. "Le Nom et le drame: Aspects de la fonction du chœur dans l'*Agamemnon* d'Eschyle." *Ecriture et théorie poétique* (1976), pp. 57-72.

Hartman, Geoffrey. *The Unmediated Vision.* 1954; rpt. New York: Harcourt, Brace, and World, Inc., 1966.

Heidegger, Martin. *Erläuterungen zu Hölderlins Dichtung.* Frankfurt am Main: Klostermann, 1951.

―――. *Poetry, Language, Thought.* Tr. Albert Hofstadter. New York: Harper and Row, 1975.

Jakobson, Roman. "Two Aspects of Language and Two Types of Aphasic Disturbances." In *Fundamentals of Language.* Ed. Roman Jakobson and Morris Halle. 2nd ed. The Hague: Mouton, 1971.

Kristeva, Julia. Σημειωτικὴ: *Recherches pour une sémanalyse.* Paris: Editions du Seuil, 1969.

Lacan, Jacques. *The Language of the Self: The Function of Language in Psychoanalysis.* Tr. and comm. Anthony Wilden. New York: Dell, 1968.

Lallot, Jean. "*Xumbola kranai*: Réflections sur la fonction du *sumbolon* dans l'*Agamemnon* d'Eschyle." *Cahiers Internationaux du symbolisme,* 26 (1974), 39-48.

Lawler, James. *The Language of French Symbolism.* Princeton: Princeton University Press, 1969.

Le Guern, Michel. *Sémantique de la métaphore et de la métonymie.* Paris: Larousse, 1972.

Lehmann, A. J. *The Symbolist Aesthetic in France.* Oxford: Blackwell, 1950.

Lévi-Strauss, Claude. *Structural Anthropology.* Tr. Claire Jacobson and Brooke Grundfest Schoepf. New York: Basic Books, 1963.

Littré, Emile. *Dictionnaire de la langue française.* Paris: Hachette, 1962.

Lukács, Georg. *The Theory of the Novel: A Historico-Philosophical Essay on the Forms of Great Epic Literature.* Tr. Anna Bostock. Cambridge: MIT Press, 1971.

Nietzsche, Friedrich. *"The Birth of Tragedy" and "The Case of Wagner."* Tr. and comm. Walter Kaufmann. New York: Vintage Books–Random House, 1967.

Pascal, Blaise. *Pensées.* Paris: Editions du Seuil, 1963.

Plato. *Cratylus.* In *Opera Omnia.* Ed. and comm. Stallbaum. London: Dulau and Co., 1857.

_____. *The Dialogues of Plato.* Tr. Benjamin Jowett. 1892; rpt. New York: Random House, 1937.

Poulet, Georges. *Etudes sur le temps humain.* Paris: Plon, 1949.

_____. *The Interior Distance.* Tr. Elliott Coleman. Ann Arbor: University of Michigan Press, 1964.

Raymond, Marcel. *De Baudelaire au Surréalisme.* Paris: Corti, 1947.

Rose, H. J. *A Handbook of Greek Mythology.* New York: E. P. Dutton, 1959.

Saussure, Ferdinand de. *Course in General Linguistics.* Tr. and comm. Wade Baskin. New York: McGraw-Hill, 1966.

Segal, Charles. "The Raw and the Cooked in Greek Literature." *Classical Journal,* 69 (April-May 1974), 289-308.

Steiner, George. *The Death of Tragedy.* 1961; rpt. New York: Oxford University Press, 1980.

Todorov, Tzvetan. *Théories du symbole.* Paris: Editions du Seuil, 1977.

Valéry, Paul. *Œuvres.* Bibliothèque de la Pléiade. Paris: Gallimard, 1957.

_____. *Le Cimetière marin.* Ed. and tr. Graham Dunstan Martin. Austin: University of Texas Press, 1971.

Vernant, Jean-Pierre. *Mythe et pensée chez les Grecs.* Paris: Librairie François Maspero, 1965.

_____. *Mythe et tragédie en Grèce Ancienne.* Paris: Librairie François Maspero, 1973.

In the PURDUE UNIVERSITY MONOGRAPHS IN ROMANCE LANGUAGES
series the following monographs have been published thus far:

1. John R. Beverley: *Aspects of Góngora's "Soledades."*
   Amsterdam, 1980. xiv, 139 pp. Bound.

2. Robert Francis Cook: *"Chanson d'Antioche," chanson de geste: Le Cycle de la Croisade est-il épique?*
   Amsterdam, 1980. viii, 107 pp. Bound.

3. Sandy Petrey: *History in the Text: "Quatrevingt-Treize" and the French Revolution.*
   Amsterdam, 1980. viii, 129 pp. Bound.

4. Walter Kasell: *Marcel Proust and the Strategy of Reading.*
   Amsterdam, 1980. x, 125 pp. Bound.

5. Inés Azar: *Discurso retórico y mundo pastoral en la "Egloga segunda" de Garcilaso.*
   Amsterdam, 1981. x, 171 pp. Bound.

6. Roy Armes: *The Films of Alain Robbe-Grillet.*
   Amsterdam, 1981. x, 216 pp. Bound.

7. *Le "Galien" de Cheltenham*, edited by David M. Dougherty and Eugene B. Barnes.
   Amsterdam, 1981. xxxvi, 203 pp. Bound.

8. Ana Hernández del Castillo: *Keats, Poe, and the Shaping of Cortázar's Mythopoesis.*
   Amsterdam, 1981. xii, 135 pp. Bound.

9. Carlos Albarracín-Sarmiento: *Estructura del "Martín Fierro."*
   Amsterdam, 1981. xx, 336 pp. Bound.

10. C. George Peale et al. (eds.): *Antigüedad y actualidad de Luis Vélez de Guevara: Estudios críticos.*
    Amsterdam, 1983. xii, 298 pp. Bound.

11. David Jonathan Hildner: *Reason and the Passions in the "Comedias" of Calderón.*
    Amsterdam, 1982. xii, 119 pp. Bound.

12. Floyd Merrell: *Pararealities: The Nature of Our Fictions and How We Know Them.*
    Amsterdam, 1983. xii, 170 pp. Bound.

13. Richard E. Goodkin: *The Symbolist Home and the Tragic Home: Mallarmé and Oedipus.*
    Amsterdam, 1983. xvi, 203 pp. Bound.

14. Philip Walker: *"Germinal" and Zola's Philosophical and Religious Thought.*
    Amsterdam, 1983. ca. 185 pp. Bound.

15. Claire-Lise Tondeur: *Gustave Flaubert, critique: Thèmes et structures.*
    Amsterdam, 1983. ca. 130 pp. Bound.